A BED OF ROSES

A BED OF ROSES

Some Press Comments

The Times says

This is a novel of undeniable insight and considerable literary skill by a writer who is interested in social problems.

The Daily News says

It is by its social purpose rather than by its artistic treatment that this painful story is justified. Victoria sums up the whole matter from the author's point of view when she says to the suffragist canvasser :

'So long as your economic system is such that there is not work for the asking, work, mark you, fitted to strength and ability, so long on the other hand as there is such uncertainty as prevents men from marrying, so long as there is a leisured class which draws luxury from the labour of other men, so long will my class endure as it endured in Athens, in Rome, in Alexandria, as it does now from St John's Wood to Pekin.'

A BED OF ROSES is a powerful and earnest 'novel of ideas,' a remarkable sociological document. It is, incidentally, a book not for fools but for serious people.

The Daily Telegraph says

The pages which describe this life are full of the deepest interest, and though it is realism all through, there is not a dull line in it. Mr. George, among other excellences, has created a character which is thoroughly human though unusual and one which holds the interest from the first page of his sincere work to the last.

The Manchester Guardian says

It is an intensely painful, arresting study of humanity's facts and if to excite pity and terror is proof of a book's power, power it certainly possesses. It fascinates and it terrifies by its merciless exactness and its truthfulness that sears. The subject is one that only utmost sincerity should touch, and Mr George deals with it seriously and altogether admirably. He spares us nothing, going deep into the woman's hampered thought. It is a book that would be intolerable if it had any sentimentality, or, worse, that pseudo-passion with which novelists like to cover the case of Victoria. Here there is no glamour on matter or manner, no relief from the grim pressure of painful truth save an occasional twist of humour as grim.

The Star (Mr James Douglas) says

A very powerful study of the economic position of woman in the present state of society. The pitiless veracity of the story blisters and burns into the social conscience. It is not a comfortable story. It is a story which will infuriate good easy folk who hate to be confronted with the facts of life as it is lived in the twentieth century. Mr George does not spare his readers. He is not sickly or noisome or prurient. He is not furtively nasty. He simply tells the truth as he sees it. . . .

A BED OF ROSES

BY

W. L. GEORGE

Author of "Engines of Social Progress," "France in the Twentieth Century," &c.

> It's not work that any woman would do for pleasure, goodness knows; though to hear the pious people talk you would suppose it was a bed of roses.
>
> (*Mrs. Warren's Profession*, by G. Bernard Shaw).

THIRTEENTH IMPRESSION

WILDSIDE PRESS

FIRST PUBLISHED	-	-	-	-	*April* 1911
SECOND IMPRESSION	-	-	-	*May* 1911
THIRD IMPRESSION	-	-	-	*July* 1911
FOURTH IMPRESSION	-	-	-	*July* 1911
FIFTH IMPRESSION	-	-	-	*Sept.* 1911
SIXTH IMPRESSION	-	-	-	*Oct.* 1911
SEVENTH IMPRESSION	-	-	-	*Nov.* 1911
EIGHTH IMPRESSION	-	-	-	*Mar.* 1912
NINTH IMPRESSION	-	-	-	*April* 1912
TENTH IMPRESSION (popular 1/- net edition)					*May* 1913
ELEVENTH IMPRESSION	ditto	-			*July* 1913
TWELFTH IMPRESSION	ditto	-			*July* 1915
THIRTEENTH IMPRESSION (cheaper cloth edition)					
					July 1915

Printed at the Ferrestone Press,
London, England.

PART I

CHAPTER I

'WE go.' The lascar meditatively pressed his face, brown and begrimed with coal dust, streaked here and there with sweat, against the rope which formed the rough bulwark. His dark eyes were fixed on the shore, near by, between which and the ship's side the water quivered quicker and quicker in little ripples, each ripple carrying an iridescent film of grey ooze. Without joy or sadness he was bidding goodbye to Bombay, his city. Those goodbyes are often farewells for lascars who must face the Bay and the Channel. But the stoker did not care.

His companion lay by his side, lazily propped up on his elbow, not deigning even to take a last look at the market place, seething still with its crowded reds and blues and golds. 'Dekko!' cried the first stoker pointing to the wharf where a white man in a dirty smock had just cast off the last rope, which came away swishing through the air.

His companion did not raise his eyes. Slowly he tilted up his pannikin and let the water flow in a thin stream into his mouth, keeping the metal away from his lips. Then, careless of the land of Akbar, he let himself sink on the deck and composed himself to sleep. India was no concern of his.

A few yards away a woman watched them absently from the upper deck. She was conscious of them, conscious too of the slow insistent buzzing of a gad-

fly. Her eyes slowly shifted to the shore, passed over
the market place, stopped at the Fort. There, in the
open space, a troop was drilling, white and speckless,
alertly wheeling at the word of command. Her eyes
were still fixed on the group as the ship imperceptibly
receded from the shore, throbbing steadily as the
boilers got up steam. A half-naked brown boy was
racing along the wharf to gain a start and beat the
vessel before she reached the military crane.

The woman turned away. She was neither tall nor
short: she did not attract attention overmuch but she
was one of those who retain such attention as they
draw. She was clad entirely in black; her face
seemed to start forward intensified. Her features were
regular; her mouth small. Her skin, darkened by the
shadow of a broad brimmed hat, blushed still darker
at the cheeks. The attraction was all in the eyes,
large and grey, suggestive of energy without emotion.
Her chin was square, perhaps too thick in the jaw.

She turned once more and leant against the bulwark.
A yard away another woman was also standing, her
eyes fixed on the shore, on a figure who waited motionless on the fast receding wharf. As the steamer kept
on her course the woman craned forward, saw once
more and then lost sight of the lonely figure. She
was small, fair, a little insignificant, and dressed all
in white drill.

The steamer had by now attained half speed. The
shore was streaming by. The second woman turned
her back on the bulwark, looked about aimlessly,
then, perceiving her neighbour, impulsively went up
to her and stood close beside her.

The two women did not speak, but remained
watching the shoals fly past. Far away a train in
Kolaba puffed up sharp bursts of smoke into the blue
air. There was nothing to draw the attention of the
beholder in that interminable shore, low-lying and
muddy, splashed here and there with ragged trees.

It was a desert almost, save for a village built between two swamps. Here and then smoke arose, brown and peaty from a bonfire. In the evening light the sun's declining rays lit up with radiance the red speck of a heavy shawl on the tiny figure of a brown girl.

Little by little, as the ship entered the fairway, the shore receded almost into nothingness. The two women still watched, while India merged into shadow. It was the second hour and, as the ship slowly turned towards the west, the women watched the great cocoanut trees turn into black specks upon Marla point. Then, slowly, the shore sank into the dark sea until it was gone and nothing was left of India save the vaguely paler night that tells of land and the even fainter white spears of the distant light.

For a moment they stood still, side by side. Then the fair woman suddenly put her hand on her companion's arm. 'I'm cold,' she said, 'let's go below.'

The dark girl looked at her sympathetically. 'Yes,' she said, 'let's, who'd have thought we wanted to see more of the beastly country than we could help. . . . I say, what's the matter, Molly?'

Molly was still looking towards the light; one of her feet tapped the deck nervously; she fumbled for her handkerchief. 'Nothing, nothing,' she said indistinctly, 'come and unpack.' She turned away from her companion and quickly walked towards the gangway.

The dark girl looked once more into the distance where even the searchlight had waned. 'Vic!' cried the fair girl querulously, half way up the deck. 'All right, I'm coming,' replied the woman in black. She looked again at the pale horizon into which India had faded, at the deck before her where a little black cluster of people had formed to look their last upon the light. Then she turned and followed her companion.

The cabin was on the lower deck, small, stuffy in the extreme. Its two grave-like bunks, its drop table, even its exiguous armchair promised no comfort. On the worn carpet the pattern had almost vanished; alone the official numerals on the edge stared forth. For half an hour the two women unpacked in silence; Molly knelt by the side of her trunk delving into it, dragging out garments which she tried to find room for on the scanty pegs. Her companion merely raised the lid of her trunk to ease the pressure on her clothes, and placed a small dressing-case on the drop table. Once she would have spoken but, at that moment, a faint sob came from Molly's kneeling form. She went up to her, put her arm about her neck and kissed her cheek. She undressed wearily, climbed into the upper berth. Soon Molly did likewise, after turning down the light. For a while she sighed and turned uneasily; then she became quieter, her breathing more measured, and she slept.

Victoria Fulton lay in her berth, her eyes wide open, glued to the roof a foot or so above her face. It was very like a coffin, she thought, perhaps a suitable enough habitation for her, but at present, not in the least tempting. A salutary capacity for optimism was enabling her to review the past three years and to speculate about the future. Not that either was very rosy, especially the future.

The steady throb of the screw pulsated through the stuffy cabin, and blended with the silence broken only by Molly's regular breathing in the lower berth. Victoria could not help remembering other nights passed also in a stuffy little cabin, where the screw was throbbing as steadily, and when the silence was broken by breathing as regular, but a little heavier. Three years only, and she was going home. But now she was leaving behind her the high hopes she had brought with her.

She was no exception to the common rule, and memories, whether bitter or sweet, had always bridged for her the gulf between wakefulness and sleep. And what could be more natural than to recall those nights, three years ago, when every beat of that steady screw was bringing her nearer to the country where her young husband was, according to his mood, going to win the V.C., trace the treasure stolen from a Begum, or become military member on the Viceroy's Council? Poor old Dicky, she thought, perhaps it was as well he did not live to see himself a major, old and embittered, with all those hopes behind him.

There were no tears in her eyes when she thought of Fulton. The good old days, the officers' ball at Lympton when she danced with him half the night, the rutty lane where they met to sit on a bank of damp moss smelling of earth and crushed leaves, and the crumbling little church where she became Fulton's wife, all that was far away. How dulled it all was too by those three years during which, in the hot moist air of the plains, she had seen him degenerate, his skin lose his freshness, his eyelids pucker and gather pouches, his tongue grow ever more bitter as he attempted to still with whisky the drunkard's chronic thirst. She could not even shudder at the thought of all it had meant for her, at the horror of seeing him become every day more stupefied, at the savage outbursts of the later days, at the last scenes, crude and physically foul. Three years had taught her brain dullness to such scenes as those.

The tragedy of Fulton was a common enough thing. Heat, idleness, temporary affluence, all those things that do not let a man see that life is blessed only by the works that enable him to forget it, had played havoc with him. He had followed up his initial error of coming into the world at all by marrying a woman who neither cajoled or coerced him. With the best of intentions she had bored him to extinction. His interest in things became slender ; he drank himself to death, and not even the ghost of his self lived to grieve by his bedside.

In spite of everything it had not been a bad life in its way. Victoria had been the belle, in spite of Mrs Major Dartle and her peroxidised tresses. And there had been polo (Dicky always would have three ponies and refused three hundred guineas for Tagrag), and regimental dances and gymkhanas and what not. Under the sleepy sun these three years had passed, not like a flash of lightning, but slowly, dreamily, in the unending routine of marches, inspections, migrations to and from the hills. The end had come quickly. One day they carried Dick Fulton all the way from the mess and laid him under his own verandah. The fourth day he died of cirrhosis of the liver. Even Mrs Major Dartle who formally called and lit up the darkened room with the meretricious glow of her curls hinted that it was a happy release. The station in general had no doubt as to the person for whom release had come.

As Victoria lay in the coffin-like berth she vainly tried to analyse her feeling for Fulton. The three years had drawn over her past something like a veil behind which she could see the dim shapes of her impressions dancing like ghostly marionettes. She knew that she had loved him with the discreet passion of an Englishwoman. He had burst in upon her ravished soul like the materialised dream of a schoolgirl; he had been adorably careless, adorably rakish. For a whole year all his foibles had been charms in so far as they made the god more human, nearer to her. Then, one night, he had returned home so drunk as to fall prostrate on the tiles of the verandah and sleep there until next morning. She had not dared to call the ayah or the butler and, as she could not rouse or lift him, she had left him lying there under some rugs and mosquito netting.

During the rest of that revolutionary night she had not slept, nor had she found the relief of tears that is given most women. Hot waves of indignation flowed over her. She wanted to get up, to stamp with rage, to kick the disgraceful thing on the tiles. She held herself down, however, or perhaps the tradition of the English counties whispered to her that anything was preferable to scandal, that crises must be noiseless. When dawn came and she at last managed to arouse Fulton by flooding his head with the contents of the water jug, the hot fit was gone. She felt cold, too aloof, too far away from him to hate him, too petrified to reproach him.

Fulton took no notice of the incident. He was still young and vigorous enough to shake off within a few hours the effects of the drink. Besides he seldom mentioned things that affected their relations; in the keep of his heart he hid the resentment of a culprit against the one who has caught him in the act. He confined his conversation to daily happenings; in moments of expansion he talked of the future. They did not, however, draw nearer one another; thus the evolution of their marriage tended inevitably to draw them apart. Victoria was no longer angry, but she was frightened because she had been frightened and she hated the source of her fear. Fulton, thick skinned as he was, felt their estrangement keenly. He grew to hate his wife; it almost made him wish to hurt her again. So he absented himself more often, drank more, then died. His wife was free. So this was freedom. Freedom, a word to conjure with, thought Victoria, when one is enslaved and meaning very little when one is free. She was able to do what she liked and wished to do nothing. Of course things would smooth themselves out: they always did, even though the smoothing process might be lengthy. They must do so, but how? There were friends of course, and Ted, and thirty pounds of Consols unless they'd gone down again, as safe investments are wont to do. She would have to do some work. Rather funny, but how jolly to draw your first month's or week's salary; everybody said it was a proud moment. Of course it would have to be earned, but that did not matter: everybody had to earn what they got, she supposed, and they ought to enjoy doing it. Old Flynn, the D.C., used to say that work was a remunerative occupation you didn't like, but then he had been twenty years in India.

Molly turned uneasily in her bunk and settled down again. Victoria's train of thought was broken and she could not detach her attention from the very gentle snore that came from the lower berth, a snore gentle but so insidious that it seemed to dominate the steady beat of the screw. Through the porthole, over which now there raced some flecks of spray, she could see nothing but the blackness of the sky, a blackness which at times turned to grey whenever the still inkier sea appeared. The cabin seemed black and empty, lit up faintly by a white skirt flung on a chair. Slowly Victoria sank into sleep, conscious of a half dream of England where so many unknowable things must happen.

CHAPTER II

'No, Molly, I don't think it's very nice of you,' said Victoria, 'we've been out four days and I've done nothing but mope and mope; it's all very well my being a widow and all that: I'm not suggesting you and I should play hop scotch on deck with the master gunner, but for four days I've been reading a three months old *Harper's* and the memoirs of Mademoiselle de I don't know what, and . . .'

'But what have I done?' cried Molly.

'I'm bored,' replied Victoria, with admirable detachment, 'and what's more, I don't intend to go on being bored for another fortnight; I'm going on deck to find somebody to amuse me.'

'You can't do that,' said Molly, 'they're washing it.'

'Very well, then, I'll go and watch and sing songs to the men.' Victoria glared at her unoffending companion, her lips tightening and her jaw growing ominously squarer.

'But my dear girl,' said Molly, 'I'm awfully sorry. I didn't know you cared; come and have a game of quoits with me and old Cairns. There's a place behind the companion which I should say nobody ever does wash.'

Victoria was on the point of answering that she hated quoits as she never scored and they were generally dirty, but the prospect of returning to the ancient *Harper's* was not alluring, so she followed Molly to the hatchway and climbed up to the upper deck still shining moist and white. Apparently they would not have to play behind the companion. Four men were leaning against the bulwarks, looking out at nothing as people do on board ship. Victoria just had time to notice a very broad flannel-clad back surmounted by a thick neck, while Molly went up to the last man and unceremoniously prodded him in the ribs.

'Wake up, Bobby,' she said, 'I'm waiting.'

The men all wheeled round suddenly. The broad man stepped forward quickly and shook hands with Molly. Then he took a critical look at Victoria. The three young men struggled for an absurd little bag which Molly always dropped at the right moment.

'How do you do, Mrs Fulton,' said the broad man stretching out his hand. Victoria took it hesitatingly.

'Don't you remember me?' he said. 'My name's Cairns. Major Cairns. You know. Travancores. Met you at His Excellency's hop.

Of course she remembered him. He was so typical. Anybody could have told his profession and his rank at sight. He had a broad humorous face, tanned over freckled pink. Since he left Wellington he had grown a little in every direction and had become a large middle aged boy. Victoria took him in at one look. A square face such as that of Cairns, distinctly chubby, framing grey blue eyes, was as easily recalled as forgotten. She took in his forehead, high and likely to become higher as his hair receded; his straight aggressive nose; his little rough moustache looking like nothing so much as a ragged strip off an Irish terrier's back.

While Victoria was wondering what to say, Molly, determined to show her that she was not going to leave her out, had thrust her three henchmen forward.

'This is Bobby,' she remarked. Bobby was a tall young man with a round head, bright brown eyes full of cheerfulness and hot temper. 'And

Captain Alastair . . . and Mr Parker.' Alastair smiled. Smiles were his method of expression. Mr Parker bowed rather low and said nothing. He had at once conceived for Victoria the mixture of admiration and dislike that a man feels towards a woman who would not marry him if she knew where he had been to school.

'I hope,' said Mr Parker slowly, 'that your. . . .' But he broke off suddenly, realising the mourning and feeling the ground to be unsafe.

'Mr Parker, I've been looking for you all the morning,' interjected Molly, with intuition. 'You've promised to teach me to judge my distance,' and she cleverly pushed Bobby between Mr Parker and Victoria. 'Come along, and you Bobby,'you can pick the rings up.'

'Right O,' said Bobby readily. She turned towards the stern followed by the obedient Bobby and Mr Parker.

Captain Alastair smiled vacuously, made as if to follow the trio, realising that it was a false start, swerved back and finally covering his confusion by sliding a few yards onwards to tell Mrs Colonel Lanning that it was blowing up for a squall.

Victoria had watched the little incident with amused detachment.

'Who is Mr Parker?' she enquired.

'Met him yesterday for the first time,' said Cairns, 'and really I can't say I want to know. Might be awkward. Must be in the stores or something. Looks to me like a cross between a mute and a parson. Bit of a worm, anyhow.'

'Oh, he didn't hurt my feelings,' remarked Victoria ; 'but some men never know what women have got on.' Cairns looked her over approvingly. Shoddy-looking mourning. Durzee made of course. But, Lord, what hands and eyes.

'I daresay not,' he said drily. 'I wish he'd keep away through. Let's walk up.'

He took a stride or two away from Alastair.
Victoria followed him. She was rather taken with
his rough simplicity, the comfort of his apparent
obtuseness. So like an uncle, she thought.

'Well, Mrs Fulton,' said Cairns, 'I suppose you're
glad to be here, as usual.'

'As usual?'

'Yes, as usual; people are always glad to be on
board. If they're going home, they're going home
and if they're going out they're thinking that it's
going to be full pay instead of half.'

'It hadn't struck me like that,' said Victoria with a
smile, 'though I suppose I am glad to go home.'

'Funny,' said the Major, 'I never found a country
like India to make people want to come to it and to
make them want to get out of it when they were
there. We had a sub once. You should have heard
him on the dead cities. Somewhere south east of
Hyderabad, he said. And native jewellery, and
fakirism, and all that. He's got a liver now and the
last I heard of him was that he put his shoulder out
at polo.'

Victoria looked out over the immense oily greenness
of the water. Far away on the skyline a twirling
wreath of smoke showed that some tramp steamer
was passing them unseen. The world was between
them; they were crawling on one side of the ball and
the tramp on the other, like flies on an orange. Was
that tramp, Bombay bound, carrying more than a
cargo of rolling stock? Perhaps the mate had
forgotten his B.S.A. fittings and was brooding, he
too, over the dead cities, somewhere south-east of
Hyderabad.

'No,' repeated Victoria slowly, 'it hadn't struck me
like that.'

Cairns looked at her curiously. He had heard of
Fulton and knew of the manner of his death. He
could not help thinking that she did not seem to

show many signs of a recent bereavement, but then she was well rid of Fulton. Of course there were other things too. Going back as the widow of an Indian officer was all very well if you could afford the luxury, but if you couldn't, well it couldn't be much catch. So, being thirty eight or so, he prudently directed the conversation towards the customary subjects discussed on board a trooper : the abominable accommodation and the appalling incompetency of the government with regard to the catering.

Victoria listened to him placidly. His ancient tittle-tattle had been made familiar to her by three years' association with his fellows, and she had learned that she need not say much, as his one wish was naturally to revile the authorities and all their work. But one item interested her.

' After all,' he said, ' I don't see why I should talk. I've had enough of it. I'm sending in my papers as soon as I've settled a small job at Perim. I'll get back to Aden and shake all that beastly Asiatic dust off my shoes.'

'Surely,' said Victoria, ' you're not going to leave the Service?' Her intonation implied that she was urging him not to commit suicide. Some women must pass twice under the yoke.

'Fed up. Simply fed up with it. Suppose I do waste another twenty years in India or Singapore or Hong Kong, how much forrarder am I? They'll retire me as a colonel or courtesy general and dump me into an England which doesn't care a hang about me with the remains of malaria, no digestion and no temper. I'll then while away my time watching the busses pass by from one of the windows of the Rag and give my daily opinion of the doings of Simla and the National Congress to men who will only listen to me so long as I stand them a whisky and soda.'

' It isn't alluring,' said Victoria, ' but it may not

be as bad as that. You can do marvels in India. My husband used to say that a man could hope for anything there.'

Cairns suppressed the obvious retort that Fulton's ideals did not seem to have materialised.

'No,' he said, 'I'm not ambitious. India's steam rollered all that. When I've done with my job at Perim, which won't be much more than a couple of months, I'm going home. Don't know that I'll do anything in particular. Farm a bit, perhaps, or have some chambers somewhere near St James' and dabble in balloons or motors. Some shooting too. All that sort of thing.'

'Perhaps you are right,' said Victoria after a pause. 'I suppose it's as well to do what one likes. Shall we join the others?'

CHAPTER III

LIFE on a trooper is not eventful. Victoria was not
so deeply absorbed in her mourning or in the pallid
literature borrowed from Molly as not to notice it.
Though she was not what is termed serious, the
perpetual quoits on the upper deck in company with
Alastair and his conversation limited by smiles, and
with Mr. Parker and his conversation limited by
uneasiness, palled about the second game. Bobby
too was a cypher. It was his fate to be known as
' Bobby,' a quantity of no importance. He belonged
to the modern school of squires of dames, ever ready
to fetch a handkerchief, to fish when he inwardly
wanted to sleep in a deck-chair or to talk when he
had a headache. Such men have their value as tame
cats and Victoria did not avoid his cheery neighbourhood. But he was summed up in the small fact
which she recalled with gentle amusement a long
time after : she had never known his name. For
her, as for the ship's company, he was ' Bobby,'
merely ' Bobby.'

The female section too could detain none but cats
and hens, as Victoria put it. She had moved too
long like a tiny satellite in the orbit of Mrs. Colonel
So-and-So to return to the little group which
slumbered all day by the funnel dreaming aloud the
petty happenings of Bombay. The heavy rains at
Chandraga, the simply awful things that had been said
about an A.D.C. and Mrs. Bryan, and the scandalous
way in which a Babu had been made a judge,

all this filled her with an extraordinary weariness. She felt, in the presence of these remains of her daily life, as she would when confronted for the third time with the cold leg of mutton.

True there was Cairns, a man right enough and jovial in spite of his cynical assumption that nothing was worth anything. He could produce passing fair aphorisms, throw doubts on the value of success and happiness. There was nothing, however, to hold on to. Victoria had not found in him a teacher or a helper. He was merely destructive of thought and epicurean in taste. Convinced that wine, woman and song were quite valueless things, he nevertheless knew the best Rüdesheimer and had an eye for the droop of Victoria's shoulders.

Cairns obviously liked Victoria. He did not shun his fellow passengers, for he considered that the dullest people are the most interesting, yet she could not help noticing from time to time that his eyes followed her round. He was a good big man and she knew that his thick hand, a little swollen and sunburnt would be a good thing to touch. But there was in him none of that subtle magnetism that grasps and holds. He was coarse, perhaps a little vulgar at heart.

Thus Victoria had roamed aimlessly over the ship, visiting even the bows where, everlastingly, a lascar seemed to brood in fixed attitudes as a Budh dreaming of Nirvana. She often wandered in the troop-deck filled with the womankind and children of the non-coms. Without disliking children she could find no attraction in these poor little faded things born to be scorched by the Indian sun. The women too, mostly yellow and faded, always recalled to her, so languid and tired were they, commonplace flowers, marigolds, drooping on their stems. Besides, the society of the upper deck found a replica on the troop deck, where it was occasionally a little shriller.

There too, she could catch snatches which told of the heavy rains of Chandraga, the goings on of Lance Corporal Maccaskie's wife and the disgrace of giving Babu clerks more than fifty rupees a month.

Perpetually the Indian ocean shimmered by, calm as the opaque eye of a shark, breaking at times into immense rollers that swelled hardly more than a woman's breast. And the days passed on.

They were nearing Aden, though nothing on the mauve horizon told of the outpost where the filth of the East begins to overwhelm the ugliness of the West. Victoria and Cairns were leaning on the starboard bulwark. She was looking vacuously into the greying sky, conscious that Cairns was watching her. She felt with extraordinary clearness that he was gazing as if spell-bound at the soft and regular rise and fall of her skin towards the coarse black openwork of her bodice. Far away in the twilight was something long and black, hardly more than a line vanishing towards the north.

'Araby,' said Cairns.

Victoria looked more intently. Far away, half veiled by the mists of night, unlit by the evening star, lay the coast. Araby, the land of manna and milk—of black-eyed women—of horses that champ strange bits. Here and there a blackened rock sprang up from the waste of sand and scrub. Its utter desolation awakened a sympathetic chord. It was lonely, as she was lonely. As the night swiftly rushed into the heavens, she let her arm rest against that of Cairns. Then his hand closed over hers. It was warm and hard ; something like a pale light of companionship struggled through the solitude of her soul.

They stood cold and silent while the night swallowed up the coast and all save here and there the foam tip of a wave. The man had put his arm round her and pressed her to him. She did not resist. The soft

B

wind playing in her hair carried a straying lock into
his eyes, half blinding him and making him catch his
breath, so redolent was it, not with the scent of flowers,
but of life, vigorous and rich in its thousand saps.
He drew her closer to him and pressed his lips on her
neck. Victoria did not resist.

From the forepeak swathed in darkness, came the
faint unearthly echoes of the stokers' song. There
were no fourths; the dominant and the subdominant
were absent. Strangely attuned to the western ear,
the sounds sometimes boomed, sometimes fell to a
whisper. The chant rose like incense into the heavens,
celebrating Durga, protector of the Motherland,
Lakshmi, bowered in the flower that in the water
grows. Cairns had drawn Victoria close against him.
He was stirred and shaken as never before. All
conspired against him, the night, the fancied scents
of Araby, the unresisting woman in his arms who
yielded him her lips with the passivity of weariness.
They did not think as they kissed, whether laying the
foundation of regret or snatching from the fleeting
hour a moment of thoughtless joy. Again a brass
drum boomed out beyond them, softly as if touched
by velvet hands. It carried the buzzing of bees, the
calls of corncrakes, in every tone the rich scents of
the jungle, where undergrowth rots in black water—
of perfumes that burn before the gods. Then the
night wind arose and swept away the crooning voices.

CHAPTER IV

VICTORIA stepped out on to the platform with a heart that bounded and yet shrank. Not even the first faint coming of the coastline had given her the almost physical shock that she experienced on this bare platform. Waterloo station lay around her in a pall of faint yellow mist that gripped and wrenched at her throat. Through the fog a thousand ungainly shapes of stairs and signals thrust themselves, some crude in their near blackness, others fainter in the distance. It might have been a dream scene but for the uproar that rose around her from the rumble of London, the voices of a great crowd. Yet all this violence of life, the darkness, the surge of men and women, all this told her that she was once more in the midst of things.

She found her belongings mechanically, fumblingly. She did not realise until then the bitterness that drove its iron into her soul. Already, when the troopship had entered the Channel she had felt a cruel pang when she realised that she must expect nothing and that nobody would greet her. She had fled from the circle near the funnel when the talk began to turn round London and waiting sisters and fathers, round the Lord Mayor's show, the play, the old fashioned Christmas. Now, as she struggled through the crowd that cried out and laughed excitedly and kissed, she knew her isolation was complete. There was nobody to meet her. The fog made her eyes smart, so they filled readily with tears.

As she sat in the cab, however, and there flashed
by her like beacons the lights of the stalls in the
Waterloo Road, the black and greasy pavement sown
with orange peel, she felt her heart beating furiously
with the excitement of home coming. She passed
the Thames flowing silently, swathed in its shroud of
mist. Then the blackness of St James's Park through
which her cab crawled timidly as if it feared things
that might lurk unknown in the fogbound thickets.

It was still in a state of feverish dreaming that
Victoria entered her room at Curran's Private Hotel,
otherwise known by a humble number in Seymour
Street. 'Curran's' is much in favour among Anglo-
Indians, as it is both central and cheap. It has
everything that distinguishes the English hotel which
has grown from a boarding-house into a superior
establishment where you may stay at so much a day.
The successful owner had bought up one after the
other three contiguous houses and had connected them
by means of a conservatory where there lived, among
much pampas grass, small ferns in pots shrouded in
pea-green paper and sickly plants to which no name
could be attached as they mostly suggested stewed
lettuce. It was impossible to walk in a straight line
from one end of the coalition of buildings to the other
without climbing and descending steps every one of
which proclaimed the fact that the leases of the houses
would soon fall in. From the three kitchens ascended
three smells of mutton. The three halls were strewn
with bicycles, gun cases in their last phase, sticks
decrepit or dandified. The three hat racks, all early
Victorian in their lines, bore a motley cargo. Dusty
bowlers hustled it with heather coloured caps and
top hats; one even bore a pith helmet and a clerical
atrocity.

Queer as Curran's is, it is comfortable enough.
Victoria looked round her room, tiny in length and
breadth, high however with all the dignity that befits

an odd corner left over by the Victorian builder. It was distinguished by its simplicity, for the walls bore nothing whatever beyond a restrained papering of brownish roses. A small black and gold bed, a wardrobe with a white handle, a washing stand with a marble top took up all the space left by the large tin trunk which contained most of Victoria's worldly goods. So this, thought Victoria, is the beginning. She pulled aside the curtain. Before her lay Seymour Street, where alone an eye of light shone faintly from the nearest lamp post. Through the fog came the warning noise of a lorry picking its way. It was cold, cold, all this, and lonely like an island.

Her meditations were disturbed by the maid who brought her hot water.

'My name is Carlotta,' said the girl complacently depositing the can upon the marble topped washstand.

'Yes?' said Victoria. 'You are a foreigner?'

'Yes. I am Italian. It is foggy,' replied the girl.

Victoria sighed. It was kind of the girl to make her feel at home, to smile at her with those flashing teeth so well set in her ugly little brown face. She went to the washstand and cried out in horror at her dirt and fog begrimed face, rimmed at the eyes, furrowed on the left by the course of that tear shed at Waterloo.

'Tell them downstairs I shan't be ready for half an hour,' she said; 'it'll take me about a week to get quite clean, I should say.'

Carlotta bared her white teeth again and withdrew gently as a cat, while Victoria courageously drenched her face and neck. The scents of England, already conjured up by the fog and the mutton, rose at her still more vividly from the warm water which inevitably exhales the traditional perfume of hot painted can.

Her dinner was a small affair but delightful. It was good to eat and drink once more things to which she had been accustomed for the first twenty years of her life. Her depression had vanished; she was merely hungry, and, like the healthy young animal she was, longing for a rare cut of roast beef, accompanied by the good old English potatoes boiled down to the consistency of flour and the flavour of nothing. Her companions were so normal that she could not help wondering, when her first hunger was sated and she was confronted with the apple tart of her fathers, whether she was not in the unchanging old board residence in Fulham where her mother had stayed with her whenever she came up to town, excited and conscious of being on the spree.

Two spinsters of no age discussed the fog. Both were immaculate and sat rigidly in correct attitudes facing their plates. Both talked quickly and continuously in soft but high tones. They passed one another the salt with the courtesy of abbés taking pinches of snuff. A young man from the Midlands explained to the owner of the clerical hat that under certain circumstances his food would cost him more. Near by a heavy man solemnly and steadily ate, wiping at times from his beard drops of gravy and of sauce, whilst his faded wife nibbled disconsolately tiny scraps of crust. These she daintily buttered, while her four lanky girls nudged and whispered.

Victoria did not stay in the conservatory after the important meal. As she passed through it, a mist of weariness gathering before her eyes, she had a vision of half a dozen men sleeping in cane chairs, or studying pink or white evening papers. The young man from the Midlands had captured another victim and was once more explaining that under certain circumstances his food would cost him more.

Victoria seemed to have reached the limits of physical endurance. She fumbled as she divested herself of her clothes; she could not even collect nough energy to wash. All the room seemed filled

with haze. Her tongue clove to her palate. Little
tingles in her eyelids crushed them together over
her pupils. She stumbled into her bed, mechanically
switching off the light by her bedside. In the very
act her arm lost its energy and she sank into a dream-
less sleep.

Next morning she breakfasted with good appetite.
The fog had almost entirely lifted and sunshine soft
as silver was filtering through the windows into the
little dining-room. Its mahoganous ugliness was
almost warmed into charm. The sideboard shone
dully through its covering of coarse net. Even the
stacked cruets remembered the days when they
cunningly blazed in a shop window. A pleasurable
feeling of excitement ran through Victoria's body,
for she was going to discover London, to have
adventures. As she closed the door behind her
with a definite little slam she felt like a buccaneer.

Buccaneering in the Edgware Road, even when it
is bathed in the morning sun, soon falls flat in
November. It came upon Victoria rather as a shock
that her Indian clothing was rather thin. As her
flying visits to town had only left in her mind a
very hazy picture of Regent Street it was quite unconsciously that she entered the emporium opposite. A
frigid young lady sacrificed for her benefit an abominable vicuna coat which, she said, fitted Victoria like
a glove. Victoria paid the twenty seven and six
with an admirable feeling of recklessness and left
the shop reflecting that she looked the complete
charwoman.

She turned into Hyde Park, where the gentle wind
was sorrowfully driving the brown and broken leaves
along the rough gravel. The thin tracery of the
trees imaged itself on the road like a giant cobweb.
Victoria looked for a moment towards the south
where the massive buildings rise, towards the east
where a cathedral thrusts into the sky a tower that

suspiciously recalls waterworks. She drank in the cold air with a gusto that can be understood by none save those who have learned to live in the floating moisture of the plains. She felt young and, in the sunshine, with her cheeks gaining colour as the wind whipped them, she looked in her long black coat and broad brimmed straw hat, like a quakeress in love.

As she walked down towards the Achilles statue the early morning panorama of London unfolded itself before her un-understanding eyes. Girls hurried by with their satchels towards the typewriting rooms of the west; they stole a look at Victoria's face but quickly turned away from her clothes. Now and then spruce young clerks walking to the Tube slackened their pace to look twice into her grey eyes; one or two looked back, not so much in the hope of an adventure, for time could not be snatched for Venus herself on the way to the office, as to see whether they could carry away with them the flattery of having been noticed.

In a sense that first day in London was for Victoria a day of revelations. Having despatched a telegram to her brother to announce her arrival she felt that the day was hers. Ted had not troubled to meet her either at Southampton or Waterloo: it was not likely that he had followed the sightings of her ship. The next day being a Saturday, however, he would probably come up from the Bedfordshire school where he proffered Latin to an ungrateful generation.

Victoria's excursions to London had been so few that she had but the faintest idea of where she was to go. Knowing, however, that one cannot lose oneself in London, she walked aimlessly towards the east. It was a voyage of discovery. Piccadilly, bathed in the pale sun, revealed itself as a land where luxury flows like rivers of milk. Victoria, being a true woman, could not pass a shop. Thus her progress was slow, so slow that when she found herself between the lions of Trafalgar Square she began to realise that she wanted her lunch.

The problem of food is cruel for all women who desire more than a bun. They risk either inattention or over attention, and if they follow other women, they almost invariably discover the cheap and bad. Victoria hesitated for a moment on the steps of an oyster shop, as nervous in the presence of her first plunge into freedom as a novice at the side door of a pawnbroker. A man passed by her into the oyster shop, smoking a pipe. She felt she would never dare to sit in a room where strange men smoked pipes. Thus she stood for a moment forlorn on the pavement, until a memory of the only decent grill in town, according to Bobby, passed through her mind.

A policeman sent her by bus to the New Gaiety, patronised by Bobby and his cronies. As Victoria went down the interminable underground staircase, and especially as she entered the enormous room where paper, carpets, and plate always seem new, her courage almost failed her. Indeed she looked round anxiously, half hoping that the anonymous Bobby might be revisiting his old haunts. But she was quite alone, and it was only by reminding herself that she must always be alone at meals now that she coerced herself into sitting down. She got through her meal with expedition. She felt frightfully small; the waiters were painfully courteous; a man laid aside his orange coloured newspaper, and embarrassed her with frequent side glances. She braced herself up however. 'I am training,' was her uppermost thought. She then wondered whether she ought to have come to the New Gaiety at all. Fortunately it was only at the very end of her lunch that Victoria realised she was the only woman sitting alone. After this discovery her nerve failed her. She got up hurriedly, and, in her confusion, omitted to tip the waiter. At the desk the last stone was heaped on the cairn of her discomfiture when the cashier politely returned to her a quarter rupee which she had given her thinking it was a sixpence.

With a sigh of satisfaction Victoria resumed her walk through London. She was a little tired already but she could think of nothing to do, nowhere to go to. She did not want to return to Curran's to sit in her box-like room, or to look at the two spinsters availing themselves of their holiday in town to play patience in the conservatory.

All the afternoon, therefore, Victoria saw the sights. Covent Garden repelled her by the massiveness of its food suggestion, and especially by the choking dirt of its lanes. After Covent Garden, Savoy court yard and its announcements of intellectual plays by unknown women. Then once more, drawn by its spaciousness guessed at through Spring Gardens, Victoria walked into Saint James's Park. She rested awhile upon a seat, watching the waterfowl strut and plume themselves, the pelicans flounder heavily in the mud. She was tired. The sun was setting early. The magic slowly faded from London; Buckingham Palace lost the fictitious grace that it has when set in a blue sky. Victoria shivered a little. She felt tired. She did not know where to go. She was alone. On the seat nearest to hers two lovers sat together, hand in hand. The man's face was almost hidden by his cap and by the blue puffs of his pipe; the girl's was averted towards the ground where, with the ferule of her umbrella, she lazily drew signs. There was no bitterness in this sight for Victoria. Her romance had come and gone so long ago that she looked quite casually at these wanderers in Arcadia. She only knew that she was alone and cold.

Victoria got up and walked out of the park. It was darkening, and little by little the lights of London were springing into life. By dint of many question-ings she managed to regain Oxford Street, that spinal column of London without which the stranger would be lost. Then her course was easy, and it was with a peculiar feeling of luxuriousness that she resigned herself to the motor bus that jolted and shook her tired body until she reached the Arch. More slowly, and with diminished optimism, she found her way up Edgware Road, where night was now falling. The emporium was dazzling with lights. Alone the public house rivalled it and thrust its glare through the settling mist. Victoria closed the door of Curran's. At once she re-entered its atmosphere; into the warm air rose the three smells of three legs of mutton.

CHAPTER V

'Mr Wren, ma'am.'

Victoria turned quickly to Carlotta. The girl's face was obtrusively demure. Some years at Curran's had not dulled in her the interest that any woman subtly feels in the meeting of the sexes.

'Ask him to come in here, Carlotta,' said Victoria. 'We shan't be disturbed, shall we?'

'Oh no! ma'am,' said Carlotta, with increasing demureness. 'There is nobody, nobody. I will show the young gentleman in.'

Victoria walked to the looking-glass which shyly peeped out from the back of the monumental side-board. She re-arranged her hair and hurriedly flicked some dust from the corners of her eyes. All this for Edward, but she had not seen him for three years. As she turned round she was confronted by her brother who had gently stolen into the dining-room. Edward's every movement was unobtrusive. He put one arm round her and kissed her cheek.

'How are you, Victoria?' he said, looking her in the eyes.

'Oh, I'm alright, Ted. I'm so glad to see you.' She was genuinely glad; it was so good to have belongings once again.

'Did you have a good passage?' asked Edward.

'Pretty good until we got to Ushant and then it did blow. I was glad to get home.'

'I'm very glad to see you,' said Edward, 'very glad.' His eyes fixed on the sideboard as if he were

mesmerised by the cruets. Victoria looked at him
critically. Three years had not made on him the
smallest impression. He was at twenty-eight what
he had been at twenty-five or for the matter of that
at eighteen. He was a tall slim figure with narrow
pointed shoulders and a slightly bowed back. His
face was pale without being unhealthy. There was
nothing in his countenance to arouse any particular
interest, for he had those average features that
commit no man either to coarseness or to intellectu-
ality. He showed no trace of the massiveness of his
sister's chin; his mouth too was looser and hung a
little open. Alone his eyes, richly grey, recalled his
relationship. Straggly fair hair fell across the left
side of his forehead. He peered through silver
rimmed spectacles as he nervously worried his watch
chain with both hands. Every movement exposed
the sharpness of his knees through his worn
trousers.

'Ted,' said Victoria, breaking in upon the silence,
'it was kind of you to come up at once.'

'Of course I'd come up at once. I couldn't leave
you here alone. It must be a big change after the
sunshine.'

'Yes,' said Victoria slowly, 'it is a big change.
Not only the sunshine. Other things, you know.'

Edward's hands played still more nervously with
his watch chain. He had not heard much of the
manner of Fulton's death. Victoria's serious face
encouraged him to believe that she might harrow
him with details, weep even. He feared any expression of feeling, not because he was hard but
because it was so difficult to know what to say. He
was neither hard nor soft; he was a schoolmaster
and could deal readily enough with the pangs of
Andromeda but what should he say to a live woman,
his sister too?

'I understand—I—you see, it's quite awful about Dick—' he stopped, lost, groping for the proper sentiment.

'Ted,' said Victoria, 'don't condole with me. I don't want to be unkind—if you knew everything—But there, I'd rather not tell you; poor Dicky's dead and I suppose it's wrong, but I can't be sorry.'

Edward looked at her with some disapproval. The marriage had not been a success, he knew that much, but she ought not to speak like that. He felt he ought to reprove her, but the difficulty of finding words stopped him.

'Have you made any plans?' he asked in his embarrassment, thus blundering into the subject he had intended to lead up to with infinite tact.

'Plans?' said Victoria. 'Well, not exactly. Of course I shall have to work; I thought you might help me perhaps.'

Edward looked at her again uneasily. She had sat down in an armchair by the side of the fire with her back to the light. In the penumbra her eyes came out like dark pools. A curl rippled over one of her ears. She looked so self-possessed that his embarrassment increased.

'Will you have to work?' he asked. The idea of his sister working filled him with vague annoyance.

'I don't quite see how I can help it,' said Victoria smiling. 'You see, I've got nothing, absolutely nothing. When I've spent the thirty pounds or so I've got, I must either earn my own living or go into the workhouse.' She spoke lightly, but she was conscious of a peculiar sinking.

'I thought you might come back with me,' said Edward, '. . . and stay with me a little . . . and look round.'

'Ted, it's awfully kind of you, but I'm not going to let you saddle yourself with me. I can't be your housekeeper; oh! it would never do. And don't you think

I am more likely to get something to do here than down in Bedfordshire ? '

' I do want you to come back with me,' said Edward hesitatingly. ' I don't think you ought to be alone here. And perhaps I could find you something in a family at Cray or thereabouts. I could ask the vicar.'

Victoria shuddered. It had never struck her that employment might be difficult to find or uncongenial when one found it. The words 'vicar' and 'Cray' suggested something like domestic service without its rights, gentility without its privileges.

' Ted,' she said gravely, ' you're awfully good to me, but I'd rather stay here. I'm sure I could find something to do.' Edward's thoughts naturally came back to his own profession.

' I'll ask the Head,' he said with the first flash of animation he had shown since he entered the room. To ask the Head was to go to the source of all knowledge. ' Perhaps he knows a school. Of course your French is pretty good, isn't it ? '

' Ted, Ted, you do forget things,' said Victoria, laughing. ' Don't you remember the mater insisting on my ṭaking German because so few girls did ? Why, it was the only original thing she ever did in her life, poor dear ! '

' But nobody wants German, for girls that is,' replied Edward miserably.

' Very well then,' said Victoria, ' I won't teach ; that's all. I must do something else.'

Edward walked up and down nervously, pushing back his thin fair hair with one hand, and with the other nervously tugging at his watch chain.

' Don't worry yourself, Ted,' said Victoria. ' Something will turn up. Besides there's no hurry. Why, I can live two or three months on my money, can't I ? '

' I suppose you can,' said Edward gloomily, ' but what will you do afterwards ? '

'Earn some more,' said Victoria. 'Now Ted, you haven't seen me for three years. Don't let us worry. Think things over when you get back to Cray and write to me. You won't go back until to-morrow, will you?'

'I'm sorry,' said Edward, 'but I didn't think you'd be back this week. I shall be in charge to-morrow. Why don't you come down?'

'Ted, Ted, how can you suggest that I should spend my poor little fortune in railway fares! Well, if you can't stay, you can't. But I'll tell you what you can do. I can't go on paying two and a half guineas a week here; I must get some rooms. You lived here when you taught at that school in the city, didn't you? Well then, you must know all about it: we'll go house-hunting.'

Edward looked at her dubiously. He disliked the idea of Victoria in rooms almost as much as Victoria at Curran's. It offended some vague notions of propriety. However her suggestion would give him time to think. Perhaps she was right.

'Of course, I'll be glad to help,' he said, 'I don't know much about it; I used to live in Gower Street.' A faint flush of reminiscent excitement rose to his cheeks. Gower Street, by the side of Cray and Lymptom, had been almost adventurous.

'Very well then,' said Victoria, 'we shall go to Gower Street first. Just wait till I put on my hat.'

She ran upstairs, not exactly light of heart, but pleased with the idea of house-hunting. There's romance in all seeking, even if the treasure is to be found in a Bloomsbury lodging-house.

The ride on the top of the motor bus was exhilarating. The pale sun of November was lighting up the streets with the almost mystic whiteness of the footlights. Edward said nothing, for his memories of London were stale and he did not feel secure enough to point out the Church of the Deaf and

Dumb, nor had he ever known his London well
enough to be able to pronounce judgment on the
shops. Besides, Victoria was too much absorbed in
gazing at London rolling and swirling beneath her,
belching out its crowds of workers and pleasure
seekers from every tube and main street. At every
shop the omnibus seemed surrounded by a swarm of
angry bees. Victoria watched them struggle with
spirit still unspoiled, wondering at the determination
on the faces of the men, at the bitterness painted on
the sharp features of the women as they savagely
thrust one another aside and, dishevelled and dusty,
successively conquered their seats. All this, the
constant surge of horse and mechanical conveyances,
the shrill cries of the newsboys flashing pink papers
like *chulos* at an angry bull, the roar of the town, made
Victoria understand the city. Something like fear
of this strong restless people crept into her as she
began to have a dim perception that she too would
have to fight. She was young, however, and the
feeling was not unpleasant. Her nerves tingled a
little as she thought of the struggle to come and the
inevitable victory at the end.

Victoria's spirits had not subsided even when she
entered Gower Street. Its immensity, its interminable length frightened her a little. The contrast
between it, so quiet, dignified and dull, and the
inferno she had just left behind her impressed her
with a sense of security. Its houses, however, seemed
so high and dirty that she wondered, looking at its
thousand windows, whether human beings could be
cooped up thus and yet retain their humanity.

Here Edward was a little more in his element.
With a degree of animation he pointed to the staid
beauty of Bedford Square. He demanded admiration
like a native guiding a stranger in his own town.
Victoria watched him curiously. He was a good
fellow but it was odd to hear him raise his voice and

c

to see him point with his stick. He had always been quiet, so she had not expected him to show as much interest as he did in his old surroundings.

'I suppose you had a good time when you were here?' she said.

'Nothing special. I was too busy at the school,' he replied. 'But, of course, you know, one does things in London. It's not very lively at Cray.'

'Wouldn't you like to leave Cray,' she said, 'and come back?'

Edward paused nervously. London frightened him a little and the idea of leaving Cray suddenly thrust upon him froze him to the bone. It was not Cray he loved, but Cray meant a life passing gently away by the side of a few beloved books. Though he had never realised that hedgerows flower in the spring and that trees redden to gold and copper in the autumn, the country had taken upon him so great a hold that even the thought of leaving it was pain.

'Oh! no,' he said hurriedly. 'I couldn't leave Cray. I couldn't live here, it's too noisy. There are my old rooms, there, the house with the torch extinguishers.'

Victoria looked at him again. What curious tricks does nature play and how strangely she pleases to distort her own work! Then she looked at the house with the extinguishers. Clearly it would be impossible, but for those aristocratic remains, to distinguish it from among half a dozen of its fellows. It was a house, that was all. It was faced in dirty brick, parted at every floor by stone work. A portico, rising over six stone steps, protected a door painted brown and bearing a brass knocker. It had windows, an area, bells. It was impossible to find in it an individual detail to remember.

But Edward was talking almost excitedly for him. 'See there,' he said, 'those are my old rooms,' pointing indefinitely at the frontage. 'They were quite decent,

you know. Wonder whether they're let. You could
have them.' He looked almost sentimentally at the
home of the Wrens.

'Why not ring and ask?' said Victoria, whose
resourcefulness equalled that of Mr Dick.

Edward took another loving look at the familiar
window, strode up the steps, followed by Victoria.

There were several bells. 'Curious,' he said, 'she
must have let it out in floors ; Wakefield and Grindlay,
don't know them. Seymour? It's Mrs Brumfit's
house : Oh! here it is.' He pressed a bell marked
'House.' Victoria heard with a curious sensation of
unexpectedness the sudden shrill sound of the electric
bell.

After an interminable interval, during which
Edward's hands nervously played, the door opened.
A young girl stood on the threshold. She wore a
red cloth blouse, a black skirt, and an unspeakably
dirty apron half loose round her waist. Her hair
was tightly done up in curlers in expectation of
Sunday.

'Mrs Brumfit,' said Edward, 'is she in?'

''oo?' said the girl.

'Mrs Brumfit, the landlady,' said Edward.

'Don't know 'er, try next 'ouse.' The girl tried to
shut the door.

'You don't understand,' cried Edward, stopping
the door with his hand. 'I used to live here.'

'Well, wot do yer want?' replied the girl. 'Can't
'elp that, can I? There ain't no Mrs Brumfit 'ere.
Only them there.' She pointed at the bells. 'Nobody but them and mother. She's the 'ousekeeper.
If yer mean the old woman as was 'ere when they
turned the 'ouse into flats, she's dead.'

Edward stepped back. The girl shut the door
with a slam. He stood as if petrified. Victoria
looked at him with amusement in her eyes, listening
to the echoes of the girl's voice singing more and

more faintly some catchy tune as she descended into the basement.

'Dead,' said Edward, 'can it be possible—?' He looked like a plant torn up by the roots. He had jumped on the old ground and it had given way.

'My dear Ted,' said Victoria gently, 'things change, you see.' Slowly they went down the steps of the house. Victoria did not speak, for a strange mixture of pity and disdain was in her. She quite understood that a tie had been severed and that the death of his old landlady meant for Edward that the past which he had vaguely loved had died with her. He was one of those amorphous creatures whose life is so interwoven with that of their fellows that any death throws it into disarray. She let him brood over his lost memories until they reached Bedford Square.

'But Ted,' she broke in, 'where am I to go?'

Edward looked at her as if dazed. Clearly he had not foreseen that Mrs Brumfit was not an institution.

'Go?' he said, 'I don't know.'

'Don't you know any other lodgings?' asked Victoria. 'Gower Street seems full of them.'

'Oh! no,' said Edward quickly, 'we don't know what sort of places they are. You couldn't go there.'

'But where am I to go then?' Victoria persisted. Edward was silent. 'It seems to me,' his sister went on, 'that I shall have to risk it. After all, they won't murder me and they can't rob me of much.'

'Please don't talk like that,' said Edward stiffly. He did not like this association of ideas.

'Well I must find some lodgings,' said Victoria, a little irritably. 'In that case I may as well look round near Curran's. I don't like this street much.'

In default of an alternative, Edward looked sulky. Victoria felt remorseful; she knew that Gower Street must have become for her brother the traveller's Mecca and that he was vaguely afraid of the West End.

'Never mind, dear,' she went on more gently,
'don't worry about lodgings any more. Do you know
what you're going to do? you're going to take me to
tea in some nice place and then I'll go with you to
St Pancras; that's the station you said you were
going back by, isn't it? and you'll put me in a bus
and I'll go home. Now, come along, it's past five
and I'm dying for some tea.'

As Victoria stood, an hour later, just outside the
station in which expires the spirit of Constantine the
Great, she could not help feeling relieved. As she
stood there, so self-possessed, seeing so clearly the
busy world, she wondered why she had been given
a broken reed to lean upon. Where had her brother
left his virility? Had it been sapped by years of
self-restraint? Had the formidable code of pretence,
the daily affectation of dignity, the perpetual giving
of good examples, reduced him to this shred of
humanity, so timid, so resourceless? As she sped
home in the tube into which she had been directed
by a policeman, she vainly turned over the problem.

Fortunately Victoria was young. As she laid her
head on the pillow, conscious of the coming of Sunday,
when nothing could be done, visions of things she
could do obsessed her. There were lodgings to find,
nice, clean, cheap lodgings, with a dear old landlady
and trees outside the window, in a pretty old-fashioned
house, very very quiet and quite near all the tubes.
She nursed the ideal for a time. Then she thought
of careers. She would read all the advertisements
and pick out the nicest work. Perhaps she could be
a housekeeper. Or a secretary. On reflection, a
secretary would be better. It might be so interesting.
Fancy being secretary to a member of Parliament.
Or to a famous author.

She too might write.

Her dreams were pleasant.

CHAPTER VI

A WEEK had elapsed and Victoria was beginning to feel the strain. She looked out from the window into the little street where fine rain fell gently as if it had decided to do so for ever. It was deserted, save by a cat who shivered and crouched under the archway of the mews. Sometimes a horse stirred. Through the open window the hot alcaline smell of the animals filtered slowly.

Victoria had found her lodgings. They were not quite the ideal, but she had not seen the ideal and this little den in Portsea Place was not without its charms. Her room, for the 'rooms' had turned from the plural into the singular, was comfortable enough. It occupied the front of the second floor in a small house. It had two windows, from which, by craning out a little, the trees of Connaught Square could be seen standing out like black skeletons against a white house. Opposite was the archway of the mews out of which came most of the traffic of the street. Under it too was the mart where the landladies who have invaded the little street exchange notes on their lodgers and boast of their ailments.

Victoria inspected her domain. She had a very big bed, a little inclined to creak; she had a table on a pedestal split so cunningly at the base that she was always table-conscious when she sat by it; she had a mahogany wash-stand, also on the triangular pedestal loved by the pre-Morrisites, enriched by a white marble top and splasher. A large armchair, smooth and rather treacherous, a small mahogany chest of drawers, every drawer of which took a minute to pull out, some chairs of no importance, completed her furniture. The carpet had been of all colours and was now of none. The tablecloth was blue serge and would have been serviceabe if it had not contracted the habit of sliding off the mahogany table whenever it was touched. Ugly as it was in every detail, Victoria could not help thinking the room comfortable ; its light paper saved it and it was not over-loaded with pictures. It had escaped with one text and the 'Sailor's Homecoming.' Besides it was restrained in colour and solid : it was comfortable like roast beef and boiled potatoes.

Victoria looked at all these things, at her few scattered books, the picture of Dick and of a group of school friends, at some of her boots piled in a corner. Then she listened and heard nothing. Once more she was struck by the emptiness, the darkness around her. She was alone. She had been alone a whole week, hardly knowing what to do. The excitement of choosing lodgings over, she had found time hang heavy on her hands. She had interminably walked in London, gazed at shop windows, read hundreds of imbecile picture postcards on bookstalls, gone continually to many places in omnibuses. She had stumbled upon South Kensington and wandered in its catacombs of stone and brick. She had discovered Hampstead, lost herself horribly near Albany Street ; she had even unexpectedly landed in the City where rushing mobs had hustled and battered her.

Faithful to her resolve she had sedulously read the morning papers and applied for several posts as housekeeper without receiving any answers. She had realised that answering advertisements must be an art and had become quite conscious that employment was not so easy to find as she thought. Nobody seemed to want secretaries, except the limited

companies, about which she was not quite clear. As
these mostly required the investment of a hundred
pounds or more she had not followed them up.

She paced up and down in her room. The afternoon was wearing. Soon the man downstairs would
come back and slam the door. A little later the
young lady in the City would gently enter the room
behind hers and, after washing in an unobtrusive
manner, would discreetly leave for an hour. Meanwhile nothing broke the silence, except the postman's
knock coming nearer and nearer along Portsea Place.
It fell unheeded even on her own front door, for
Victoria's ears were already attuned to the sound. It
meant nothing.

She walked up and down nervously. She looked
at herself in the glass. She was pretty she thought,
with her creamy skin and thick hair; her eyes too
were good; what a pity her chin was so thick. That's
why Dicky used to call her 'Towzer.' Poor old
Dicky!

Shuffling footsteps rose up the stairs. Then a
knock. At Victoria's invitation, a woman entered.
It was Mrs Bell, the landlady.

'Why, ma'am, you're sitting in the dark! Let me
light the lamp,' cried Mrs Bell, producing a large
wooden box from a capacious front pocket. She lit
the lamp and a yellow glow filled the room, except
the corners which remained in darkness.

'Here's a letter for you, ma'am,' said Mrs Bell
holding it out. As Victoria took it, Mrs Bell beamed
on her approvingly. She liked her new lodger. She
had already informed the gathering under the archway that she was a real lady. She had a leaning for
real ladies, having been a parlourmaid previous to
marrying a butler and eking out his income by
letting rooms.

'Thank you, Mrs Bell,' said Victoria, 'it was kind
of you to come up.'

'Oh! ma'am, no trouble I can assure you,' said Mrs Bell, with a mixture of respect and patronage. She wanted to be kind to her lodger, but she found a difficulty in being kind to so real a lady.

Victoria saw the letter was from Edward and opened it hurriedly. Mrs Bell hesitated, looking with her black dress, clean face and grey hair, the picture of the respectable maid. Then she turned and struggled out on her worn shoes, the one blot on her neatness. Victoria read the letter, bending perilously over the lamp which smoked like a funnel. The letter was quite short; it ran:

My dear Victoria,—I am sorry I could not write before now, but I wanted to have some news to give you. I am glad to say that I have been able to interest the vicar on your behalf. He informs me that if you will call at once on Lady Rockham, 7a Queen's Gate, South Kensington, S.W., she may be in a position to find you a post in a family of standing. He tells me she is most capable and kind. He is writing to her. I shall come to London and see you soon.—Yours affectionately,

EDWARD.'

Victoria fingered the letter lovingly: Perhaps she was going to have a chance after all. It was good to have something to do. Indeed it seemed almost too good to be true; she had vaguely resigned herself to unemployment. Of course something would ultimately turn up, but the what and when and how thereof were dangerously dim. She hardly cared to face these ideas; indeed she dismissed them when they occurred to her with a mixture of depression and optimism. Now, however, she was buoyant again. The family of standing would probably pay well and demand little. It would mean the theatres, the shops, flowers, the latest novels, no end of nice things. A little work too, of course, driving in the Park with a dear dowager with the most lovely white hair.

She ate an excellent and comparatively expensive dinner in an Oxford Street restaurant and went to bed early for the express purpose of making plans until she fell asleep. She was still buoyant in the morning. Connaught Square looked its best and even South Kensington's stony face melted into smiles when it caught sight of her. Lady Rockham's was a mighty house, the very house for a family of standing.

Victoria walked up the four steep steps of the house where something of her fate was to be decided. She hesitated for an instant and then, being healthily inclined to take plunges, pulled the bell with a little more vigour than was in her heart. It echoed tremendously. The quietude of Queen's Gate stretching apparently for miles towards the south, increased the terrifying noise. Victoria's anticipations were half pleasureable, half fearsome; she felt on the brink of an adventure and recalled the tremor with which she had entered the New Gaiety for the first time. Measured steps came nearer and nearer from the inside of the house; a shape silhouetted itself vaguely on the stained glass of the door.

She mustered sufficient coolness to tell the butler that she wished to see Lady Rockham, who was probably expecting her. As the large and solid man preceded her along an interminable hall, she felt rather than saw the thick Persian rug stretching along the crude mosaic of the floor, the red paper on the walls almost entirely hidden by exceedingly large and new pictures. Over her head a ponderous iron chandelier carrying many electric lamps blotted out most of the staircase.

For some minutes she waited in the dining-room into which she had been shown; for the butler was not at all certain, from a look at the visitor's mourning, that she was quite entitled to the boudoir. Victoria's square chin and steady eyes saved her, however, from

having to accommodate her spine to the exceeding
perpendicularity of the high-backed chairs in the hall.
The dining-room, ridiculous thought, reminded her
of Curran's. In every particular it seemed the same.
There was the large table with the thick cloth of
indefinite design and colour. The sideboard too was
there, larger and richer perhaps, of Spanish mahogany
not an inch of which was left bare of garlands of
flowers or archangelic faces. It carried Curran's
looking-glass; Curran's cruets were replaced by a
number of cups which proclaimed that Charles
Rockham had once won the Junior Sculls, and more
recently, the spring handicap of the Kidderwick Golf
Club. The walls were red as in the hall and profusely decorated with large pictures representing
various generations having tea in old English gardens,
decorously garbed Roman ladies basking by the side
of marble basins, and such like subjects. Twelve
chairs, all high backed and heavily groined, were
ranged round the walls, with the exception of a
large carving chair, standing at the head of the table,
awaiting one who was clearly the head of a household.
Victoria was looking pensively at the large black
marble clock representing the temple in which the
Lares and Penates of South Kensington usually dwell,
when the door opened and a vigorous rustle entered
the room.

'I am very glad to see you, Mrs Fulton,' remarked
the owner of the rustle. 'I have just received a
letter from Mr Meaker, the vicar of Cray. A most
excellent man. I am sure we can do something for
you. Something quite nice.'

Victoria looked at Lady Rockham with shyness and
surprise. Never had she seen anything so majestic.
Lady Rockham had but lately attained her ladyhood
by marrying a knight bachelor whose name was a
household word in the wood-paving world. She felt
at peace with the universe. Her large silk clad

person was redolent with content. She did not
vulgarly beam. She merely was. On her capacious
bosom large brooches rose and fell rhythmically.
Her face was round and smooth as her voice. Her
eyes were almost severely healthy.

'I am sure it is very kind of you,' said Victoria.
'I don't know anybody in London, you see.'

'That will not matter; that will not matter at all,'
said Lady Rockham. 'Some people prefer those whose
connections live in the country, yes, absolutely
prefer them: Why, friends come to me every day,
and they are clamouring for country girls, absolutely
clamouring. I do hope you are not too particular.
For things are difficult in London. So very
difficult.'

'Yes, I know,' murmured Victoria, thinking of her
unanswered applications. 'But I'm not particular at
all. If you can find me anything to do, Lady
Rockham, I should be so grateful.'

'Of course, of course. Now let me see. A young
friend of mine has just started a poultry farm in
Dorset. She is doing very well. Oh! very well. Of
course you want a little capital. But such a very
nice occupation for a young woman. The capital is
often the difficulty. Perhaps you would not be prepared to invest much?'

'No, I'm afraid I couldn't,' faltered Victoria,
wondering at what figure capital began.

'No, no, quite right,' purred Lady Rockham, 'I
can see you are quite sensible. It is a little risky too.
Yet my young friend is doing well, very well, indeed.
Her sister is in Johannesburg. She went out as a
governess and now she is married to a mine manager.
There are so few girls in the country. Oh! he is
quite a nice man, a little rough, I should say, but
quite suitable.'

Victoria wondered for a moment whether her Lady-
ship was going to suggest sending her out to Johan-

nesburg to marry a mine manager, but the Presence resumed.

'No doubt you would rather stay in London. Things are a little difficult here, but very pleasant, very pleasant indeed.'

'I don't mind things being difficult,' Victoria broke in, mustering a little courage. 'I must earn my own living and I don't mind what I do ; I'd be a nursery governess, or a housekeeper, or companion. I haven't got any degrees, I couldn't quite be a governess, but I'd try anything.'

'Certainly, certainly, I'm sure we will find something very nice for you. I can't think of anybody just now but leave me your address. I'll let you know as soon as I hear of anything.' Lady Rockham gently crossed her hands over her waistband and benevolently smiled at her protégée.

Victoria wrote down her address and listened patiently to Lady Rockham who discoursed at length on the imperfections of the weather, the noisiness of London streets and the prowess of Charless Rockham on the Kidderwick links. She felt conscious of having to return thanks for what she was about to receive.

Lady Rockham's kindness persisted up to the door to which she showed Victoria. She dismissed her with the Parthian shot that 'they would find something for her, something quite nice.'

Victoria walked away ; cold gusts of wind struck her, chilling her to the bone, catching and furling her skirts about her. She felt at the same time cheered and depressed. The interview had been inconclusive. However, as she walked over the Serpentine bridge, under which the wind was angrily ruffling the black water, a great wave of optimism came over her ; for it was late, and she remembered that in the Edgware Road, there was a small Italian restaurant where she was about to lunch.

It was well for Victoria that she was an optimist and
a good sleeper, for November had waned into December
before anything happened to disturb the tenor of her
life. For a whole fortnight she had heard nothing
from Lady Rockham or from Edward. She had
written to Molly but had received no answer. All
day long the knocker fell with brutal emphasis upon
the doors of Portsea Place and brought her nothing.
She did not think much or hope much. She did
nothing and spent little. Her only companion was
Mrs Bell, who still hovered round her mysterious
lodger, so ladylike and so quiet.

She passed hours sometimes at the window watching the stream of life in Portsea Place. The stream
did not flow very swiftly; its principal eddies
vanished by midday with the milkman and the
butcher. The postman recurred more often but he
did not count. Now and then the policeman passed
and spied suspiciously into the archway where the
landladies no longer met. Cabs trotted into it now
and then to change horses.

Victoria watched alone. Beyond Mrs Bell, she
seemed to know nobody. The young man downstairs
continued to be invisible, and contented himself with
slamming the door. The young lady in the back room
continued to wash discreetly and to snore gently at
night. Sometimes Victoria ventured abroad to be
bitten by the blast. Sometimes she strayed over the
town in the intervals of food. She had to exercise
caution in this, for an aspect of the lodging house
fire had only lately dawned upon her. If she did not
order it at all she was met on the threshold by darkness and cold; if she ordered it for a given time she
was so often late that she returned to find it dead or
kept up wastefully at the rate of sixpence a scuttle.
This trouble was chronic; on bitter days it seemed to
dog her footsteps.

She had almost grown accustomed to loneliness.

Alone she watched at her window or paced the streets. She had established a quasi-right to a certain seat at the Italian restaurant where the waiters had ceased to speculate as to who she was. The demoralisation of unemployment was upon her. She did not cast up her accounts ; she rose late, made no plans. She slept and ate, careless of the morrow.

It was in the midst of this slow settling into despond that a short note from Lady Rockham arrived like a boomshell. It asked her to call on a Mrs Holt who lived in Finchley Road. It appeared that Mrs Holt was in need of a companion as her husband was often away. Victoria was shaken out of her torpor. In a trice her optimism crushed out of sight the flat thoughts of aimless days. She feverishly dressed for the occasion. She debated whether she would have time to insert a new white frill into the neck of a black blouse. Heedless of expenditure she spent two and eleven pence on new black gloves, and twopence on the services of a shoeblack who whistled cheerful tunes, and smiled on the coppers. Victoria sallied out to certain victory. The wind was blowing balmier. A fitful gleam of sunshine lit up and reddened the pile of tangerines in a shop window.

CHAPTER VII

'I'm very sorry you can't come,' said Mrs Holt. 'Last Sunday, Mr Baker was so nice. I never heard anything so interesting as his sermon on the personal devil. I was quite frightened. At least I would have been if he had said all that at Bethlehem. You know, when we were at Rawsley we had such nice lantern lectures. I do miss them.'

Victoria looked up with a smile at the kindly red face. 'I'm so sorry,' she said, 'I've got such a headache. Perhaps it'll pass over if I go for a little walk while you are at Church.' She was not unconscious, as she said this, of the subtle flattery that the use of the word 'church' implies when used to people who dare not leave their chapel.

'Do, Victoria, I'm sure it will do you good,' said Mrs Holt, kindly. 'If the sun keeps on, we'll go to the Zoo this afternoon. I do like to see the children in the monkey house.'

'I'm sure I shall be glad to go,' said Victoria quietly. 'It's very kind of you to take me.'

'Nonsense, my dear,' replied Mrs Holt, gently beaming. 'You are like the sunshine, you know Dear me! I don't know what I should have done if I hadn't found you. You can't imagine the woman who was here before you. She was the daughter of a clergyman, and I did get so tired of hearing how they lost their money. But, there, I'm worrying you when you've got a headache. I do wish you'd try Dr Eberman's pills. All the papers are simply full

of advertisements about them. And these German
doctors are so clever. Oh, I shall be so late.'

Victoria assured her that she was sure her head
would be better by dinner time. Mrs Holt fussed
about the room for a moment, anxiously tested the
possible dustiness of a bracket, pulled the curtains
and picked up the Sunday papers from the floor.
She then collected a small canvas bag decorated with
a rainbow parrot, a hymn and service book, her
spectacle case, several unnecessary articles which
happened to be about and left the room with the
characteristic rustle which pervades the black silk
dresses of well-to-do Rawsley dames.

Victoria sat back in the large leather armchair.
Her head was not very bad but she felt just enough
in her temples a tiny passing twinge to shirk chapel
without qualms. She toyed with a broken backed
copy of *Charlton on Book-Keeping* which lay in her
lap. It was a curious fate that had landed her into
Charlton's epoch making work. Mrs Holt, that prince
of good fellows, had a genius for saving pennies and
had been trained in the school of a Midland household, but the fortunes of her husband had left her
feebly struggling in a backwash of pounds. So
much had this been the case that Mr Holt had
discovered joyfully that he had at last in his house a
woman who could bring herself to passing an account
for twenty pounds for stabling. Little by little
Victoria had established her position. She was
Mrs Holt's necessary companion and factotum. She
could apparently do anything and do it well; she
could even tackle such intricate tasks as checking
washing or understanding Bradshaw. She was
always ready and always bright. She had an
unerring eye for a good quality of velvet; she could
time the carriage to a nicety for the Albert Hall
concert. Mrs Holt felt that without this pleasant
and competent young woman she would be quite lost.

D

Mr Holt, too, after inspecting Victoria grimly every day for an entire month, had decided that she would do and had lent her the work on book-keeping, hoping that she would be able to keep the house accounts. In three months he had not addressed her twenty times beyond wishing her good morning and good night. He had but reluctantly left Rawsley and his beloved cement works to superintend his ever growing London business. He was a little suspicious of Victoria's easy manners; suspicious of her intentions, too, as the northerner is wont to be. Yet he grudgingly admitted that she was level headed, which was 'more than Maria or his fool of a son would ever be.'

Victoria thought for a moment of Holt, the book-keeping, the falling due of insurance premiums; then of Mrs Holt who had just stepped into her carriage which was slowly proceeding down the drive, crunching into the hard gravel. A gleam of sunshine fitfully lit up the polished panels of the clumsy barouche as it vanished through the gate.

This then was her life. It might well have been worse. Mr Holt sometimes let a rough kindness appear through an exterior as hard as his own cement. Mrs Holt, stout, comfortable and good-tempered, quite incompetent when it came to con-trolling a house in the Finchley Road, was not of the termagent type that Victoria had expected when she became a companion. Her nature, peaceful as that of a mollusc, was kind and had but one out-standing feature; her passionate devotion to her son Jack.

Victoria thought that she might well be content to pass the remainder of her days among these good folk. From the bottom of her heart mild discontent rose every now and then. It was a little dull. Tuesday was like Monday and probably like the Tuesday after next. The glories of the town, which

she had caught sight of during her wanderings,
before she floated into the still waters of the Finchley
Road, haunted her at times. The motor buses too,
which perpetually carried couples to the theatre, the
crowds in Regent Street making for the tea-shops,
while the barouche trotted sedately up the hill, all
this life and adventure were closed off.

Victoria was not unhappy. She drifted in that
singular psychological region where the greatest
possible pain is not suffering and where the acme
of possible pleasure is not joy. She did not realise
that this negative condition was almost happiness,
and yet did not precisely repine. The romance of
her life, born at Lympton, now slept under the
tamarinds. The stupefaction of the search for work,
the hopes and fears of December, all that lay far
away in those dark chambers of the brain into which
memory cannot force a way but swoons on the
threshold.

Yes, she was happy enough. Her eyes, casting
through the bay window over the evergreens, trimly
stationed and dusty, strayed over the low wall. On
the other side of the road stood another house, low
and solid as this one, beautiful though ugly in its
strength and worth. It is not the house you live in
that matters, thought Victoria, unconsciously committing plagiarism, but the house opposite. The
house she lived in was well enough. Its inhabitants
were kind, the servants respectful, even the mongrel
Manchester terrier with the melancholy eyes of some
collie ancestor did not gnaw her boots.

She let her hands fall into her lap and, for a minute,
sat staring into space, seeing with extraordinary
lucidity those things to come which a movement
dispels and swathes with the dense fog of forgetful-
ness. With terrible clarity she saw the life of the
last three months and the life to come, as it was in
the beginning ever to be.

The door opened softly. Before she had time to turn round two hands were clapped over her eyes. She struggled to free herself, but the hands grew more insistent and two thumbs softly touched her cheeks.

'Dimple, dimple,' said a voice, while one of the thumbs gently dwelled near the corner of her mouth.

Victoria struggled to her feet, a little flushed, a strand of hair flying over her left ear.

'Mr Jack,' she said rather curtly, 'I don't like that. You know you mustn't do that. It's not fair. I really don't like it.' She was angry; her nostrils opened and shut quickly; she glared at the good looking boy before her.

'Naughty temper,' he remarked, quite unruffled. 'You'll take a fit one of these days, Vicky, if you don't look out.'

'Very likely if you give me starts like that. Not that I mind that so much, but really it's not nice of you. You know you wouldn't do that if your mother was looking.'

'Course I wouldn't,' said Jack, 'the old mater's such a back number, you know.'

'Then,' replied Victoria with much dignity, 'you ought not to do things when we're alone which you wouldn't do before her.'

'Oh Lord! morals again,' groaned the youth. 'You are rough on me, Vicky.'

'And you mustn't call me Vicky,' said Victoria. 'I don't say I mind, but it isn't the thing. If anybody heard you I don't know what they'd think.'

'Who cares!' said Jack in his most dare devil style, putting his hand on the back of hers and stroking it softly. Victoria snatched her hand away and went to the window, where she seemed absorbed in the contemplation of the evergreens. Jack looked a little nonplussed. He was an attractive youth and looked about twenty. He had the fresh complexion

and blue eyes of his father but differed from him by
a measure of delicacy. His tall body was a little
bent; his face was all pinks and whites set off by the
blackness of his straight hair. He well deserved his
school nickname of Kathleen Mavourneen. His long
thin hands, which would have been aristocratic but
for the slight thickness of the joints, branded him a
poet. He was not happy in the cement business.

Jack stepped up to the window. 'Sorry,' he said,
as humbly as possible. Victoria did not move.

'Won't never do it again,' he said, pouting like a
scolded child.

'It's no good,' answered Victoria, 'I'm not going to
make it up.'

'I shall go and drown myself in the Regent Canal,'
said Jack dolefully.

'I'd rather you went for a walk along the banks,'
said Victoria.

'I will if you'll come too,' answered Jack.

'No, I'm not going out. I've got a headache.
Look here, I'll forgive you on condition that you
go out now and if you'll do that perhaps you can
come with your mother and me to the Zoo this
afternoon.'

'All right then,' grumbled the culprit, 'you're
rather hard on me. Always knew you didn't like
me. Sorry.'

Victoria looked out again. A minute later Jack
came out of the house and, pausing before the window,
signed to her to lift up the sash.

'What do you want now?' asked Victoria, thrusting
her head out.

'It's a bargain about the Zoo, isn't it?'

'Yes, of course it is, silly boy. I've got several
children's tickets.'

Jack made a wry face, but walked away with a
queer little feeling of exultation. 'Silly boy.' She
had called him 'silly boy.' Victoria watched him

go with some perplexity. The young man was
rather a problem. Not only did his pretty face and
gentle ways appeal to her in themselves, but he had
told her something of his thoughts and they did not
run on cement. His father had thrust him into his
business as men of his type naturally force their sons
into their own avocation whatever it be. Victoria
knew that he was not happy and was sorry for him;
how could she help feeling sorry for this lonely youth
who had once printed a rondeau in the *Westminster
Gazette*.

Jack had taken to her at once. All that was
delicate and feminine in him called out to her square
chin and steady eyes. Often she had seen him look
hungrily at her strong hands where bone and muscle
plainly showed. But, in his wistful way, Jack had
begun to embarrass her. He was making love to her
in a sense, sometimes sportively, sometimes plaintively,
and he was difficult to resist.

Victoria saw quite well that trouble must ensue.
She would not allow the boy to fall in love with her
when all she could offer was an almost motherly
affection. Besides, they could not marry; it would
be absurd. She was puzzled as to what to do.
Everything tended to complicate the situation for
her. She had once been to the theatre with Jack
and remembered with anxiety how his arm had rested
against hers in the cab and how, when he leaned
over towards her to speak, she had felt him slowly
inhaling the scents of her hair.

She had promised herself that Jack should be
snubbed. And now he played pranks on her. It
must end in their being caught in an ambiguous
attitude and then she would be blamed. She might
tell Mrs Holt, but then what would be her position in
the household? Jack would sulk and Mrs Holt
would watch them suspiciously until the situation
became intolerable and she had to leave. Leave!

no, no, she couldn't do that. With sudden vividness Victoria pictured the search for work, the silence of Portsea Place, the Rialto-like archway, Mrs Bell, and the cold, the loneliness. Events must take their course.

Like the rasp of a corncrake she heard the wheels of the barouche on the gravel. Mrs Holt had returned from the discourse on the personal devil.

CHAPTER VIII

'THOMAS,' said Mrs Holt with some hesitation.

'Yes,' said Mr Holt. 'What is it?'

'Oh! nothing,' said Mrs Holt, 'Just a queer idea. Nothing worth talking about.'

'Well, come again when it is worth talking about,' growled Mr Holt, relapsing into his newspaper.

'Of course there's nothing in it,' remarked Mrs Holt pertinaciously.

'Nothing in what?' her husband burst forth. 'What do you mean, Maria? Have you got anything to say or not? If you have, let's have it out.'

'I was only going to say that Jack . . . of course I don't think that Victoria sees it, but you understand he's a very young man, but I don't blame her, he's such a funny boy,' said Mrs Holt lucidly.

'Good heavens, Maria,' cried her husband, 'do you want me to smash something?'

'How you do go on,' remarked Maria placidly. 'What I meant to say is that don't you think Jack's rather too attentive to Victoria?'

Mr Holt dropped his paper suddenly. 'Attentive?' he growled, 'haven't noticed it.'

'Oh! you men never notice things,' replied Mrs Holt with conscious superiority. 'Don't say I didn't warn you, that's all.'

'Now look here, Maria,' said Mr Holt, his blue eyes darkening visibly, 'I don't want any more of this tittle tattle. You can keep it for the next P.S.A. I can tell you that if the young cub is "attentive" to

Mrs Fulton, well, so much the better : it'll teach him something worth knowing if he finds out that there's somebody else in the world who's worth doing something for beyond *his* precious self.'

'Very well, very well,' purred Mrs Holt. 'If you take it like that, I don't mind, Thomas. Don't say I didn't warn you if anything happens. That's all.'

Mr Holt got up from the leather chair and left the room. There were moments when his wife roused in him the fury that filled him when once, in his young days, he had dropped steel bolts into the cement grinders to gratify a grudge against an employer. The temper that had made him rejoice over the sharp cracks speaking of smashed axles was in him still. He had got above the social stratum where husbands beat their wives, but innuendoes and semi-secrets goaded him almost to paroxysm.

Mrs Holt heard the door slam and coolly took up her work. She was engaged in the congenial task of disfiguring a piece of Morris chintz. She had decided that the little bag given her by an æsthetic friend was too flat and she was busily employed in embroidering the 'eyebright' pattern, with coloured wool in the most approved early Victorian manner. 'At any rate,' she thought, 'Thomas has got the idea in his head.'

Mrs Holt had not arrived at her determination to awaken her husband's suspicions without much thought. She had begun to realise that 'something was wrong' one Sunday afternoon at the Zoo. She had taken Jack and Victoria in the barouche, putting down to a fit of filial affection the readiness of Jack to join them. She had availed herself of the opportunity to drive round the Circle ; so as to show off her adored son to the Bramleys, who were there in their electric, to the Wilsons, who were worth quite fifty thousand a year, to the Wellensteins too, who seemed to do so wonderfully well on the

Stock Exchange. Jack had taken it very nicely indeed.

All the afternoon Jack had remained with them; he had bought animal food, found a fellow to take them into the pavilion, and even driven home with them. It was when he helped his charges into the carriage that Mrs Holt had noticed something. He first handed his mother in and then Victoria. Mrs Holt had seen him put his hand under Victoria's forearm, which was quite ordinary, but she had also seen him hold her in so doing by the joint of her short sleeve and long glove where a strip of white skin showed and slip two fingers under the glove. This was not so ordinary and Mrs Holt began to think.

When a Rawsley dame begins to think of things such as these, her conscience invariably demands of her that she should know more. Mrs Holt therefore said nothing, but kept a watchful eye on the couple. She could urge nothing against Victoria. Her companion remained the cheerful and competent friend of the early days; she was no more amiable to Jack than to his father : she talked no more to him than to the rest of the household; she did not even look at him much. But Jack was always about her; his eyes followed her round the room, playing with every one of her movements. Whenever she smiled his lips fluttered in response.

Mrs Holt passed slowly through the tragic stages that a mother goes through when her son loves. She was not very anxious as to the results of the affair, for she knew Jack, though she loved him. She knew that his purpose was never strong. Also she trusted Victoria. But, every day and inevitably, the terrible jealousy that invades a mother's soul crept further into hers. He was her son and he was wavering from an allegiance the pangs of childbirth had entitled her to.

Mrs Holt loved her son, and, like most of those who love, would torture the being that was all in all for her. She would have crushed his thoughts if she had felt able to do so, so as to make him more malleable ; she rejoiced to see him safely anchored to the cement business, where nothing could distract him ; she even rejoiced over his weakness, for she enjoyed the privilege of giving him strength. She would have ground to powder his ambitions, so that he might be more fully her son, hers, hers only.

The stepping in of the other woman, remote and subtle as it was, was a terrible thing. She felt it from afar as the Arabian steed hears the coming simoon moaning beyond the desert. With terrible lucidity she had seen everything that passed for a month after that fatal day at the Zoo, when Jack touched Victoria's arm. She saw his looks, stolen from his mother's face, heard the softness of his voice which was often sharp for her. Like gall, his little attentions, the quick turn of his face, a flush some- times, entered into and poisoned her soul. He was her son ; and, with all the ruthless, entirely animal cruelty of the mother, she had begun to swear to herself that he should be hers and hers only, and that she would hug him in her arms, aye, hug him to death if need be, if only in her arms he died.

Savagely selfish as a good mother, however, Mrs Holt remembered that she must go slowly, collect her evidence, allow the fruit to ripen before she plucked it. Thus she retained her outward kindnesses for Victoria, spoke her fair, threw her even into frequent contact with her son. And every day she tortured herself with all the tiny signs that radiate from a lover's face like aerolites from the blazing tail of a comet. Now her case was complete. She had seen Jack lean over Victoria while she was on her knees dusting some books, and let his hand dwell on hers. She had seen his face all alight, his mouth a little open, breathing in the fragrance of this woman, the intruder. And the iron had entered into the mother's heart so sharply that she had to hurry away unseen for fear she should cry out.

Mrs Holt dropped her little work bag. She wondered whether her husband would see. Would she have to worry him placidly for months as she usually had to when she wanted her own way? Or would he understand and side with her? She did not know that women are intuitive, for she knew nothing either of women or men, but she felt perfectly certain that she was cleverer than Thomas Holt. If he would not see, then she would have to show him, even if she had to plot for her son's sake.

The door opened suddenly. Thomas Holt entered. His face was perturbed, his jaw setting grimly between the two deep folds in his cheeks. That was the face of his bad days.

'Well, Thomas?' ventured his wife hesitatingly.

'You were right, Maria,' answered Holt after a pause. 'Jack's a bigger fool than I thought him.'

'Ah!' said Mrs Holt with meaning, her heart beating a sharp tatoo.

'I was standing on the first landing,' Holt went on. 'I saw them at the door of the smoke-room. He asked her for a flower from her dress; she wouldn't give it him; he reached over and pulled one away.'

'Yes?' said Mrs Holt, everything in her quivering.

'Put his arm round her, though she pushed him off, and kissed her.'

Mrs Holt clasped her hands together. A sharp pang had shot through her. 'What are you going to do?' she asked.

'Do?' said Holt. 'Sack her of course. Send him up to Rawsley. Damn the young fool.'

CHAPTER IX

BREAKFAST is so proverbially dismal, that dismalness becomes good form; humanity feels silent and liverish, so it grudges Providence its due, for it cannot return thanks for the precocious blessings of the day. Such was breakfast at Finchley Road, and Victoria would not have noticed it on that particular morning had the silence not somehow been eloquent. She could feel, if not see storm clouds on the horizon.

Mr Holt sat over his eggs and bacon, eating quickly with both hands, every now and then soiling the napkin tightly tucked into the front of his low collar. There was nothing abnormal in this, except perhaps that he kept his eyes more closely glued than usual to the table cloth; moreover, he had not unfolded the paper. Therefore he had not looked up the prices of Industrials. This was singular. Mrs Holt never said much at breakfast, in deference to her husband, but this morning her silence was somewhat ostentatious. She handed Victoria her tea. Victoria passed her the toast and hardly heard her 'thank you.'

Jack sat more abstracted than ever. He was feeling very uncomfortable. He wavered between the severe talking to he had received from Victoria the previous afternoon and the sulkiness of his parents. Of course he was feeling depressed, but he could not tell why. Victoria's mere nod of acceptance when he offered her the salt, and his mother's curt refusal of the pepper did not contribute to make him easier in his mind. Mrs Holt cleared her throat: 'Blowing up for rain, Thomas,' she said. Mr Holt did not move a muscle. He helped himself to marmalade. Stolid silence once more reigned over the breakfast table. Jack stole a sidelong glance at Victoria. Her eyes were fixed upon her hands crossed before her. Jack's eyes dwelled for a moment on their shapely strength, then upon the firm white nape of her bent neck. An insane desire possessed him to jump up, seize her in his arms, crush his lips into that spot where the dark tendrils of her hair began. He repressed it, and considered the grandfather's clock which had once ticked in a peasant Holt's kitchen. To-day it ticked with almost horrible deliberation.

Jack found that he had no appetite. Forebodings were at work with him. Perhaps Vic had told. Of course not, she couldn't be such a fool. What a beastly room it was! Sideboard must weigh a ton. And those red curtains! awful, simply awful. Good God, why couldn't he get out of the damned place and take Vic with him. Couldn't do that yet of course, but couldn't stick it much longer. He'd be off to the City now. Simply awful here. Jack rose to his feet suddenly, so suddenly that his chair tilted and fell over.

Mrs Holt looked up. 'I wish you wouldn't be so noisy, Jack,' she said.

'Sorry, mater,' said Jack, going round to her and bending down to kiss her, 'I'm off.'

'You're in a fine hurry,' remarked Mr Holt grimly, looking up and speaking for the first time.

'Left some work over,' said Jack, in a curt manner, making for the door.

'Hem! you've got work on the brain,' retorted his father in his most sardonic tone.

Jack opened the door without a word.

'One minute, Jack,' said Mrs Holt placidly, 'you

needn't go yet, your father and I have something to
say to you.'

Jack stood rooted to the ground. His knees almost
gave way beneath him. It, it, it was it. They knew.
Victoria's face, the pr file of which he could see
outlined like a plaster cast against the red wall paper
did not help him. Her face had set, rigid like a
mask. Now she knew why the previous evening had
gone by in silence. She rose to her feet, a strange
numb feeling creeping all over her.

'Don't go, Mrs Fulton,' said Mr Holt sharply, 'this
concerns you.'

For some seconds the party remained silent. Mr
and Mrs Holt had not moved from the table. Jack and
Victoria stood right and left, like prisoners at the bar.

'Victoria,' said Mrs Holt, 'I'm very sorry to have
to say it, but I'm afraid you know what I'm going to
tell you. Of course I don't say I blame you. It's
quite natural at your age and all that.' She stopped,
for a flush was rising in Victoria's face, the cheekbones showing two little red patches. Mr Holt had
clasped his hands together and kept his eyes fixed
on Victoria's with unnatural intensity.

'You see, Victoria,' resumed Mrs Holt, 'it's always
difficult when there's a young man in the house ; of
course I make allowances, but, really, you see it's so
complicated and things get so annoying. You know
what people are . . .'

'That'll do, Maria,' snarled Mr Holt, jumping to
his feet. 'If you don't know what you have to say,
I do. Look here, Mrs Fulton. Last night I saw
Jack kissing you. I know perfectly well you didn't
encourage him. You'd know better. However, there
it is. I don't pretend I like what I've got to do, but
this must be stopped. I can't have philandering
going on here. You, Jack, you're going back to the
works at Rawsley and don't let me see anything of
you this side of the next three months. As for you,

Mrs Fulton, I'm sorry, but Mrs Holt will have to find another companion. I know it's hard on you to ask you to leave without notice, but I propose to give you an indemnity of twenty pounds. I should like to keep you here, but you see that after what has happened it's impossible. I suppose you agree to that?'

Victoria stood silent for a moment, her hands tightly clenched. She knew Holt's short ways, but the manner of the dismissal was brutal. Everything seemed to revolve round her, she recovered herself with difficulty.

'Yes,' she said at length, 'you're quite right.'

Jack had not moved. His hands were nervously playing with his watch chain. Victoria, in the midst of her trouble, remembered Edward's familiar gesture. They were alike in a way, these two tall weedy men, both irresolute and undeveloped.

'Very well then,' continued Holt; 'perhaps you'll make your arrangements at once. Here is the cheque.' He held out a slip of blue paper.

Victoria looked at him for a moment dully. Then revolt surged inside her. 'I don't want your indemnity,' she said coldly, 'you merely owe me a month's wages in lieu of notice.'

The shadow of a smile crept into Holt's face. The semi-legal, semi-commercial phrase pleased him.

Mrs Holt rose from the table and went to Victoria. 'I'm so sorry,' she said, speaking more gently than she had ever done. 'You must take it. Things are so hard.'

'Oh, but I say, dad . . .' broke in Jack.

'That will do, do you hear me, sir?' thundered the father violently, bringing down his fist on the table. 'I'm not asking you for your opinion? You can stay and look at your work but you just keep a silent tongue in your head. D'you hear?'

Jack stood cowed and dumb.

'There's nothing more to say, is there?' growled Mr Holt, placing the cheque on the table before Victoria.

'Not much,' said Victoria. 'I've done no wrong. Oh! I'm not complaining. But I begin to understand things. Your son has persecuted me. I didn't want his attentions. You turn me out. Of course it's my fault, I know.'

'My dear Victoria,' interposed Mrs Holt, 'nobody says it's your fault. We all think . . .'

'Indeed? it's not my fault, but you turn me out.'

Mrs Holt dropped her hands helplessly.

'I see it all now,' continued Victoria. 'You don't blame me, but you're afraid to have me here. So long as I was a servant all was well. Now I'm a woman and you're afraid of me.' She walked up and down nervously. 'Now understand, I've never encouraged your son. If he had asked me to marry him I wouldn't have done it.' A look of pain passed over Jack's face but aroused no pity in Victoria. She felt frozen.

'Oh! but there was no question of that,' cried Mrs Holt, plaintively.

'No doubt,' said Victoria ruthlessly. 'You couldn't think of it. Nobody could think of an officer's widow marrying into the Rawsley Works. From more than one point of view it would be impossible. Very good. I'll leave in the course of the morning. As for the cheque, I'll take it. As you say, Mrs Holt, things are hard. I've learned that and I'm still learning.'

Victoria took up the blue slip. The flush on her face subsided somewhat. She picked up her handkerchief, a letter from Molly and a small anthology lying on the dumb waiter. She made for the door, avoiding Jack's eyes. She felt through her downcast lids the misery of his looks. A softer feeling went through her, and she regretted her outburst. As she placed her hand on the handle she turned round and faced Mrs Holt, a gentler look in her eyes.

'I'm sorry I was hasty,' she stammered. 'I was taken by surprise. It was . . . vulgar.'

The door closed softly behind her.

E

CHAPTER X

VICTORIA went up to her room and locked the door behind her. She sat down on her small basket trunk and stared out of the dormer window. She was still all of a tingle ; her hands, grasping the rough edges of the trunk, trembled a little. Yet she felt, amid all her perturbation, the strange gladness that overcomes one who has had a shock ; the contest was still upon her.

'Yes,' she said aloud, 'I'm free. I'm out of it.' She hated the dullness and ugliness which the Holts had brought with them from the Midlands. The feeling came over her almost like a spasm. Through the dormer window she could see the white frontage of the house opposite. It was repellent like Mrs Holt's personal devil.

The feeling of exultation suddenly subsided in Victoria's breast. She realised all of a sudden that she was once more adrift, that she must find something to do. It might not be easy. She would have to find lodgings. The archway in Portsea Place materialised crudely. She could hear the landlady from 84 detailing the last phase of rheumatics to the slatternly maid who did for the grocer. Awful, awful. Perhaps she'd never find another berth. What should she do?

Victoria pulled herself together with a start. 'This will never do,' she said, 'there's lots of time to worry in. Now I must pack.' She got up, drew the trunk into the middle of the room, opened it and took out the tray. Then, methodically, as she had been taught

to do by her mother, she piled her belongings on the
bed. In a few minutes it was filled with the nondescript possessions of the nomad. Skirts, books, boots,
underclothing, an inkpot even, jostled one another in
dangerous proximity. Victoria surveyed the heap
with some dismay; all her troubles had vanished in
the horror that comes over every packer: she would
never get it all in. She struggled for half an hour,
putting the heavy things at the bottom, piling blouses
on the tray, cunningly secreting scent bottles in shoes,
stuffing handkerchiefs into odd corners. Then she
dropped the tray in, closed the lid and sat down upon
it. The box creaked a little and gave way. Victoria
locked it and got up with a little sigh of satisfaction.
But she suddenly saw that the cupboard door was
ajar and that in it hung her best dress and a
feather boa; on the floor stood the packer's plague,
shoes. It was quite hopeless to try and get them in.

Victoria surveyed the difficulty for a moment; then
she regretfully decided that she must ask Mrs Holt
for a cardboard box, for her hat-box was already
mortgaged. A nuisance. But rather no, she would
ask the parlourmaid. She went to the door and was
surprised to find it locked. She turned the key
slowly, looking round at the cheerful little room,
every article of which was stupid without being
offensive. It was hard, after all, to leave all this,
without knowing where to go.

Victoria opened the door and jumped back with
a little cry. Before her stood Jack. He had stolen
up silently and waited. His face had flushed as he
saw her; in his eyes was the misery of a sorrowful
dog. His mouth, always a little open, trembled with
excitement.

'Jack,' cried Victoria, 'oh! what do you want?'

'I've come to say . . . oh! Victoria . . .' Jack
broke down in the middle of his carefully prepared
sentence.

'Oh! go away,' said Victoria faintly, putting her hand on her breast. 'Do go away. Can't you see I've had trouble enough this morning?'

'I'm sorry,' muttered Jack miserably. 'I've been a fool. Vic, I've come to ask you if you'll forgive me. It's all my fault. I can't bear it.'

'Don't talk about it,' said Victoria becoming rigid. 'That's all over. Besides you'll have forgotten all about it to-morrow,' she added cruelly.

Jack did not answer directly, though he was stung. 'Vic,' he said with hesitation, 'I can't bear to see you go, all through me. Listen, there's something you said this morning. Did you mean it?'

'Mean what?' asked Victoria uneasily.

'You said, if I'd asked you to marry me you . . . I know I didn't, but you know, Vic, I wanted you the first time I saw you. Oh! Vic, won't you marry me now?'

Victoria looked at him incredulously. His hands were still trembling with excitement. His light eyes stared a little. His long thin frame was swaying. 'I'd do anything for you. You don't know what I could do. I'd work for you. I'd love you more than you've ever been loved.' Jack stopped short; there was a hardness that frightened him in the set of Victoria's jaw.

'You didn't say that yesterday,' she answered.

'No, I was mad. But I wanted to all along, Vic. You're the only woman I ever loved. I don't ask more of you than to let me love you.'

Victoria looked at him more gently. His likeness to her brother grew plainer than ever. Kind but hopelessly inefficient. Poor boy, he meant no harm.

'I'm sorry, Jack,' she said after a pause, 'I can't do it. 'You know you couldn't make a living . . .'

'Oh, I could, I could!' cried Jack clinging at the straw, 'if I had you to work for. You can't tell what it means for me.'

'Perhaps you could work,' said Victoria with a wan little smile, 'but I can't marry you, Jack, you see. I like you very much, but I'm not in love with you. It would't be fair.'

Jack looked at her dully. He had not dared to expect anything but defeat, yet defeat crushed him.

'There, you must go away now,' said Victoria, 'I must go downstairs. Let me pass please.' She squeezed between him and the wall and made for the stairs.

'No, I can't let you go,' said Jack hoarsely. He seized her by the waist and bent over her. Victoria looked the space of a second into his eyes where the tiny veins were becoming bloodshot. She pushed him back sharply and, wrenching herself away, ran down the stairs. He did not follow her.

Victoria looked up from the landing. Jack was standing with bent head, one hand on the banister. 'The only thing you can do for me is to go away,' she said coldly. 'I shall come up again in five minutes with Effie. I suppose you will not want us to find you outside my bedroom door.'

She went downstairs. When she came up again with the maid, who carried a large brown cardboard box, Jack was nowhere to be seen.

A quarter of an hour later she followed the butcher's boy who was dragging her box down the stairs, dropping it with successive thuds from step to step. As she reached the hall, while she was hesitating as to whether she should go into the dining-room to say good-bye to Mrs Holt, the door opened and Mrs Holt came out. The two women looked at one another for the space of a second, like duellists about to cross swords. Then Mrs Holt held out her hand.

'Good-bye, Victoria,' she said, 'I'm sorry you're going. I know you're not to blame.'

'Thank you,' said Victoria icily. 'I'm sorry also, but it couldn't be helped.'

Mrs Holt heaved a large sigh. 'I suppose not,' she said.

Victoria withdrew her hand and went towards the door. The butcher's boy had already taken her box down, marking the whitened steps with two black lines.

'Shall I call a cab, mum?' he asked.

'Yes please,' said Victoria dreamily.

The youth went down the drive, his heels crunching into the gravel. Victoria stood at the top of the steps, looking out at the shrubs, one or two of which showed pale buds, standing sharp like jewels on the black stems. Mrs Holt came up behind her softly.

'I hope we don't part in anger, Victoria,' she said guiltily.

Victoria looked at her with faint amusement. True, anger is a cardinal sin.

'Oh! no, not at all,' she answered. 'I quite understand.'

'Don't be afraid to give me as a reference,' said Mrs Holt.

'Thank you,' said Victoria. 'I shan't forget.'

'And if ever you're in trouble, come to me.'

'You're very kind,' said Victoria. Mrs Holt was kind, she felt. She understood her better now. Much of her sternness oozed out of her. A mother defending her son knows no pity, thought Victoria; perhaps it's wrong to resent it. It's nature's way of keeping the young alive.

The cab came trotting up the drive and stopped. The butcher's boy was loading the trunk upon the roof. Victoria turned to Mrs Holt and took her hand.

'Good-bye,' she said, 'you've been very good to me. Don't think I'm so bad as you thought me this morning. Your son has just asked me to marry him.'

Mrs Holt dropped Victoria's hand; her face was distorted by a spasm.

'I refused him,' said Victoria.

She stepped into the cab and directed the cabman
to Portsea Place. As they turned into the road she
looked back. At the head of the steps Mrs Holt
stood frozen and amazed. Victoria almost smiled
but, her eyes wandering upwards, she saw, at her
dormer window, Jack's head and shoulders. His
blue eyes were fixed upon her with unutterable longing. A few strands of hair had blown down upon his
forehead. For the space of a second they gazed into
each other's eyes. Then the wall blotted him out
suddenly. Victoria sighed softly and sank back upon
the seat of the cab.

At the moment she had no thought. She was at
such a point as one may be who has turned the last
page of the first volume of a lengthy book : the next
page is blank. Nothing remained even of that last
look in which Jack's blue eyes had pitifully retold
his sorry tale. She was like a rope which has parted
with many groans and wrenchings ; broken and its
strands scattering, its ends float lazily at the mercy
of the waves, preparing to sink. She was going more
certainly into the unknown than if she had walked
blindfold into the darkest night.

The horse trotted gently, the brakes gritting on the
wheels as it picked its way down the steep. The
fresh air of April drove into the cab, stinging a little
and yet balmy with the freshness of latent spring.
Victoria sat up, clasped her hands on the doors and
craned out to see. There was a little fever in her
blood again ; the spirit of adventure was raising its
head. As fitful gleams of sunshine lit up and irradi-
ated the puddles a passionate interest in the life
around seemed to overpower her. She looked almost
greedily at the spire, far down the Wellington Road,
shining white like molten metal with almost Italian
brilliancy against a sky pale as shallow water. The
light, the young wind, the scents of earth and buds,
the men and women who walked with springy step

intent on no business, all this, and even the horse who seemed to toss his head and swish his tail in sheer glee, told her that the world was singing its alleluia, for, behold, spring was born unto it in gladness, with all its trappings and its sumptuous promise.

Everything was beautiful ; not even the dreary waste of wall which conceals Lords from the vulgar, nor the thousand tombs of the churchyard where the dead jostle and grab land from one another were without their peculiar charm. It was not until the cab crossed the Edgware Road that Victoria realised with a start that, though the world was born again, she did not share its good fortune. Edgware Road had dragged her down to the old level ; a horrible familiarity, half pleasurable, half fearful, overwhelmed her. This street, which she had so often paced carrying a heart that grew heavier with every step, had never led her to anything but loneliness, to the cold emptiness of her room. Her mood had changed. She saw nothing now but tawdry stationer's shops, meretricious jewellery and, worse still, the sickening plenty of its monster stores of clothing and food. The road had seized her and was carrying her away towards its summit, where the hill melts into the skies between the houses that grow lower as far as the eye can see.

Victoria closed her eyes. She was in the grip once more ; the wheels of the machine were not moving yet but she could feel the vibration as it got up steam. In a little the flywheel would slowly revolve and then she would be caught and ground up. Yes, ground up, cried the Edgware Road, like thousands of others as good as you, ground into little bits to make roadmetal of, yes, ground, ground fine.

The cab stopped suddenly. Victoria opened her eyes. Yes, this was Portsea Place. She got out. It had not changed. The curtains of the house opposite were as dirty as ever. The landlady from the corner was standing just under the archway, dressed as usual

in an expansive pink blouse in which her flowing
contours rose and fell. She interrupted the voluble
comments on the weather which she was addressing
to the little faded colleague, dressed in equally faded
black, to stare at the newcomer.

'There ain't no more room at Bell's,' she remarked.

'She is very fortunate,' said the faded little woman.
'Dear me, dear me. It's a cruel world.'

'Them lidies' maids allus ketches on,' said the
large woman savagely. 'Tell yer wot, though, p'raps
they wouldn't if they was to see Bell's kitching. Oh,
Lor'! There ain't no black-beetles. I don't think.'

The little faded woman looked longingly at Victoria
standing on the steps. A loafer sprung from thin air
as is the way of his kind and leant against the area
railings, touching his cap whenever he caught
Victoria's eye, indicating at times the box on the roof
of the cab. From the silent house came a noise that
grew louder and louder as the footsteps drew nearer
the door. Victoria recognised the familiar shuffle.
Mrs Bell opened the door.

'Lor, mum,' she cried, 'I'm glad to see you again.'
She caught sight of the trunk. 'Oh, are you moving,
mum?'

'Yes, Mrs Bell,' said Victoria. 'I'm moving and I
want some rooms. Of course I thought of you.'

Mrs Bell's face fell. 'Oh, I'm so sorry, mum. The
house is full. If you'd come last week I had the first
floor back.' She seemed genuinely distressed. She
liked her quiet lodger and to turn away business of
any kind was always depressing.

Victoria felt dashed. She remembered Edward's
consternation on discovering the change in Gower
Street and, for the first time, sympathised.

'Oh, I'm so sorry too, Mrs Bell. I should like to
have come back to you.'

'Couldn't you wait until next month, mum!' said
Mrs Bell, reluctant to turn her away. 'The gentleman

in the second floor front, he's going away to Rhodesia. It's your old room, mum.'

'I'm afraid not,' said Victoria with a smile. 'In fact I must find lodgings at once. Never mind, if I don't like them I'll come back here. But can't you recommend somebody?'

Mrs Bell looked right and left, then into the archway. The little faded woman had disappeared. The landlady in the billowy blouse was still surveying the scene. Mrs Bell froze her with a single look.

'No, mum, can't say I know of anybody, leastways not here,' she said slowly. 'It's a nice neighbourhood of course, but the houses here, they look all right, but oh, mum, you should see their kitchens! Dirty ain't the word, mum. But wait a bit, mum, if you wouldn't mind that, I've got a sister who's got a very nice room. She lives in Castle Street, mum, near Oxford Circus. It's a nice neighbourhood, of course not so near the Park,' added Mrs Bell with conscious superiority.

'I don't mind, Mrs Bell,' said Victoria. 'I'm not fashionable.'

'Oh, mum,' cried Mrs Bell, endeavouring to imply together the superiority of Portsea Place and the respectability of any street patronised by her family, 'I'm sure you'll like it. I'll give you the address.'

In a few minutes Victoria was speeding eastwards. Now she was rooted up for good. She was leaving behind her Curran's and Mrs Bell, slender links between her and home life, links still, however. The pageant of London rolled by her, heaving, bursting with rich life. The sunshine around her bade her be of good cheer. Then the cab turned a corner and, with the suddenness of a stage effect, it carried its burden into the haunts of darkness and malodour.

CHAPTER XI

'*Telegraph*, mum,' said a voice.

Victoria started up from the big armchair with a suddenness that almost shot her out of it. It was the brother of the one in Portsea Place and shared its constitutional objection to being sat upon. It was part of the 'sweet' which Miss Briggs had divided with Mrs Bell when their grandmother died.

'Thanks, Miss Briggs,' said Victoria. 'By the way, I don't think that egg is quite fresh. And why does Hetty put the armchair in front of the cupboard every day so that I can't open it?'

'The slut, I don't see there's anything the matter with it,' remarked Miss Briggs, simultaneously endorsing the complaint against Hetty and defending her own marketing.

'Oh, yes there is, Miss Briggs,' snapped Victoria with a sharpness which would have been foreign to her some months before. 'Don't let it happen again or I'll do my own catering.'

Miss Briggs collapsed on the spot. The profits on the three and sixpence a week for 'tea, bread and butter and anything that's going,' formed quite a substantial portion of her budget.

'Oh, I'm sorry, mum,' she said, 'it's Hetty bought 'em this week. The slut, I'll talk to her.'

Victoria took no notice of the penitent landlady and opened the *Telegraph*. She absorbed the fact that Consols had gone up an eighth and that contangoes were in process of arrangement, without

interest or understanding. She was thinking of
something else. Miss Briggs coughed apologetically.
Victoria looked up. Miss Briggs reflectively tied
knots in her apron string. She was a tall, lantern-
jawed woman of no particular age; old looking for
thirty-five perhaps or young looking for fifty. Her
brown hair, plentifully sprinkled with grey, broke
out in wisps over each ear and at the back of the
neck. Her perfectly flat chest allowed big bags of
coarse black serge to hang over her dirty white
apron. Her hands played mechanically with the
strings, while her water-coloured eye fixed upon the
Telegraph.

'You shouldn't read that paper, mum,' she remarked.

' Why not ? ' asked Victoria, with a smile, ' isn't it
a good one ? '

' Oh, yes, mum, I don't say that,' said Miss Briggs
with the respect that she felt for the buyers of penny
papers. 'There's none better. Mine's the *Daily Mail*
of course and just a peep into *Reynolds* before the
young gent on the first floor front. But you shouldn't
have it. *Tizer's* your paper.'

' *Tizer* ? ' said Victoria interrogatively.

' *Morning Advertiser*, mum; that's the one for
advertisements.'

' But how do you know I read the advertisements,
Miss Briggs ? ' asked Victoria still smiling.

' Oh, mum, excuse the liberty,' said Miss Briggs in
great trepidation. 'It's the only sheet I don't find
when I comes up to do the bed. *Tizer's* the one
for you, mum; I had a young lady 'ere, once. Got
a job at the Inverness Lounge, she did. Married a
clergyman, they say. He's divorced her now.'

'That's an encouraging story, Miss Briggs,' said
Victoria with a twinkle in her eye. 'How do you
know I want to be a barmaid, though ? '

' Oh, one has to be what one can, mum,' said Miss
Briggs sorrowfully. 'Sure enough, it ain't all honey

and it ain't all jam keeping this house. The bells,
they rings all day and it's the breakfast that's bad
and their ain't blankets enough, and I never 'ad a
scuttle big enough to please 'em for sixpence. But
you ain't doing that, mum,' she added after a pause
devoted to the consideration of her wrongs. 'A young
lady like you, she ought to be behind the bar.'

Victoria laughed aloud. 'Thanks for the hint,
Miss Briggs,' she said, 'I'll think it over. To-day
however, I'm going to try my luck on the stage.
What do you think of that?'

'Going on tour?' cried Miss Briggs in a tone of
tense anxiety.

'Well, not yet,' said Victoria soothingly. 'I'm
going to see an agent.'

'Oh, that's all right,' said Miss Briggs with ghoulish
relief. 'Hope yer'll get a job,' she added as confidently as a man offering a drink to a teetotaller.
At that moment a fearful clattering on the stairs
announced that Hetty and the pail had suddenly
descended to the lower landing. Liquid noises
followed. Miss Briggs rushed out. Victoria jumped
up and slammed her door on the chaotic scene. She
returned to the *Telegraph*. The last six weeks in the
Castle Street lodging house had taught her that these
were happenings quite devoid of importance.

Victoria spread out the *Telegraph*, ignored the
foreign news, the leaders and the shocking revelations
as to the Government's Saharan policy; she dallied
for a moment over 'gowns for débutantes,' for she
was a true woman, and passed on to the advertisements. She was getting quite experienced as a
reader and could sift the wheat from the chaff with
some accuracy. She knew that she could safely
ignore applications for lady helps in 'small families,'
at least unless she was willing to clean boots and
blacklead grates for five shillings a week and meals
when an opportunity occurred; her last revelation as

to the nature of a post of housekeeper to an elderly
gentleman who had retired from business into the
quietude of Surbiton had not been edifying. The
'Financial and Businesses' column left her colder
than she had been when she left Mrs Holt with nearly
thirty-seven pounds. Then she was a capitalist and
pondered longingly over the proposals of tobacconists,
fancy goods firms, and stationers, who were prepared
to guarantee a fortune to any person who could
muster thirty pounds. Fortunately Miss Briggs had
undeceived her. In her variegated experience, she
herself had surrendered some sixty golden sovereigns
to the persuasive owner of a flourishing newsagent's
business. After a few weeks of vain attempts to
induce the neighbourhood to indulge in the news of
the day, she had been glad to sell her stock of sweets
for eighteen shillings, and to take half a crown for a
hundred penny novelettes.

Victoria turned to the 'Situations Vacant.' Their
numbers were deceptive. She had never realised
before how many people live by fitting other people
for work they cannot get. Two thirds of the
advertisements offered wonderful opportunities for
sons of gentlemen in the offices of architects and
engineers on payment of a premium ; she also found
she could become a lady gardener if she would only
follow the courses in some dukery and meanwhile
live on air ; others would teach her shorthand, typewriting or the art of the secretary. All these she
now calmly skipped. She was obviously unfitted to
be the matron of an asylum for the feeble-minded.
Such experience had not been hers, nor had she the
redoubtable record which would open the gates of
an emporium. An illegible hand would exclude her
from the City.

'No,' thought Victoria, 'I'm an unskilled labourer ;
that's what I am.' She wearily skimmed the agencies ;
as a matter of habit noted the demand for two com-

panions and one nursery governess and put the paper aside. There was not much hope in any of these, for one was for Tiverton, the other for Cardiff, which would make a personal interview a costly business; the third, discreetly cloaked by an initial, suggested by its terseness a companionship probably undue in its intimacy. The last six weeks had opened Victoria's eyes to the unpleasant aspects of life, so much so that she wondered whether there were any other. She felt now that London was waiting for her outside, waiting for her to have spent her last copper, when she would come out to be eaten so that she might eat.

Whatever her conceit might have been six months before, Victoria had lost it all. She could do nothing that was wanted and desired everything she could not get. She had tried all sources and found them dry. Commercialism, philanthropy, and five per cent. philanthropy had failed her. What can you do? was their cry. And, the answer being 'nothing,' their retort had been 'No more can we.'

Victoria turned over in her mind her interview with the Honorary Secretary of the British Women's Imperial Self Help Association. 'Of course,' said the Secretary, 'we will be glad to register you. We need some references and, as our principle is to foster the independence and self-respect of those whom we endeavour to place in positions such as may befit their social status, we are compelled to demand a fee of five shillings.'

'Oh, self help, I see,' said Victoria sardonically, for she was beginning to understand the world.

'Yes,' replied the Honorary Secretary, oblivious of the sneer, for his mind was cast in the parliamentary mould, 'by adhering to our principle and by this means only can we hope to stem the tide of pauperism to which modern socialistic tendencies are—are— spurring the masses.' Victoria had paid five shillings for this immortal metaphor and within a week had received an invitation to attend a meeting presided over by several countesses.

The B. W. I. S. H. A., (as it was called by its intimates) had induced in Victoria suspicions of societies in general. She had, however, applied also to the Ladies' Provider. Its name left one in doubt whether it provided ladies with persons or whether it provided ladies to persons who might not be ladies. The Secretary in this case, was not Honorary. The inwardness of this did not appear to Victoria; for she did not then know that plain secretaries are generally paid, and try to earn their salary. Their interview had, however, not been such as to convert her to the value of corporate effort.

The Secretary in this case was a woman of forty, with a pink face, trim grey hair, spectacles, amorphous clothing, capable hands. She exhaled an atmosphere of respectability, and the faint odour of almonds which emanates from those women who eschew scent in favour of soap. She had quietly listened to Victoria's history, making every now and then a shorthand note. Then she had coughed gently once or twice. Victoria felt as in the presence of an examiner. Was she going to get a pass?

' I do not say that we cannot do anything for you, Mrs Fulton,' she said, ' but we have so many cases similar to yours.'

Victoria had bridled a little at this. ' Cases ' was a nasty word.

' I'm not particular,' she had answered, ' I'd be a companion any day.'

' I'm sure you'd make a pleasant one,' said the Secretary graciously, ' but before we go any further, tell me how it was you left your last place. You were in the . . . in the Finchley Road, was it not?' The Secretary's eyes travelled to a map of London where Marylebone, South Paddington, Kensington, Belgravia, and Mayfair, were blocked out in blue.

Victoria had hesitated, then fenced. 'Mrs Holt will give me a good character,' she faltered.

'No doubt, no doubt,' replied the Secretary, her eyes growing just a little darker behind the glasses. 'Yet, you see, we are compelled by the nature of our business to make enquiries. A good reference is a very good thing, yet people are a little careless sometimes; the hearts of employers are often rather soft.'

This was a little too much for Victoria. 'If you want to know the truth,' she said bluntly, 'the son of the house persecuted me with his attentions, and I couldn't bear it.'

The Secretary made a shorthand note. Then she looked at Victoria's flashing eyes, heightened colour, thick piled hair.

'I am very sorry,' she began lamely. . . .

What dreadful things women are, thought Victoria, folding up the *Telegraph*. If Christ had said: Let *her* who hath never sinned. . . the woman would have been stoned. Victoria got up, went to the looking-glass and inspected herself. Yes, she was very pretty. She was prettier than she had ever been before. Her skin was paler, her eyes larger; her thick eyebrows almost met in an exquisite gradation of short dark hairs over the bridge of the nose. She watched her breast rise and fall gently, flashing white through the black lacework of her blouse, then falling away from it, tantalising the faint sunshine that would kiss it. As she turned, another looking-glass set in the lower panels of a small cupboard told her that her feet were small and high arched. Her openwork stockings were drawn so tight that the skin there also gleamed white.

Victoria took from the table a dirty visiting card. It bore the words 'Louis Carrel, Musical and Theatrical Agent, 5 Soho Place.' She had come by it in singular manner. Two days before, as she left the offices of the 'Compleat Governess Agency' after

F

having realised that she could not qualify in either
French, German, Music, Poker work or Swedish drill,
she had paused for a moment on the doorstep,
surveying the dingy court where they were concealed, the dirty panes of an unlet shop opposite,
the strange literature flaunting in the showcase of
some publisher of esoterics. A woman had come up
to her, rising like the loafers from the flagstones.
She had realised her as between ages and between
colours. Then the woman had disappeared as
suddenly as she came without having spoken, leaving
in Victoria's hand the little square of pasteboard.

Victoria looked at it meditatively. She would
have shrunk from the idea of the stage a year before,
when the tradition of Lympton was still upon her.
But times had changed; a simple philosophy was
growing in her; what did anything matter? would
it not be all the same in a hundred years? The
discovery of this philosophy did not strike her as
commonplace. There are but few who know that
this is the philosophy of the world.

Victoria put down the card and began to dress.
She removed the old black skirt and ragged lace
blouse and, as she stood before the glass in her short
petticoat, patting her hair and setting a comb, she
reflected with satisfaction that her arms were shapely
and white. She looked almost lovingly at the long
thin dark hairs, fine as silk, that streaked her fore-
arms; she kissed them gently, moved to self-adoration
by the sweet scent of femininity that rose from her.

She tore herself away from her self-worship and
quickly began to dress. She put on a light skirt in
serge, striped black and white, threading her head
through it with great care for fear she should damage
her fringe net. She drew on a white blouse, simple
enough though cheap. As it fastened along the side
she did not have to call in Miss Briggs; which was
fortunate, as this was the time when Miss Briggs

carried coals. Victoria wriggled for a moment to settle the uncomfortable boning of the neck and, having buckled and belted the skirt over the blouse, completed her toilet with her little black and white jacket to match the skirt. A tiny black silk cravat from her neck was discarded, as she found that the fashionable ruffle, emerging from the closed coat, produced an *effet mousquetaire*. Lastly she put on her hat; a lapse from the fashions perhaps, but a lovable, flat, almost crownless, dead black, save a vertical group of feathers.

Victoria drew her veil down, regretting the thickness of the spots, pushed it up to repair with a dab of powder the ravage of a pod on the tip of her nose. She took up her parasol and white gloves, a glow of excitement already creeping over her as she realised how cleverly she must have caught the spirit of the profession to look the actress to the life and yet remain in the note of the demure widow.

Soho Place is neither one of the ' good ' streets nor one of the 'bad.' The police do not pace it in twos and threes in broad daylight, yet they hardly like to venture into it singly by night. On one side it ends in a square; on the other it turns off into an unobtrusive side street, the reputation of which varies yard by yard according to the distance from the main roads. It is dirty, dingy; yet not without dignity, for its good Georgian and Victorian houses preserve some solidity and are not yet of the tenement class. They are still in the grade of office and shop which is immediately below their one-time status of dwellings for well-to-do merchants.

Victoria entered Soho Place from the square, so that she was not too ill impressed. She walked in the middle of the pavement, unconsciously influenced by the foreign flavour of Soho. There men and women stand all day in the street, talking, bargaining, quarrelling and making love ; when a cab rattles by they move aside lazily, as a Neapolitan stevedore rolls away on the wharf from the wheels of a passing cart.

Victoria paused for a second on the steps. No 5 Soho Place was a good house enough. The ground floor was occupied by a firm of auctioneers; a gentleman describing himself as A.R.I.B.A. exercised his profession on the third floor; below his plate was nailed a visiting-card similar to the one Victoria took from her reticule. She went up the staircase feeling a little braced by the respectability of the house, though she had caught sight through the area railings of an unspeakably dirty kitchen where unwashed pots flaunted greasy remains on a liquor stained deal table. The staircase itself, with its neutral and stained green distemper, was not over encouraging. Victoria stopped at the first landing. She had no need to enquire as to the whereabouts of the impresario for, on a door which stood ajar, was nailed another dirty card. Just as she was about to push it, it opened further to allow a girl to come out. She was very fair; her cheeks were a little flushed; a golden lock or two fell like keepsake ringlets on her low lace collar. Victoria just had time to see that the blue eyes sparkled and to receive a cheerful smile. The girl muttered an apology and, smiling still, brushed past her and lightly ran down the stairs. 'A successful candidate,' thought Victoria, her heart rising once more.

She entered the room and found it empty. It was almost entirely bare of furniture, for little save an island of chairs in the middle and faded red cloth curtains relieved the uniform dirtiness of the wall paper which once was flowered. One wall was entirely covered by a large poster where half a dozen impossibly charming girls of the biscuit box type were executing a cancan so symmetrically as to recall an Egyptian frieze. The mantlepiece was bare save for the signed photograph of some magnificent foreign-looking athlete, nude to the waist. Victoria waited for a moment, watching a door which led into an inner room, then went towards it. At once the sound of a chair being pushed back and the fall of some small article on the floor told her that the occupant had heard her footsteps. The door opened suddenly.

Victoria looked at the apparition with some surprise. In a single glance she took in the details of his face and clothes, all of which were pleasing. The man was obviously a foreigner. His face was pale, clean shaven save for a small black moustache closely cropped at the ends; his eyes were brown; his eyebrows, as beautifully pencilled as those of a girl, emphasized the whiteness of his high forehead from which the hair receded in thick waves. His lips, red and full, were parted over his white teeth in a pleasant smile. Victoria saw too that he was dressed in perfect taste, in soft grey tweed, fitting well over the collar and loose everywhere else; his linen was immaculate; in fact nothing about him would have disgraced the Chandraga mess, except perhaps a gold ring with a large diamond which he wore on the little finger of his right hand.

'Mr Carrel?' said Victoria in some trepidation.

'Yes, Mademoiselle,' said the man pleasantly. 'Will you have the kindness to enter?' He held the door open and Victoria, hesitating a little, preceded him.

The inner room was almost a replica of the outer. It too was scantily furnished. On a large table heaps of dusty papers were stacked. An ash-tray overflowed over one end. In a corner stood a rickety-looking piano. The walls were profusely decorated with posters and photographs, presumably of actors and actresses, some highly renowned. Victoria felt respect creeping into her soul.

Carrel placed a chair for her before the table and

resumed his own. For the space of a second or two
he looked Victoria over. She was a little too conscious
of his scrutiny to be quite at ease, but she was
not afraid of the verdict.

'So, Mademoiselle,' said the man gently, 'you wish
for an engagement on the stage?'

Victoria had not expected such directness. 'Yes,
I do,' she said. 'That is, I was thinking of it since
I got your card.'

'My card?' said Carrel, raising his eyebrows a
little. 'How did you get my card?'

Victoria told him briefly how the card had been
thrust into her hand, how curious it was and how
surprised she had been as she did did not know the
woman and had never seen her again. Then she
frankly confessed that she had no experience of the
stage but wanted to earn her living and that . . .
She stopped aghast at the tactical error. But Carrel
was looking at her fixedly, a smile playing on his lips
as he pulled his tiny moustache with his jewelled
hand.

'Yes, certainly, I understand,' he said. 'Experience is very useful, naturally. But you must begin
and you know: *il n'y a que le premier pas qui coûte.*
Now perhaps you can sing? It would be very
useful.'

'Yes, I can sing,' said Victoria doubtfully, suppress-
ing 'a little,' remembering her first mistake.

'Ah, that is good,' said Carrel smiling. 'Will you
sit down to the piano? I have no music; ladies
always bring it but do you not know something by
heart?'

Victoria got up, her heart beating a little and went
to the piano. 'I don't know anything French,' she
said.

'It does not matter,' said Carrel, 'you will learn
easily.' He lowered the piano stool for her. As she
sat down the side of his head brushed her shoulder

lightly. A faint scent of heliotrope rose from his hair.

Victoria dragged off her gloves nervously, felt for the pedals and with a voice that trembled a little sang two ballads which had always pleased Lympton. The piano was frightfully out of tune. Everything conspired to make her nervous. It was only when she struck the last note that she looked at the impresario.

'Very good, very good,' cried Carrel. '*Magnifique*. Mademoiselle, you have a beautiful voice. You will be a great success at Vichy.'

'Vichy?' echoed Victoria, a little overwhelmed by his approval of a voice which she knew to be quite ordinary.

'Yes, I have a troupe to sing and dance at Vichy and in the towns, Clermont Ferrand, Lyon, everywhere. I will engage you to sing and dance,' said Carrel, his dark eyes sparkling.

'Oh, I can't dance,' cried Victoria despairingly.

'But I assure you, it is not difficult,' said Carrel. 'We will teach you. There, I will show you the contract. As you have not had much experience my syndicate can only pay you one hundred and fifty francs a month. But we will pay the expenses and the costumes.'

Victoria looked doubtful for a moment. To sing, to dance, to go to France where she had never been, all this was sudden and momentous.

'*Voyons*,' said Carrel, 'it will be quite easy. I am taking four English ladies with you and two do not understand the theatre. You will make more money if the audience like you. Here is the contract.' He drew a printed sheet out of the drawer and handed it to her.

It was an impressive document with a heavy headline; *Troupe de Théâtre Anglaise*. It bore a French revenue stamp and contained half-a-dozen clauses in French which she struggled through painfully;

she could only guess at their meaning. So far as
she could see she was bound to sing and dance
according to the programme which was to be fixed
by the *Directeur*, twice every day including Sundays.
The *syndicat* undertook to pay the railway fares and
to provide costumes. She hesitated, then crossed
the Rubicon.

'Fill in the blanks, please,' she said unsteadily.
' I accept.'

Carrel took up a pen and wrote in the date and
cent cinquante francs. ' What name will you adopt ? '
he asked, ' and what is your own name ? '

Victoria hesitated. 'My name is Victoria Fulton,'
she said. ' You may call me . . . Aminta Ormond.'

Carrel smiled once more. 'Aminta Ormond ? I
do not think you will like that. It is not English.
It is like Amanda. No! I have it, Gladys Oxford,
it is excellent.'

Before she could protest he had begun writing.
After all, what did it matter ? She signed the document without a word.

'*Voilà*,' said Carrel smoothly, locking the drawer
on the contract. ' We leave from Charing Cross on
Wednesday evening. So you have two days to
prepare yourself. *Monsieur le Directeur* will meet
you under the clock at a quarter past eight. The
train leaves at nine. We will take your ticket when
you arrive. Please come here at four on Wednesday
and I will introduce you to the *Directeur*.'

Victoria got up and mechanically shook hands.
Carrel opened the door for her and ceremoniously
bowed her out. She walked into Soho place as in a
dream, every pulse in her body thrilling with
unwonted adventure. She stared at a dirty window
pane and wondered at the brilliance it threw back
from her eyes.

CHAPTER XII

VICTORIA had forgotten her latchkey. Miss Briggs opened the door for her. Her sallow face brightened up.

'There's a gentleman waiting, mum,' she said, and ''ere's a telegram.' Came jest five minutes after you left. I've put him in the front room what's empty, mum. Thought you'd rather see him there. Been 'ere 'arf an 'our, mum.'

Victoria did not attempt to disentangle the hours of arrival of the gentleman and the telegram; she tore open the brown envelope excitedly. It only heralded the coming of Edward who was doubtless the gentleman.

'Thanks, Miss Briggs,' she said, ' it's my brother.'

'Yes, mum, nice young gentleman. He's all right; been reading the *New Age*, mum, this 'arf hour, what belongs to the lady on the third.'

Victoria smiled and went into the dining-room, where none dine in lodging houses save ghosts. Edward was standing near the mantlepiece immersed in the paper.

'Why, Ted, this is nice of you,' cried Victoria going up to him and taking his hand.

'I had to come up to town suddenly,' said Edward, 'to get books for the Head. I'm going back this afternoon but I thought I'd look you up. Did you get the telegram.'

'Just got it now,' said Victoria, showing it, ' so you might have saved the sixpence.'

'I'm sorry,' said Edward. 'I didn't know until this morning.'

'It doesn't matter. I'm so glad to see you.'

There was an awkward pause. Edward brushed away the hair from his forehead. His hands flew back to his watch-chain. Victoria had briefly written to him to tell him why she left the Holts. Fearful of all that touches women, he was acutely conscious that he blamed her and yet knew her to be blameless.

'It's a beautiful day,' he said suddenly.

'Isn't it?' agreed Victoria, looking at him with surprise. There was another pause.

'What are you doing just now, Vic?' Edward breathed more freely, having taken the plunge.

'I've just got some work,' said Victoria. 'I begin on Wednesday.'

'Oh, indeed?' said Edward with increasing interest. 'Have you got a post as companion?'

'Well, not exactly,' said Victoria. She realised that her story was not very easy to tell a man like Edward. He looked at her sharply. His face flushed. His brow puckered. With both hands he grasped his watch-chain.

'I hope, Victoria,' he said severely, 'that you are not adopting an occupation unworthy of a lady. I mean I know you couldn't,' he added, his severity melting into nervousness.

'I suppose nothing's unworthy,' said Victoria; 'the fact is, Ted, I'm afraid you won't like it much, but I'm going on the stage.'

Edward started and flushed like an angry boy. 'On the . . . the stage?' he gasped.

'Yes,' said Victoria quietly. 'I've got an engagement for six months to play at Vichy and other places in France. I only get six pounds a month but they pay all the expenses. I'll have quite thirty pounds clear when I come back. What do you think of that?'

'It's . . . it's awful,' cried Edward losing all self-consciousness. 'How can you do such a thing, Vic? If it were in London, it would be different. You simply can't do it.'

'Can't?' asked Victoria, raising her eyebrows. 'Why?'

'It's not done. No really Vic, you can't do it,' Edward was evidently disturbed. Fancy a sister of his . . . It was preposterous.

'I'm sorry, Ted,' said Victoria, 'but I'm going on Wednesday. I've signed the agreement.'

Edward looked at her almost horror-struck. His spectacles had slid down to the sharp tip of his nose.

'You are doing very wrong, Victoria,' he said, resuming his pedagogic gravity. 'You could have done nothing that I should have disapproved of as much. You should have looked out for something else.'

'Looked out for something else?' said Victoria with the suspicion of a sneer. 'Look here, Ted. I know you mean well, but I know what I'm doing; I haven't been in London for six months without finding out that life is hard on women like me. I'm no good because I'm too good for a poor job and not suitable for a superior one. So I've just got to do what I can.'

'Why didn't you try for a post as companion?' asked Edward with a half snarl.

'Try indeed! Anybody can see you haven't had to try, Ted. I've tried everything I could think of, agencies, societies, papers, everything. I can't get a post. I must do something. I've got to take what I can get. I know it now; we women are just raw material. The world uses as much of us as it needs and throws the rest on the scrap heap. Do you think I don't keep my eyes open? Do you think I don't see that when you want somebody to do double work at half rates you get a woman? And she thanks God and struggles for the work that's too dirty or too hard for a man to touch.'

Victoria paced up and down the small room, carried away by her vehemence. Edward said nothing. He was much upset and did not know what to say ; he had never seen Victoria like this and he was constitutionally afraid of vigour.

'I'm sorry, Ted,' said Victoria, stopping suddenly. She laid her hand on his sleeve. 'There, don't sulk with me. Let's go out to lunch and I'll go and choose your books with you after. Is it a bargain ? '

'I don't want to discuss the matter again,' replied Edward with as much composure as he could muster. 'Yes, let's go out to lunch.'

The rest of the day passed without another word on the subject of Victoria's downfall. She saw Edward off at St. Pancras. After he had said good-bye to her, he suddenly leaned out of the window of the railway carriage as if to speak, then changed his mind and sank back on the seat. Victoria smiled at her victory.

Next morning she broke the news to Miss Briggs. The landlady seemed amazed as well as concerned.

'You seem rather taken aback,' said Victoria.

'Well, mum, you see it's a funny thing the stage ; young ladies all seems to think it's easy to get on. And then they don't get on. And there you are.'

'Well, I *am* on,' said Victoria, 'so I shall have to leave on Wednesday.'

'Sorry to lose you, mum,' said Miss Briggs. ' 'ope yer'll 'ave a success. In course, as you 'aven't given me notice, mum, it'll 'ave to be a week's money more.'

'Oh, come, Miss Briggs, this is too bad,' cried Victoria, 'why, you've got a whole floor vacant ! What would it have mattered if I had given you notice ? '

'Might have let it, mum. Besides, it's the law,' said Miss Briggs, placing her arms akimbo, ready for the fray.

'Very well then,' said Victoria coldly, 'don't let's say anything more about it.'

Miss Briggs looked at her critically. 'No offence meant, mum,' she said timidly, 'it's a 'ard life, lodgers.'

'Indeed?' said Victoria without any show of interest.

'You wouldn't believe it, mum, all I've got to put up with. There's Hetty now . . .'

'Yes, yes, Miss Briggs,' said Victoria impatiently, 'you've told me about Hetty.'

'To be sure, mum,' replied Miss Briggs, humbly. 'It ain't easy to make ends meet. What with the rent and them Borough Council rates. There ain't no end to it, mum. I lives in the basement, mum, and that means gas all the afternoon, mum.'

Victoria looked at her again. This was a curious outlook. The poor troglodyte had translated the glory of the sun into cubic feet of gas.

'Yes, I suppose it is hard,' she said reflectively.

'To be sure, mum,' mused Miss Briggs. 'Sometimes you can't let at all. I've watched through the area railings, mum, many a long day in August, wondering if the legs I can see was coming 'ere. They don't mostly, mum.'

'Then why do you go on?' asked Victoria hardening suddenly.

'What am I to do, mum? I just gets my board and lodging out of it, mum. Keeps one respectable; always been respectable, mum. That ain't so easy in London, mum. Ah, when I was a young girl, might have been different, mum; you should have seen me 'air. Curls like anything, mum, when I puts it in papers. 'Ad a bit of a figure too, mum.'

'Deary me!'

Victoria looked with sympathy at the hard thin face, the ragged hair. Yes, she was respectable enough, poor Miss Briggs! Women have a hard life. No wonder they too are hard. You cannot afford to be earthenware among the brass pots.

'What will you do when you can't run the house any more?' she asked more gently.

'Do, mum? I dunno.'

Yet another philosophy.

'Miss Briggs,' came a man's voice from the stairs.

'Coming, sir,' yelled Miss Briggs in the penetrating tone that calling from cellar to attic teaches.

'Where are my boots?' said the voice on the stairs.

'I'll get 'em for you, sir,' cried Miss Briggs shuffling to the door on her worn slippers.

Life is a hard thing, thought Victoria again. Another woman for the scrap heap. Fourteen hours work a day, nightmares of unlet rooms, boots to black and coals to carry, dirt, loneliness, harsh words and at the end 'I dunno.' Is that to be my fate? she wondered.

However her blood soon raced again; she was an actress, she was going abroad, she was going to see the world, to enslave it, to have adventures, live. It was good. All that day Victoria trod on air. She no longer felt her loneliness. The sun was out and aglow, bringing in its premature exuberance joyful moisture to her temples. She, with the world, was young. In a fit of extravagance she lunched at a half crown table d'hote in Oxford Street, where pink shades softly diffuse the light on shining glass and silver. The coffee was almost regal, so strong, so full of sap. The light of triumph was in her eyes, making men turn back, sometimes follow and look into her face, half appealing, half insolent. But Victoria was unconscious of them, for the world was at her feet. She was the axis of the earth. It was in such a frame of mind that, the next day, she climbed the steps of Soho Place, careless of the view into the underground kitchen, of the two dogs who under the archway fought, growling, fouling the air with the scents of their

hides, over a piece of offal. She ran up the stairs
lightly. The door was still ajar.

Two men were sitting in the anteroom, both
smoking briar pipes. The taller of the two got up.

'Yes?' he said interrogatively.

'I . . . you . . . is Mr Carrel here?' asked
Victoria nervously.

'No Miss,' said the man calmly, 'he's just gone to
Marlborough Street.'

'Oh,' said Victoria, still nervous, 'will he be long?'

'I should say so, miss,' replied the man, 'perhaps
twelve months, perhaps more.'

Victoria gasped. 'I don't understand,' she said,
but her heart began to beat.

'Don't s'pose you would, miss,' said the short man,
getting up. 'Fact is, miss, we're the police and
we've had to take him; just about time we did, too.
Leaving for France to-night with a batch of girls.
S'pose you're one of them?'

'I was going to-night,' said Victoria faintly.

'May I have your name?' asked the tall man
politely, taking out a pocket book.

'Fulton,' she faltered. 'Victoria Fulton.'

'M'yes, that's it. 'Gladys Oxford,' said the tall
man turning back a page. 'Well Miss, you can
thank your stars you're out of it.'

'But what has he done?' asked Victoria with an
effort.

'Lord, Miss, you're from the country, I can see,'
said the short man amiably. 'I thought everybody
knew that little game. Take you over to Vichy, you
know. Make you dance and sing. Provide
costumes.' He winked at his companion.

'Costumes,' said Victoria, 'what do you mean?'

'Costumes don't mean much, Miss, over there,' said
the tall man. 'Fact is you'd have to wear what they
like and sing what they like when you pass the plate
round among the customers.'

Something seemed to freeze in Victoria.

'He said it was a theatre of varieties,' she gasped.

'Quite true,' said the tall man with returning cynicism. 'A theatre right enough, but you'd have supplied the variety to the customers.'

Victoria clenched her hands on the handle of her parasol. Then she turned to fly.

The short man stopped her and demanded her address, informing her that she was to attend at Marlborough Street next day at eleven thirty.

'Case mayn't be called before twelve,' he added. 'Sorry to trouble you, Miss. You won't hear any more about it unless it's a case for the Sessions.'

Victoria ran down the steps, through the alley and into Charing Cross Road as if something was tracking her, tracking her down. So this was the end of the dream. She had stretched her hand out to the roses, and the gods, less merciful to her than to Tantalus, had filled her palm with thorns. It was horrible, horrible. She had imagination, and a memory of old prints after Rowlandson which her father had treasured came back to her with almost nauseating force. She pictured the French *café chantant* like the Cave of Harmony; rough boards on trestles, laden with tankards of foaming beer, muddy lights, a foulness of tobacco smoke, a raised stage with an enormous woman singing on it, her eye frightfully dilated by belladonna, her massive arms and legs gleaming behind the dirty footlights and everywhere around men smoking, with noses like snouts, bodies like swine's, hairy hands—hands, ye gods !

She walked quickly away from the place of revelation. She hurried through the five o'clock inferno of Trafalgar Square, careless of the traffic, escaping death ten times. She hurried down the spaces of Whitehall, and only slackened her pace at Westminster Bridge. There she stopped for a moment; the sun was setting and gilded and empurpled the

foreshores. The horror of the past half hour seemed
to fade away as she watched the roses and mauves
bloom and blend, the deep shadows of the embank-
ments rise and fall. Near by, a vagrant, every inch
of him clothed in rags, the dirt of his face mimicking
their colour, smoked a short clay pipe, puffing at long
intervals small wreaths of smoke into the blue air.
And as Victoria watched them form, rise and vanish
into nothingness, the sun kiss gently but pitilessly
the old vagrant hunched up against the parapet, the
horror seemed to melt away. The peace of the
evening was expelling it, but another dread visitor
was heralded in. Victoria felt like lead in her heart,
the return of uncertainty. Once more she was an
outcast. No work. Once more she must ask herself
what to do and find no answer.

The river glittered and rose and fell, as if inviting
her. Victoria shuddered. It was not yet time for
that. She turned back and, with downcast eyes,
made for St James's Park. There she sat for a
moment watching a pelican flop on his island, the
waterfowl race and dive. The problem of life was
upon her now and where was the solution? Must I
tread the mill once more? thought Victoria. The
vision of agencies again, of secretaries courteous or
rude, of waits and hopes and despairs, all rushed at
her and convinced her of the uselessness of it all.
She was alone, always alone, because she wanted to
be free, to be happy, to live. Perhaps she had been
wrong after all to resist the call of the river. She
shuddered once more. A couple passed her with
hands interlocked, eyes gazing into eyes. No, life
must hold forth to her something to make it worth
while. She was cold. She got up and, with nervous
determination, walked quickly towards the gate.

The first thing to be done was to get quit of all the
horrors of the day, to cut away the wreckage. She
dared not stay at Castle Street. She would be

G

tracked. She would have to give evidence. She couldn't do it. She couldn't. Victoria having regained her coolness was in no wise uncertain as to her course of action. The first thing to do was for her to lose herself in London, aud that so deep that none could drag her out and force her to tell her story. She must change her lodgings then. Nothing could be easier, as she had already given Miss Briggs notice. In fact the best thing to do would be to keep up the fiction of her departure for France.

CHAPTER XIII

VICTORIA entered her room. It was in the condition that speaks of departure. Her trunks were packed and corded, all save a small suitcase which still gaped, showing spaces among the sundries that the skilled packer collects in the same bundle. Every drawer was open; the bed was unmade; the room was littered with newspapers and nondescript articles discarded at the last moment. Victoria rang her bell and quickly finished packing the suitcase with soap, washing gloves, powder-puffs and such like. As she turned the key Miss Briggs opened the door.

'Oh, Miss Briggs,' said Victoria quietly, 'I find that I must go down by an earlier train; I must be at Charing Cross in an hour; I'm going now.'

'Yes, mum,' said Miss Briggs without interest. 'Shall I tell the greengrocer to come now, mum?'

'Yes please, Miss Briggs; here are the seven shillings.'

Miss Briggs accepted the money without a word. It had formed the basis of a hot argument between her and her tenant; she considered herself entitled to one week's rent in lieu of notice but Victoria's new born sense of business had urged the fact that she had had two days notice; this had saved her three shillings. Miss Briggs laboured under a sense of injury, so she did not see Victoria to the door.

This was well, for Victoria was able to pay the greengrocer and to get rid of him in an artistic manner by sending him to post an empty envelope

addressed to an imaginary person, while she directed
the cabman to Paddington; this saved her awkward
questions and would leave Miss Briggs under the
impression that she had gone to Charing Cross.

At Paddington station she left her luggage in the
cloak-room and went out to find lodgings. Her quest
was short, for she had ceased to be particular, so that
within an hour she was installed in an imposing
ground floor front in the most respectable house in
Star Street. The district was not so refined as
Portsea Place, but the house seemed clean and the
quarters were certainly cheaper; eleven and six
covered both them and the usual breakfast.

Victoria surveyed the room in a friendly manner;
there was nothing attractive or repulsive in it; it
was clean; the furniture was almost exactly similar
to that which graced her lodgings in Portsea Place
and in Castle Street. The landlady seemed a friendly
body, and had already saved Victoria a drain on her
small store by sending her son, an out-of-work
furrier's hand, to fetch the luggage in a handcart
Remembering that she was a fugitive from justice
she gave her name as Miss Ferris.

Victoria returned from a hurried tea, unpacked
with content the trunk that should have followed
her to France. She was almost exhilarated by the
feeling of safety which enveloped her like comforting
warmth. The day was blithe in unison. She felt
quite safe, every movement of her flight having been
so skilfully calculated; she was revelling therefore
in her escape from danger, the deepest and truest
of all joys.

The next morning, however, found her in the
familiar mood of wondering what was to become of
her. After an extremely inferior breakfast which
brought down upon the already awed Mrs Smith
well deserved reproaches, Victoria investigated the
Telegraph columns with the usual negative results and,

in the resultant acid frame of mind, went through her accounts and discovered that her possessions amounted to twelve pounds, eight shillings and four pence. This was a terrible blow; the outfit for the interview with Carrel and the trip to France had dug an enormous hole in Victoria's resources.

'I must hurry up and find something,' said Victoria to herself. 'Twelve pounds eight and fourpence— say twelve weeks—and then?'

The next morning reconciled her a little to her fate. True, the paper yielded no help, but a lengthy account of Carrel's preliminary examination occupied three quarters of a column in the police court report. It was apparently a complicated case, for Carrel had been remanded and bail refused. The report did not yield her much information. Apparently Carrel was indicted for other counts than the exporting of the dancing girls to Vichy, for nine women had appeared. Victoria had quite a thrill of horror when she read the line in which the well schooled reporter dismissed the evidence of Miss 'S,' by saying that 'Miss S——here gave an account of her experience in the green room of the Folichon-Palace in 1902.' The baldness of the statement was appaling in its suggestiveness. She had been called, apparently, but no comment was made on her non-appearance.

'That's all over,' said Victoria with decision, throwing the newspaper down. She rose from the armchair, shook herself and opened the window to let out the smell of breakfast. Then she put on her hat and gloves and decided to have a walk to cheer herself up. Mindful that she was in a sense a fugitive, she avoided the Marble Arch and made for the Park through the desolate respectability of Lancaster Gate.

She made for the South East, unconsciously guided by the hieratic shot tower of Westminster. It was early; the freshness of May still bejewelled with dew drops the crisp new grass; the gravel, stained dark by moisture, hardly crunched under her feet, but gave like springy turf. Forgetting her depleted exchequer Victoria stepped briskly as if on business bent, looking at nothing but absorbing as through her skin the kisses of the western wind. At Hyde Park Corner she turned into St James's Park, and, passing the barracks, received with an old familiar thrill a covert smile from the handsome sentry. After all she was young, and it was good somehow to be once more smiled at by a soldier. Soldiers, soldiers—stupid perhaps, but could one help liking them? Victoria let her thoughts run back to Dicky—poor old wasted Dicky—and the Colonel and his liver, and Bobby, who would never be anything but Bobby, and Major Cairns too. Victoria felt a tiny pang as she thought of the Major. He was hardly young or handsome but strong, reassuring. She suddenly felt his lips on her neck again as she gazed rapidly at the dark lift on the horizon of the coast of Araby. He was a good fellow, the Major. She would like to meet him again.

She had reached Westminster Bridge. Her thoughts fell away from the comfortable presence of Major Cairns. Hunched up against the parapet sat the old vagrant she had seen there before, motionless, his rags lifting in the breeze, puffs of smoke coming at long intervals from his short clay pipe. Victoria shuddered; it seemed as if her life were bound to a wheel which brought her back inexorably to the same spot until the time came for her to lose there energy and life itself. She turned quickly towards the Embankment, and, as she rounded the curve, caught a glimpse of the old vagrant. The symbol of time had not moved.

Another twenty minutes of quick walking had brought her to the City. She was no longer fearful of it; indeed she almost enjoyed its surge and roar.

Log that she was, tossed on a stormy sea, she could not help feeling the joy of life in its buffeting. Not even the dullness and eternal length of Queen Victoria Street, which seems in the City, like Gower Street, indefinite and interminable, robbed her of the curious exultation which she felt whenever she entered the precincts. Here at least was life and doing; ugly doing perhaps, but things worthy of the name of action. At Mansion House she stopped for a moment to look at the turmoil: drays, motorbuses, cabs, cycles, entangled and threatening everywhere the little running black mites of humanity.

As Victoria passed the Bank and walked up Princes Street she felt hungry, for it was nearly one o'clock. She turned up a lane and stopped before a small shop which arrested her attention by its name above the door. It was called 'The Rosebud Café,' every letter of its name being made up of tiny roses; all the woodwork was painted white; the door was glazed and faced with pink curtains; pink half blinds lined the two small windows, nothing appearing through them except, right and left, two tall palms. 'The Rosebud,' had a freshness and newness that pleased her; and, as it boldly announced luncheons and teas, she pushed the white door open and entered. The room was larger than the outside gave reason to think, for it was all in depth. It was pretty in a style suggesting a combination of Watteau, Dresden China, and the top of a biscuit tin. All the woodwork was white, relieved here and there by pink drapery and cunningly selected water colours of more or less the same tint. From the roof, at close intervals, hung little baskets of paper roses. The back part of the room was glazed over, which showed that it lay below the well of a tall building. Symmetrically ranged were little tables, some large enough for four persons, mostly however meant for two, but Victoria noticed that they were all untenanted; in fact the room was empty, save for a woman who on her hands and knees was loudly washing the upper steps of a staircase leading into a cellar, and for a tall girl who stood on a ladder at the far end of the room critically surveying a picture she had just put up.

Victoria hesitated for a moment. The girl on the ladder looked round and jumped down. She was dressed in severe black out of which her long white face, mantling pink at the cheeks, emerged like a flower; indeed Victoria wondered whether she had been selected as an attendant because she was in harmony with the colour scheme of the shop. The girl was quite charming out of sheer insignificance; her fair hair untidily crowned her with a halo marred by flying wisps. Her little pink mouth, perpetually open and pouting querulous over three white upper teeth, showed annoyance at being disturbed.

'We aren't open,' she said with much decision. It was clearly quite bad enough to have to look forward to work on the morrow without anticipating the evil.

'Oh,' said Victoria, 'I'm sorry, I didn't know.'

'We open on Monday,' said the fair girl. 'Sharp.'

'Yes?' answered Victoria vaguely interested as one is in things newly born. 'This is a pretty place, isn't it?'

A flicker of animation. The fair girl's blue eyes opened wider. 'Rather,' she said. 'I did the water colours,' she explained with pride.

'How clever of you!' exclaimed Victoria. 'I couldn't draw to save my life.'

'Coloured them up, I mean,' the girl apologised grudgingly. 'It was a long job, I can tell you.'

Victoria smiled. 'Well,' she said, 'I must come back on Monday and see it finished if I'm in the City.'

'Oh, aren't you in the City?' asked the girl. 'West End?'

'No, not exactly West End,' said Victoria. 'I'm not doing anything just now.'

The fair girl gave her a glance of faint suspicion.

'Oh, aye, I see,' she said slowly, thoughtfully considering the rather full lines of Victoria's figure.

Victoria had not the slightest idea of what she saw. 'I'm looking out for a berth,' she remarked casually.

'Oh, are you?' said the girl with renewed animation. 'What's your line?'

'Anything,' said Victoria. She looked round the pink and white shop. A feeling of weariness had suddenly come over her. The woman at the top of the steps had backed away a little, and was rhythmically swishing a wet rag on the linoleum. Under her untidy hair her neck gleamed red and fleshy, touched here and there with beads of perspiration. Victoria took her in as unconsciously as she would an ox patiently straining at the yoke. To and fro the woman's body rocked, like a machine wound up to work until its parts drop out worn and useless.

'Ever done any waiting?' The voice of the girl almost made Victoria jump. She saw herself being critically inspected.

'No, never,' she faltered. 'That's to say, I would, if I got a billet.'

'Mm,' said the girl, eyeing her over. 'Mm.'

Victoria's heart beat unreasonably. 'Do you know where I can get a job?' she asked.

'Well,' said the girl very deliberately, 'the fact of the matter is, that we're short here. We had a letter this morning. One of our girls left home yesterday. Says she can't come. They don't know where she is.'

'Yes,' said Victoria, too excited to speculate as to the implied tragedy.

'If you like, you can see the manager,' said the girl. 'He's down there.' She pointed to the cellar.

'Thank you so much,' said Victoria, 'it's awfully kind of you.' The fair girl walked to the banisters. 'Mr Stein,' she cried shrilly into the darkness.

There was a rumble, a sound like the upsetting of

a chair, footsteps on the stairs. A head appeared on a level with the floor.

'Vat is it?' growled a voice.

'New girl; wants to be taken on.'

'Vell, take her on,' growled the voice. 'You are ze 'ead vaitress, gn, you are responsible.'

Victoria had just time to see the head, perfectly round, short-haired, white faced, cloven by a turned up black moustache, when it vanished once more. The Germanic 'gn' at the end of the first sentence puzzled her.

'Sulky beast,' murmured the girl. 'Anyhow, that's settled. You know the wages, don't you? Eight bob a week and your lunch and tea.'

'Eight . . .' gasped Victoria. 'But I can't live on that.'

'My, you are a green 'un,' smiled the girl. 'With a face like that you'll make twenty-five bob in tips by the time we've been on for a month.' She looked again at Victoria not unkindly.

'Tips,' said Victoria reflectively. Awful. But after all, what did it matter.

'All right,' she said, 'put me down.'

The girl took her name and address. 'Half-past eight sharp on Monday,' she said, ''cos it's opening day. Usual time half-past nine, off at four two days a week. Other days seven. Nine o'clock mid and end.'

Victoria stared a little. This was a business woman.

'Sorry,' said the girl, 'must leave you. Got a lot more to do to-day. My name's Laura. It'll have to be Lottie though. Nothing like Lottie to make fellows remember you.'

'Remember you?' asked Victoria puzzled.

'Lord, yes, how you going to make your station if they don't remember you?' said Lottie snappishly. 'You'll learn right enough. You let

'em call you Vic. Tell 'em to. You'll be all right.
And get yourself a black business dress. We supply
pink caps and aprons; charge you sixpence a week
for washing. You get a black openwork blouse,
mind you, with short sleeves. Nothing like it to
make your station.'

'What's a station?' asked Victoria, more bewildered than ever.

'My, you *are* a green 'un! A station's your
tables. Five you get. We'll cut 'em down when
they begin to come in. What you've got to do
is to pal up with the fellows; then they'll stick
to you, see? Regulars is what you want. The sort
that give no trouble 'cos you know their orders right
off and leave their twopence like clockwork, see?
But never you mind: you'll learn.' Thereupon
Lottie tactfully pushed Victoria towards the door.

Victoria stepped past the cleaner, who was now
washing the entrance. Nothing could be seen of
her save her back heaving a little in a filthy blue
bodice and her hands, large, red, ribbed with flowing
rivulets of black dirt and water. As her left hand
swung to and fro, Victoria saw upon the middle
finger the golden strangle of a wedding ring deep in
the red cavity of the swollen flesh.

CHAPTER XIV

'You come back with me, Vic, don't you?'

'You silly,' said Victoria, witheringly, 'I don't go off to-day, Gertie, worse luck.'

'Worse luck! I don't think,' cried Gertie. 'I'll swap with you, if you like. As if yer didn't know it's settling day. Why there's two and a kick in it!'

'Shut it,' remarked a fat, dark girl, placidly helping herself to potatoes, 'some people make a sight too much out of settling day.'

'Perhaps yer'll tell me wot yer mean, Miss Prodgitt,' snarled Gertie, her brown eyes flashing, her cockney accent attaining a heroic pitch.

'What I say,' remarked Miss Prodgitt, with the patronising air that usually accompanies this enlightening answer.

'Ho, indeed,' snapped Gertie, 'then p'raps yer'll keep wot yer've got ter sye to yersel, *Miss* Prodgitt.'

The fat girl opened her mouth, then, changing her mind, turned to Victoria and informed her that the weather was very cold for the time of the year.

'That'll do, Gertie,' remarked Lottie, 'you leave Bella alone and hook it.'

Gertie glowered for a moment, wasted another look of scorn on her opponent and flounced out of the room into a cupboard-like dark place, whence issued sounds like the growl of an angry cat. Something had obviously happened to her hat.

Victoria looked round aimlessly. She had no appetite; for half-past three, the barbarous lunch hour of the Rosebud girls, seemed calculated to limit the food bill. By her side Bella was conscientiously absorbing the potatoes that her daintier companions had left over from the Irish stew. Lottie was deeply engrossed in a copy of *London Opinion*, left behind by a customer. Victoria surveyed the room, almost absolutely bare save in the essentials of chairs and tables. It was not unsightly, excepting the fact that it was probably swept now and then but never cleaned out. Upon the wall opposite was stuck a penny souvenir which proclaimed the fact that the Emperor of Patagonia had lunched at the Guildhall. By its side hung a large looking glass co-operatively purchased by the staff. Another wall was occupied by pegs on which hung sundry dust coats and feather boas, mostly smart. Gertie, in the corner, was still fumbling in the place known as 'Heath's' because it represented the 'Hatterie.' It was a silent party enough, this; even the two other girls on duty downstairs would not have increased the animation much. Victoria sat back in her chair, and, glancing at the little watch she carried on her wrist in a leather strap, saw she still had ten minutes to think.

Victoria watched Gertie, who had come out of 'Heath's' and was poising her hat before the glass. She was a neat little thing, round everywhere, trim in the figure, standing well on her toes; her brown hair and eyes, pursed up little mouth, small, sharp nose, all spoke of briskness and self-confidence.

'Quarter to four, doin' a bunk,' she remarked generally over her shoulder.

'Mind Butty doesn't catch you,' said Victoria.

'Oh, he's all right,' said Gertie, 'we're pals.'

Fat Bella, chewing the cud at the table, shot a malevolent glance at her. Gertie took no notice of

her, tied on her veil with a snap, and collected her
steel purse, parasol, and long white cotton gloves.

'Bye, everybody,' she said, 'be good. Bye, Miss
Prodgitt; wish yer luck with yer perliceman, but you
take my tip; all what glitters isn't coppers.'

Before Miss Prodgitt could find a retort to this
ruthless exposure of her idyll, Gertie had vanished
down the stairs. Lottie dreamily turned to the last
page of *London Opinion* and vainly attempted to
sound the middle of her back; she was clearly disturbed by the advertisement of a patent medicine.
Victoria watched her amusedly.

They were not bad sorts, any of them. Lottie, in
her sharp way, had been a kindly guide in the early
days, explained the meaning of 'checks,' shown her
how to distinguish the inflexion on the word 'bill,' that
tells whether a customer wants the bill of fare or the
bill of costs, imparted too the wonderful mnemonics
which enable a waitress to sort four simultaneous
orders. Gertie, the only frankly common member of
the staff, barked ever but bit never. As for Bella,
poor soul, she represented neutrality. The thread of
her life was woven; she would marry her policeman
when he got his stripe, and bear him dull company to
the grave. Gertie would no doubt look after herself.
Not being likely to marry, she might keep straight
and end as a manageress, probably save nothing and
end in the workhouse, or go wrong and live somehow,
and then die as quickly as a robin passing from the
sunshine to the darkness. Lottie was a greater
problem; in her intelligence lay danger; she had
imagination, which in girls of her class is a perilous
possession. Her enthusiasm might take her anywhere, but very much more likely to misery than to
happiness. However, as she was visibly weak-chested,
Victoria took comfort in the thought that the air of
the underground smoking-room would some day
settle her troubles.

Victoria did not follow up her own line of life because as for all young things, there was no end for her—nothing but mist ahead, with a rosy tinge in it. Sufficient was it that she was in receipt of a fairly regular income, not exactly overworked, neither happy nor miserable. Apart from the two hours rush in the middle of the day, there was nothing to worry her. After two months she had worked up a fair connection; she could not rival the experienced Lottie, nor even Gertie whose forward little ways always 'caught on,' but she kept up an average of some fourteen shillings a week in tips. Thus she scored over Gladys and Cora, whose looks and manners were unimpressive, lymphatic Bella being of course outclassed by everybody. Twenty-one and six a week was none too much for Victoria, whose ideas of clothes were fatally upper middle class; good, and not too cheap. Still, she was enough of her class to live within her income, and even add a shilling now and then to her little hoard.

A door opened downstairs. 'Four o'clock!' Come down! Vic! Bella! Lottie! Vat are you doing? gn?'

Bella jumped up in terror, her fat cheeks quivering like jelly. 'Coming, Mr Stein, coming,' she cried, making for the stairs. Victoria followed more slowly. Lottie, secure in her privileges as head waitress, did not move until she heard the door below slam behind them.

Victoria lazily made for her tables. They were unoccupied save by a youth of the junior clerk type.

'Small tea toasted scone, Miss,' said the monarch with an approving look at Victoria's eyes. As she turned to execute his order he threw himself back in the bamboo arm chair. He joined his ten finger tips, and, crossing his legs, negligently displayed a purple sock. He retained this attitude until the return of Victoria.

'Kyou,' she said, depositing his cup before him.
She had unconsciously acquired this incomprehensible
habit of waitresses.

The young man availed himself of the wait for the
scone to inform Victoria that it was a cold day.

'We don't notice it here,' she said graciously
enough.

'Hot place, eh,' said the customer with a wink.

Victoria smiled. In the early days she would have
snubbed him, but she had heard the remark before
and had a stereotyped answer ready which, with a
new customer, invariably earned her a reputation
for wit.

'Oh, the hotter the fewer.' She smiled negligently,
moving away towards the counter. When she returned
with the scone, the youth held out his hand for the
plate, and, taking it, touched the side of hers with
his finger tips. She gave him a faint smile and sat
down a couple of yards away on a chair marked
'Attendant.'

The youth congratulated her upon the prettiness
of the place. Victoria helped him through his scone
by agreeing with him generally. She completed her
conquest by lightly touching his shoulder as she
gave him his check.

'Penny?' asked Bella, as the youth gone, Victoria
slipped her fingers under the cup.

'Gent,' replied Victoria, displaying three coppers.

Bella sighed. 'You've got all the luck, don't often
get a twopenny; never had a gent in my life.'

'I don't wonder you don't,' said Cora from the other
side of the room, 'looking as pleasant as if you were
being photographed. You got to give the boys some
sport.'

Bella sighed. 'It's all very well, Cora, I'm an
ugly one, that's what it is.'

'Get out; I'm not a blooming daisy. Try washing
your hair . . .'

'It's wrong,' interposed Bella ponderously.

'Oh, shut it, *Miss* Prodgitt, I've no patience with you.'

Cora walked away to the counter where Gladys was brewing tea. There was a singular similarity between these two; both were short and plump; both used henna to bring their hair up to a certain hue of redness; both had complexions obviously too dark for the copper of their locks, belied as it was already by their brown eyes. Indeed their resemblance frequently created trouble, for each maintained that the other ruined her trade by making her face cheap.

'Can't help it if you've got a cheap face,' was the invariable answer from either. 'You go home and come back when the rhubarb's out,' usually served as a retort.

The July afternoon oozed away. It was cool; now and then an effluvium of tea came to Victoria, mingled with the scent of toast. Now and then too the rumble of a dray or the clatter of a hansom filtered into the dullness. Victoria almost slept.

The inner door opened. A tall, stout, elderly man entered, throwing a savage glance round the shop. There was a little stir among the girls. Bella's rigidity increased tenfold. Cora and Gladys suddenly stopped talking. Alone Victoria and Lottie seemed unconcerned at the entrance of Butty, for 'Butty' it was.

'Butty,' otherwise Mr Burton, the chairman of 'Rosebud, Ltd.,' continued to glare theatrically. He wore a blue suit of a crude tint, a check black and white waistcoat, a soft fronted brown shirt and, set in a shilling poplin tie, a large black pearl. Under a grey bowler set far back on his head his forehead sloped away to his wispy greying hair. His nose was large and veined, his cheeks pendulous and touched with rosacia; his hanging underlip revealed

H

yellow teeth. The heavy dullness of his face was somewhat relieved by his little blue eyes, piercing and sparkling like those of a snake. His face was that of a man who is looking for faults to correct.

Mr Burton strode through the shop to the counter where Cora and Gladys at once assumed an air of rectitude while he examined the cash register. Then, without a word, he returned towards the doorway, sweeping Lottie's tables with a discontented glance, and came to a stop before one of Bella's tables.

'What's this? what the devil do you mean by this?' thundered Butty, pointing to a soiled plate and cup.

'Oh, sir, I'm sorry, I . . .' gasped Bella, 'I . . .'

'Now look here, my girl,' hissed Butty, savagely, 'don't you give me any of your lip. If I ever find anything on a table of yours thirty seconds after a customer's gone, it's the sack. Take it from me.'

He walked to the steps and descended into the smoking-room. Cora and Gladys went into fits of silent mirth, pointing at poor Bella. Lottie, unconcerned as ever, vainly tried to extract interest from the shop copy of 'What's On.'

'Victoria,' came Butty's voice from below. 'Where's Mr Stein? Come down.'

'He's washing, sir,' said Victoria, bending over the banisters.

'Oh, washing is he? first time I've caught him at it,' came the answer with vicious jocularity. 'Here's a nice state of things; come down.'

Victoria went down the steps.

'Now then, why aren't these salt cellars put away? It's your job before you come up.'

'If you please, sir, it's settling day,' said Victoria quietly, 'we open this room again at six.'

'Oh, yes, s'pose you're right. I don't blame you. Never have to,' said Butty grudgingly, then ingratiatingly.

'No, sir,' said Victoria.

'No, you're not like the others,' said Butty
negligently coming closer to her.

Victoria smiled respectfully, but edged a little
away. Butty eyed her narrowly, his lips smiling
and a little moist. Then his hand suddenly shot
out and seized her by the arm, high up, just under
the short sleeve.

'You're a nice girl,' he said, looking into her eyes.

Victoria said nothing, but tried to free herself.
She tried harder as she felt on her forearm the moist
warmth of the ball of Butty's thumb softly caressing it.

'Let me go, sir,' she whispered, 'they can see you
through the banisters.'

'Never you mind, Vic,' said Butty drawing her
towards him.

Victoria slipped from his grasp, ran to the stairs,
but remembered to climb them in a natural and
leisurely manner.

'Cool, very cool,' said Butty, approvingly, 'fine
girl, fine girl.' He passed his tongue over his lips,
which had suddenly gone dry.

When Victoria returned to her seat Lottie had not
moved ; Bella sat deep in her own despair, but, behind
the counter, Cora and Gladys were fixing two stern
pairs of eyes upon the favourite.

CHAPTER XV

'YES, sir, yes sir; I've got your order,' cried Victoria to a middle aged man, whose face reddened with every minute of waiting. 'Steak, sir? Yes, sir, that'll be eight minutes. And sautées, yes sir. Gladys, send Dicky up to four. What was yours, sir? Wing twopence extra. No bread? Oh, sorry, sir, thought you said Worcester.'

Victoria dashed away to the counter. This was the busy hour. In her brain a hurtle of food stuffs and condiments automatically sorted itself out.

'Now then, hurry up with that chop,' she snapped, thrusting her head almost through the kitchen window.

''Oo are you,' growled the cook over her shoulder. 'Empress of Germany? I don't think.'

'Oh, shut it, Maria, hand it over; now then Cora, where you pushing to?' Victoria edged Cora back from the window, seized the chop and rushed back to her tables.

The bustle increased; it was close on one o'clock, an hour when the slaves drop their oars, and for a while leave the thwarts of many groans. The Rosebud had nearly filled up. Almost every table was occupied by young men, most of them reading a paper propped up against a cruet, some a Temple Classic, its pages kept open by the weight of the plate edge. A steady hum of talk came from those who did not read, and, mingled with the clatter of knives and forks, produced that atmosphere of mongrel sound that floats into the ears like a restless wave.

Victoria stepped briskly between the tables, collecting orders, deftly making out bill after bill, smoothing tempers ruffled here and there by a wrongful attribution of food.

'Yes sir, cutlets. No veg? Cauli? Yes sir.'

She almost ran up and down as half-past one struck and the young men asked for coffees, small coffees, small blacks, china teas. From time to time she could breathe and linger for some seconds by a youth who audaciously played with the pencil and foil suspended from her waist. Or she exchanged a pleasantry.

'Now then, Nevy, none of your larks.' Victoria turned round sharply and caught a hand engaged in forcing a piece of sugar into her belt.

Nevy, otherwise Neville Brown, laughed and held her hand the space of a second. 'I love my love with a V . . .' he began, looking up at her, his blue eyes shining.

'Chuck it or I'll tell your mother,' said Victoria, smiling too. She withdrew her hand and turned away.

'Oh, I say, Vic, don't go, wait a bit,' cried Neville, 'I want, now what did I want?'

'Sure I don't know,' said Victoria, 'you never said what you wanted. Want me to make up your mind for you?'

'Do, Vic, let our minds be one,' said Neville.

Victoria looked at him approvingly. Neville Brown deserved the nickname of 'Beauty,' which had clung to him since he left school. Brown wavy hair, features so clean cut as to appear almost effeminate, a broad pointed jaw, all combined to make him the schoolgirl's dream. Set off by his fair and slightly sunburnt face, his blue eyes sparkled with mischief.

'Well, then, special and cream. Sixpence and serve you right.'

She laughed and stepped briskly away to the counter.

'You're in luck, Beauty,' said his neighbour with a sardonic air.

'Oh, it's no go, James,' replied Brown, 'straight as they make them.'

'Don't say she's not. But if I weren't a married man, I'd go for her baldheaded.'

'Guess you would, Jimmy,' said Beauty, laughing, 'but you'd be wasting your time. You wouldn't get anything out of her.'

'Don't you be too sure,' said Jimmy meaningly. He passed his hand reflectively over his shaven lips.

'Well, well,' said Brown, 'p'raps I'm not an Apollo like you, Jimmy.'

Jimmy smiled complacently. He was a tall slim youth, well groomed about the head, doggy about the collar and tie, neatly dressed in Scotch tweed. His steady grey eyes and firm mouth, a little set and rigid, the impeccability of all about him, had stamped business upon his face as upon his clothes.

'Oh, I can't queer your pitch, Beauty,' he said a little grimly. 'I know you, you low dog.'

Beauty laughed at the epithet. 'You've got no poetry about you, you North Country chaps, when a girl's as lovely as Victoria—'

'As lovely as Victoria,' he repeated a little louder as Victoria laid the cup of coffee before him.

'I know all about that,' said Victoria coolly, 'you don't come it over me like that, Nevy.'

'Cruel, cruel girl,' sighed Neville. 'Ah, if you only knew what I feel——'

Victoria put her hand on the tablecloth and, for a moment, looked down into Neville's blue eyes.

'You oughtn't to be allowed out,' she pronounced, 'you aren't safe.'

Jimmy got up as if he had been sitting on a suddenly released spring

'Spoon away both of you,' he said smoothly, 'I'm going over to Parsons' to buy a racquet. Coming, Beauty? No, thought as much. Ta-ta, Vic. Excuse me. Steak and kidney pie is tenpence, not a shilling. Cheer oh! Beauty.'

'He's a rum one,' said Victoria, reflectively, as Jimmy passed the cash desk.

'Jimmy? oh, he's all right,' said Neville, 'but look here Vic, I want to speak to you. Let's go on the bust to-night. Dinner at the New Gaiety and the theatre. What d'you think?'

Victoria looked at him for a second.

'You are a cure, Nevy,' she said.

'Then that's a bargain?' said Brown, eagerly snapping up her non-refusal. 'Meet me at Strand Tube Station half-past seven. You're off to-night, I know.'

'Oh you know, do you,' said Victoria smiling. 'Been pumping Bella I suppose, like the rest. She's a green one, that girl.'

Neville looked up at her appealingly. 'Never mind how I know,' he said, 'say you'll come, we'll have a ripping time.'

'Well, p'raps I will and p'raps I won't,' said Victoria. 'Your bill, Sir? Yessir.'

Victoria went to the next table. While she wrote she exchanged chaff with the customers. One had not raised his eyes from his book; one stood waiting for his bill; the other two, creatures about to be men, raised languid eyes from their coffee cups. One negligently puffed a jet of tobacco smoke upwards towards Victoria.

'Rotten,' she said briefly, 'I see you didn't buy those up West.'

'That's what *you* think, Vic,' said the youth, 'fact is I got them in the Burlington. Have one?'

'No thanks. Don't want to be run in.'

'Have a match then.' The young man held up a

two inch vesta. 'What price that, eh? pinched 'em
from the Troc' last night.'

'You are a toff, Bertie,' said Victoria with unction.
'I'll have it as a keepsake.' She took it and stuck it
in her belt.

Bertie leaned over to his neighbour. 'It's a mash,'
he said confidently.

'Take her to Kew,' said his friend, 'next stop
Brighton.'

'Can't run to it, old cock,' said the youth. 'However we shall see.'

'Vic, Vic,' whispered Neville. But Victoria had
passed him quickly and was answering Mr Stein.

'Vat you mean by it,' he growled, 'making de
gentleman vait for his ticket, gn?'

'Beg your pardon, Mr Stein, I did nothing of the
kind. The gentleman was making *me* wait while he
talked to his friend.'

Victoria could now lie coolly and well. Stein looked
at her savagely and slowly walked away along the
gangway between the tables, glowering from right to
left, looking managerially for possible complaints.

Victoria turned back from the counter. There,
behind the coffee urn where Cora presided, stood
Burton, in his blue suit, tiny beads of perspiration
appearing on his forehead. His little blue eyes fixed
themselves upon her like drills seeking in her being
the line of least resistance where he could deliver his
attack. She almost fled, as if she had seen a snake,
every facet of her memory causing the touch of his
hot warm hand to materialise.

'Vic,' said Neville's voice softly as she passed, 'is
it yes?'

She looked down at the handsome face.

'Yes, Beauty Boy,' she whispered, and walked
away.

CHAPTER XVI

'SILLY ass,' remarked Victoria angrily. She threw Edward's letter on the table. Unconsciously she spoke the 'Rosebud' language, for contact had had its effect upon her; she no longer awoke with a start to the fact that she was speaking an alien tongue, a tongue she would once have despised.

Edward had expressed his interest in her welfare in a letter of four pages covered with his thin writing, every letter of which was legible and sloped at the proper angle. He 'considered it exceedingly undesirable for her to adopt a profession such as that of waitress.' It was comforting to know that 'he was relieved to see that she had the common decency to change her name, and he trusted. . . .' Here Victoria had stopped.

'I can't bear it,' she said. 'I can't, can't, can't. Twopenny little schoolmaster lecturing me, me who've got to earn every penny I get by fighting for it in the dirt, so to say.' Every one of Edward's features came up before her eyes, his straggling fair hair, his bloodless face, his fumbling ineffective hands. This pedagogue who had stepped from scholardom to teacherdom dared to blame or eulogise the steps she took to earn her living, to be free to live or die as she chose. It was preposterous. What did he know of life?

Victoria seized a pen and feverishly scribbled on a crumpled sheet of paper.

'My dear Edward,—What I do's my business. I've

got to live and I can't choose. And you can be sure that so long as I can keep myself I shan't come to you for help or advice. Perhaps you don't know what freedom is, never having had any. But I do and I'm going to keep it even if it costs me the approval of you people who sit at home comfortably and judge people like me who want to be strong and free. But what's the good of talking about freedom to you.— Your affectionate sister,

VICTORIA.

She addressed the envelope and ran out hatless to post it at the pillar box in Edgware Road. As she crossed the road homewards a horse bus rumbled by. It carried an enormous advertisement of the new musical comedy *The Teapot Girl*. 'A fine comedy indeed,' she thought, suddenly a little weary.

As she entered her room, where a small oil lamp diffused a sphere of graduated light, she was seized as by the throat by the oppression of the silent summer night. The wind had fallen; not even a whirl of dust stirred in the air. Alone and far away a piano organ in a square droned and clanked Italian melody. She thought of Edward and of her letter. Perhaps she had been too sharp. Once upon a time she would not have written like that : she was getting common.

Victoria sat down on a little chair, her hands clasped together in her lap, her eyes looking out at the blank wall opposite. This, nine o'clock, was the fatal hour when the ghosts of her dead past paced like caged beasts up and down in her small room, and the wraith of the day's work rattled its chains. There had been earlier times when, in the first flush of independence, she had sat down to gloat over what was almost success, her liberty, her living earned by her own efforts. The rosiness of freedom then wrapped around the dinge with wreaths of fancy, wreaths that curled incessantly into harmonious shapes. But

Victoria had soon plumbed the depths of speculation
and found that the fire of imagination needs shadowy
fuel for its shadowy combustion. Day by day her
brain had become less lissome. Then, instead of
thinking for the joy of thought, she had read some
fourpenny-halfpenny novel, a paper even, picked up
in the Tube. Her mind was waking up, visualising,
realising, and in its troublous surgings made for
something to cling to to steady itself. But months
rolled on and on, inharmonious in their sameness,
unrelieved by anything from the monotony of work
and sleep. Certain facts meant certain things and
recurred eternally with their unchanging meaning;
the knock that awoke her, a knock so individual and
habitual that her sleepy brain was conscious on
Sundays that she need not respond; the smell of
food which began to assail her faintly as she entered
the 'Rosebud,' then grew to pungency and reek at
midday, blended with tobacco, then slowly ebbed
almost into nothingness : the dying day that was
grateful to her eyes when she left to go home, when
things looked kindly round her.

When Victoria realised all of a sudden her loneliness
in her island in Star Street, something like the fear of
the hunted had driven her out into the streets. She
was afraid to be alone, for not even books could save
her from her thoughts, those hounds in full cry. In
such moods she had walked the streets quickly,
looking at nothing, maintaining her pace over hills.
Now and then she had suddenly landed on a slum,
caught sight of, all beery and bloody, through the
chink of a black lane. But she shunned the flares,
the wet pavement, the orange peel that squelched
beneath her boots, afraid of the sight of too vigorous
life. Unconsciously she had sought the drug of
weariness, and the cunning bred of her dipsomania
told her that the living were poor companions for her
soul. And, when at times a man had followed her,

his eye arrested by the lines of her face lit up by
a gas lamp, he had soon tired of her quick walk and
turned away towards weaker vessels.

But even weariness, when abused, loses its power
as a sedative. The body, at once hardened and
satiated, demands more every day as it craves for
increasing dozes of morphia, for more food, more
drink, more kisses, more, ever more. Thus Victoria
had reached her last stage when, sitting alone in
her room, she once more faced the emptiness where
the ghosts of her dead past paced like caged
beasts and the wraith of the day's work rattled its
chains.

From this, now a state of mental instead of physical
exhaustion, she was seldom roused ; and it needed an
Edward come to judgment to stir her sleepy brain
into quick passion. Again and again the events of
the day would chase round and round maddeningly
with every one of their little details sharp as crystals.
Victoria could almost mechanically repeat some
conversations, all trifling, similar, confined to half a
dozen topics ; she could feel, too, but casually as an
odalisque, the hot wave of desire which surrounded
her all day, evidenced by eyes that glittered, fastened
on her hands as she served, on her face, the curve of
her neck, her breast, her hips ; eyes that devoured
and divested her of her meretricious livery. And,
worse perhaps than that big primitive surge which
left her cold but unangered, the futility of others who
bandied with her the daily threadbare joke, who
wearied her mind with questions as to food, compelled her to sympathise with the vagaries of the
weather or were arch, flirtatious and dragged out of
her tired mind the necessary response. Even Butty
and the moist warmth of him, even Stein with his
flaccid surly face, were better in their grossness than
these vapid youths, thoughtless, incapable of thought,
incapable of imagining thought, who set her down

as an inferior, as a toy for games that were not even
those of men.

'Beauty' had been a disappointment. She had
met him two or three times since their first evening
out. That night Neville, who was a young man of the
world, had pressed his suit so delicately, preserving
in so cat-like a manner his lines of retreat, that she
had not been able to snub him when inclined to. He
had a small private income and knew how to make
the best of his good looks by means of gentle manners
and smart clothes. In the insurance office where he
was one of those clerks who have lately evolved from
the junior stage, he was nothing in particular and
earned ten pounds a month. He had furnished two
rooms on the Chelsea edge of Kensington, belonged to
an inexpensive club in St James's, had been twice
to Brussels and once to Paris; he smoked Turkish
cigarettes, deeming Virginia common; he subscribed
to a library in connection with Mudie's, and knew
enough of the middle classes to exaggerate his impression of them into the smart set. Perhaps he tried
a little too much to be a gentleman.

Neville Brown was strongly attracted to Victoria.
He had vainly tried to draw her out, and scented the
lie in her carefully concocted story. He knew enough
to feel that she was at heart one of those women he
met 'in society,' perhaps a little better. Thus she
puzzled him extremely, for she was not even facile;
he could hold her hand; she had not refused him
kisses, but he was afraid to secure his grip on her as
a man carrying a butterfly stirs not a finger for fear
it should escape.

Victoria turned all this over lazily. Her instinct
told her what manner of man was Neville, for he
hardly concealed his desires. Indeed their relations
had something of the charm of a masqued ball. She
saw well enough that Neville was not likely to remain
content with kisses, and viewed the inevitable battle

with mixed feelings. She liked him; indeed, in certain moods and when his blue eyes were at their bluest, he attracted her magnetically. The reminiscent scent of Turkish tobacco on her lips always drew her back towards him; and yet she was of her class, shy of love, of all that is illicit because unacknowledged. She knew very well that Neville would hardly ask her to marry him and that she would refuse if he did; she knew less well what she would do if he asked her to love him. When she analysed their relation she always found that all lay on the lap of the gods.

In the loneliness of night her thoughts would fasten on him more intently. He was youth and warmth and friendliness, words for the silent, a hand to touch; better still he was a figment of Love itself, with all its tenderness and crudity, its heat, all the quivers of its body; he was soft scented as the mysterious giver of passionate gifts. So, when Victoria lay down to try and sleep she rocked in the trough of the waves of doubt. She could not tell into what hands she would give, if she gave, her freedom, her independence of thought and deed, all that security which is dear to the sheltered class from which she came. So, far into the night she would struggle for sight, tossing from right to left and left to right, thrusting away and then recalling the brown face, the blue eyes and their promise.

CHAPTER XVII

THE days rolled on, and on every one, as their scroll revealed itself, Victoria inscribed doings which never varied. The routine grew heavier as she found that the events of a Monday were so similar to those of another Monday that after a month she could not locate happenings. She no longer read newspapers. There was nothing in them for her; not even the mock tragedy of the death of an heir presumptive or the truer grimness of a shipwreck could rouse in her an emotion. She did not care for adventure : not because she thought that adventure was beneath her notice, but because it could not affect her. A revolution could have happened, but she would have served boiled cod and coffees to the groundlings, wings of chicken to the luxurious, without a thought for the upheaval, provided it did not flutter the pink curtains beyond which hummed the world.

At times, for the holiday season was not over and work was rather slack, Victoria had time to sit on her 'attendant' chair and to think awhile. Reading nothing and seeing no one save Beauty and Mrs Smith, she was thinking once more and thinking dangerously much. Often she would watch Lottie, negligently serving, returning the ball of futility with a carelessness that was almost grace, or Cora talking smart slang in young lady-like tones.

'To what end?' thought Victoria. 'What are we doing here, wasting our lives, I suppose, to feed these boys. For what's the good of feeding them so that they may scrawl figures in books and catch trains and perhaps one day, unless they've got too old, marry some dull girl and have more children than they can keep? We girls, we're wasted too.' So strongly did she feel this that, one day, she prospected the unexplored ground of Cora's mind.

'What are you worrying about?' remarked Cora, after Victoria had tried to inflame her with noble discontent. 'I don't say it's all honey, this job of ours, but you can have a good time pretty well every night, can't you, let alone Sundays?'

'But I don't want a good time,' said Victoria, suddenly inspired. 'I want to feel I'm alive, do something.'

'Do what?' said Cora.

'Live, see things, travel.'

'Oh, we don't get a chance, of course,' said Cora. 'I'll tell you how it is, Vic, you want too much. If you want anything in life you've got to want nothing, then whatever you get good seems jolly good.'

'You're a pessimist, Cora,' said Victoria smiling.

'Meaning I see the sad side? Don't you believe it. Every cloud has a silver lining, you know.'

'And every silver lining has a cloud,' said Victoria, sadly.

'Now, Vic,' answered Cora crossly, 'don't you go on like that. You'll only mope and mope. And what's the good of that, I'd like to know.'

'Oh, I don't know,' said Victoria, 'I like thinking of things. Sometimes I wish I could make an end of it. Don't you?'

'Lord, no,' said Cora, 'I make the best of it. You take my tip and don't think too much.'

Victoria bent down in her chair, her chin upon her open palm. Cora slapped her on the back.

'Cheer up,' she said, 'we'll soon be dead.'

Victoria had also attempted Gladys, but had discovered without surprise that her association with

Cora had equalised their minds as well as the copper of their hair. Lottie never said much when attacked on a general subject, while Bella never said anything at all. Since the day when Victoria had attempted to draw her out on the fateful question 'What's the good of anything?' Bella Prodgitt had looked upon Victoria as a dangerous revolutionary. At times she would follow the firebrand round the shop with frightened and admiring eyes. For her Victoria was something like the brilliant relation of whom the family is proud without daring to acknowledge him.

It fell to Gertie's lot to enlighten Victoria further on the current outlook of life. It came about in this way. One Saturday afternoon Victoria and Bella were alone on duty upstairs, for the serving of lunch is then at a low ebb; the City makes a desperate effort to reach the edge of the world to lunch peacefully and cheaply in its homes and lodgings. Lottie and Gertie were taking the smoking room below.

It was nearly three o'clock. At one of the larger tables sat two men, both almost through with their lunch. The elder of the two, a stout, cheery-looking man, pushed away his cup, slipped two pennies under the saucer and, taking up his bill, which Victoria had made out when she gave him his coffee, went up to the cash desk. The other man, a pale-faced youth in a blue suit, sat before his half emptied cup. His hand passed nervously round his chin as he surveyed the room; his was rather the face of a ferret, with a long upper lip, watery blue eyes, and a weak chin. His forehead sloped a little and was decorated with many pimples.

Victoria passed him quickly, caught up the stout man, entered the cash desk and took his bill. He turned in the doorway.

'Well, Vic,' he said, 'when are we going to be married?'

I

'29th of February, if it's not a leap year,' she laughed.

'Too bad, too bad,' said the stout man, looking back from the open door out of which he had already passed, 'you're the third girl who's said that to me in a fortnight.'

'Serve you right,' said Victoria, looking into the mirror opposite, 'you're as bad as Henry the . . . .'

The door closed. Victoria did not finish her sentence. Her eyes were glued to the mirror. In it she could only see a young man with a thin face, decorated with many pimples, hurriedly gulping down the remains of his cup of coffee. But a second before then she had seen something which made her fetch a quick breath. The young man had looked round, marked that her head was turned away; he had thrown a quick glance to the right and the left, to the counter which Bella had left for a moment to go into the kitchen; then his hand had shot out and, with a quick movement, he had seized the stout man's pennies and slipped them under his own saucer.

The young man got up. Victoria came up to him and made out his bill. He took it without a word and paid it at the desk, Victoria taking his money.

'Well, he didn't steal it, did he?' said Gertie, when Victoria told her of the incident.

'No, not exactly. Unless he stole it from the first man.'

''Ow could he steal it if he didn't take it?' snapped Gertie.

'Well he made believe to tip me when he didn't, and he made believe that the first man was mean when it was he who was,' said Victoria. 'So he stole it from the first man to give it me.'

'Lord, I don't see what yer after,' said Gertie. 'You ain't lost nothing. And the first fellow he ain't lost nothing either. He'd *left* his money.'

Victoria struggled for a few sentences. The little Cockney brain could not take in her view. Gertie could only see that Victoria had had twopence from somebody instead of from somebody else, so what was her trouble?

'Tell yer wot,' said Gertie summing up the case, 'seems ter me the fellow knew wot he was after. Dodgy sort of thing to do. Oughter 'ave thought of the looking-glass though.'

Victoria turned away from Gertie's crafty little smile. There was something in the girl that she could not understand; nor could Gertie understand her scruple. Gertie helped her a little though to solve the problem of waste; this girl could hardly be wasted, thought Victoria, for of what use could she be? She had neither the fine physique that enables a woman to bear big stupid sons, nor the intelligence which breeds a cleverer generation; she was sunk in the worship of easy pleasure, and ever bade the fleeting joy to tarry yet awhile.

'She isn't alive at all,' said Victoria to Lottie. 'She merely grows older.'

'Well, so do we,' replied Lottie in matter of fact tones.

Victoria was compelled to admit the truth of this, but she did not see her point clearly enough to state it. Lottie, besides, did nothing to draw her out. In some ways she was Victoria's oasis in the desert, for she was simple and gentle, but her status lymphaticus was permanent. She did not even dream.

Victoria's psychological enquiries did not tend to make her popular. The verdict of the 'Rosebud' was that she was a 'rum one,' perhaps a 'deep one.' The staff were confirmed in their suspicions that she was a 'deep one' by the obvious attentions that Mr Burton paid her. They were not prudish, except Bella, who objected to 'goings on'; to be distinguished by Butty was rather disgusting, but it was flattering too.

'He could have anybody he liked, the dirty old tyke,' remarked Cora. 'Of course I'm not taking any,' she added in response to a black look from Bella Prodgitt.

Victoria was not 'taking any' either, but she every day found greater difficulty in repelling him. Burton would stand behind the counter near the kitchen door during the lunch hour, and whenever Victoria had to come up to it, he would draw closer, so close that she could see over the whites of his little eyes a fine web of blood vessels. Every time she came and went her skirts brushed against his legs ; on her neck sometimes she felt the rush of his bitter scented breath.

One afternoon, in the change room, as she was dressing alone to leave at four, the door opened. She had taken off her blouse and turned with a little cry. Burton had come in suddenly. He walked straight up to her, his eyes not fixed on hers but on her bare arms. A faintness came over her. She hardly had the strength to repel him, as without a word he threw one arm round her waist, seizing her above the elbow with his other hand. As he tried to draw her towards him she saw a few inches from her face, just the man's mouth, red and wet, like the sucker of a leech, the lips parted over the yellow teeth.

'Let me go!' she hissed, throwing her head back.

Burton ground her against him, craning his neck to touch her lips with his.

'Don't be silly,' he whispered, 'I love you. You be my little girl.'

'Let me go.' Victoria shook him savagely.

'None of that.' Burton's eyes were glittering. The corners had pulled upwards with rage.

'Let me go, I say.'

Burton did not answer. For a minute they wrestled.
Victoria thrust him back against the wall. She
almost turned sick as his hand, slipping round her,
flattened itself on her bare shoulder. In that moment
of weakness Burton won, and, bending her over,
kissed her on the mouth. She struggled, but Burton
had gripped her behind the neck. Three times he
kissed her on the lips. A convulsion of disgust and
she lay motionless in his embrace. There was a step
on the stairs. A few seconds later Burton had
slipped out by the side door.

' What's up ? ' said Gladys suspiciously.

Victoria had sunk upon a chair, breathless, dishevelled, her face in her hands.

' Nothing . . . I . . . I feel sick,' she faltered.
Then she savagely wiped her mouth with her
feather boa.

Victoria was getting a grip of things. The brute,
the currish brute. The words rang in her head like
a chorus. For days, the memory of the affray did
not leave her. She guarded, too, against any recurrence of the scene.

Her hatred for Burton seemed to increase the
fascination of Neville. She did not think of them
together, but it always seemed to happen that,
immediately after thrusting away the toad-like
picture of the chairman, she thought of the blue-eyed
boy. Yet her relations with Neville were ill-fated.
Some days after the foul incident in the change room,
Neville took her for one of his little ' busts.' As it
was one of her late nights he called for her at a
quarter past nine. They walked towards the west
and, on the stroke of ten, Neville escorted her into
one of the enormous restaurants that the Refreshment
Rendezvous, known to London as the Ah-Ah, runs as
anonymously as it may.

Victoria was amused. The R. R. was the owner
of a palace, built, if not for the classes, certainly not

for the masses. Its facing was of tortured Portland
stone, where Greek columns, Italian, Louis XIV and
Tudor mouldings blended with rich Byzantine gild-
ings and pre-Raphaelite frescoes. Inside too, it was
all plush, mainly red; gold again; palms, fountains,
with goldfish and tin ducks. The restaurant was
quite a fair imitation of the Carlton, but a table
d'hôte supper was provided for eighteen pence,
including finger bowls in which floated a rose petal.

Neville and Victoria sat at a small table made for
two. She surrendered her feet to the clasp of his.
Around her were about two hundred couples and a
hundred family parties. Most of the young men
were elaborately casual; they wore blue or tweed
suits, a few, frock coats marred by double collars;
they had a tendency to loll and to puff the insolent
tobacco smoke of virginias towards the distant roof.
Their young ladies talked a great deal and looked
about. There was much wriggling of chairs, much
giggling, much pulling up of long gloves over bare
arms. In a corner, all alone, a young man in well-
fitting evening clothes was consuming in melancholy
some chocolate and a sandwich.

Neville plied Victoria with the major part of a
half bottle of claret.

'Burgundy's the thing,' he said. 'More body
in it.'

'Yes, it is good, isn't it? I mustn't have any more,
though.'

'Oh, you're all right,' said Neville indulgently.
'Let's have some coffee and a liqueur.'

'No, no liqueur for me.'

'Well, coffee then. Here, waiter.'

Neville struggled for some minutes. He utterly
failed to gain the ear of the waiters.

'Let's go, Beauty,' said Victoria. 'I don't want
any coffee. No, really, I'd rather not. I can't sleep
if I take it.'

The couple walked up Regent Street, then along Piccadilly. Neville held Victoria's arm. He had slipped his fingers under the long glove. She did not withdraw her arm. His touch tickled her senses to quiescence if not to satisfaction. They turned into the Park. Just behind the statue of Achilles they stepped upon the grass and at once Neville threw his arm round Victoria. It was a little chilly ; mist was rising from the grass. The trees stood blackly out of it, as if sawn off a few feet from the ground. Neville stopped. A little smile was on his lips.

'Beauty boy,' said Victoria.

He drew her towards him and kissed her. He kissed her on the forehead, then on the cheek, for he was a sybarite, in matters of love something of an artist, just behind the ear, then passionately on the lips. Victoria closed her eyes and threw one arm round his neck. She felt exhilarated, as if gently warmed. They walked further westwards, and with every step the fog thickened.

'Let's stop, Beauty,' said Victoria, after they had rather suddenly walked up to a thicket. 'We'll get lost in the wilderness.'

'And wilderness were paradise enow,' murmured Neville in her ear.

Victoria did not know the hackneyed line. It sounded beautiful to her. She laughed nervously and let Neville draw her down by his side on the grass.

'Oh, let me go, Beauty,' she whispered. 'Suppose someone should come.'

Neville did not answer. He had clasped her to him. His lips were more insistent on hers. She felt his hand on her breast.

'Oh, no, no, Beauty, don't, please don't,' she said weakly.

For some minutes she lay passive in his grasp. He had undone the back of her blouse. His hand, cold and dry, had slipped along her shoulder, seeking warmth.

Slowly his clasp grew harder; he used his weight. Victoria bent under it. Something like faintness came over her.

'Victoria, Victoria, my darling.' The voice seemed far away. She was giving way more and more. Not a blade of grass shuddered under its shroud of mist. From the road came the roar of a motorbus, like a muffled drum. Then she felt the damp of the grass on her back through the opening of her blouse.

A second later she was sitting up. She had thrust Neville away with a savage push under the chin. He seized her once more. She fought him, seeing nothing to struggle with but a silent dark shadow.

'No, Beauty, no, you mustn't,' she panted.

They were standing then, both of them.

'Vic, darling, why not?' pleaded Neville gently. still holding her hand.

'I don't know. Oh, no, really I can't, Beauty.'

She did not know it, but generations of clean living were fighting behind her, driving back and crushing out the forces of nature. She did not know that, like most women, she was not a free being but the great-granddaughter of a woman whose forbears had taught her that illegal surrender is evil.

'I'm sorry, Beauty, . . . it's my fault,' she said.

'Oh, don't mention it,' said Neville icily, dropping her hand. 'You're playing with me, that's all.'

'I'm not,' said Victoria, tears of excitement in her eyes. 'Oh, Beauty, don't you understand. We women, we can't do what we like. It's so hard. We're poor, and life is so dull and we wish we were dead. And then a man comes like you and the only thing he can offer, we mustn't take it.'

'But why, why?' asked Beauty.

'I don't know,' said Victoria. 'We mustn't. At

any rate I mustn't. My freedom is all I've got and I can't give it up to you like that. I like you, you know that, don't you, Beauty?'

Neville did not answer.

'I do, Beauty. But I can't, don't you see. If I were a rich woman it would be different. I'd owe nobody anything. But I'm poor; it'd pull me down and . . . when a woman's down, men either kick or kiss her.'

Neville shrugged his shoulders.

'Let's go,' he said,

Silently, side by side, they walked out of the park.

CHAPTER XVIII

OCTOBER was dying, its russet tints slowly merging into grey. Thin mists, laden with fine specks of soot, had penetrated into the 'Rosebud.' Victoria, in her black business dress, under which she now had to wear a vest which rather killed the tip-drawing power of her openwork blouse, was setting her tables, quickly crossing red cloths over white, polishing the glasses, arranging knives and forks in artistic if inconvenient positions. It was ten o'clock, but business had not begun, neither Mr Stein nor Butty having arrived.

'Cold, ain't it?' remarked Gertie,

'Might be colder.' said Bella Prodgitt.

Victoria came towards them, carrying a trayful of cruets.

''Ow's Beauty?' asked Gertie.

Victoria passed by without a word. This romance had not added to the popularity of the chairman's favourite. Cora and Gladys were busy dusting the counter and polishing the urns. Lottie, in front of a wall glass, was putting the finishing touches to the set of her cap. The door opened to let in Mr Stein, strapped tight in his frock coat, his top hat set far back on his bullet head. He glared for a moment at the staff in general, then without a word took a letter addressed to him from a rack bearing several addressed to customers, and passed into the cash desk. The girls resumed their polishing more busily. Quickly the night wrappings fell from the chandeliers; the rosebud baskets were teased into shape; the tables, loaded swiftly with their sets, grew more becoming. Victoria, passing from table to table set on each a small vase full of chrysanthemums.

'I say, Gladys, look at Stein,' whispered Cora to her neighbour. Gladys straightened herself from under the counter and followed the direction of Cora's finger.

'Lord,' she said, 'what's up?'

Bella's attention was attracted. She too was interested in her bovine way. Mr Stein's attitude was certainly unusual. He held a sheet of paper in one hand, his other hand clutching at his cheek so hard as to make one of his eyes protrude. Both his eyes were fixed on the sheet of paper, incredulous and horror-stricken.

'I say, Vic, what's the matter with the little swine?' suddenly said Lottie, who had at length noticed him.

Victoria looked. Stein had not moved. For some seconds all the girls gazed spellbound at the frozen figure in the cashbox. The silence of tragedy was on them, a silence which arrests gesture and causes hearts to beat.

'Lord, I can't stick this,' whispered Cora, 'there's something wrong.' Quickly diving under the counter flap she ran towards the pay box where Stein still sat unmoving, as if petrified. The little group of girls watched her. Bella's stertorous breathing was plainly heard.

Cora opened the glass door and seized Stein by the arm.

'What's the matter, Mr Stein?' she said excitedly, 'are you feeling queer?'

Stein started like a somnabulist suddenly awakened and looked at her stupidly, then at the motionless girls in the shop.

'Nein, nein, lassen sie doch,' he muttered.

'Mr Stein, Mr Stein,' half-screamed Cora.

'Oh, get out, I'm all right, but the game's up. He's gone. The game's up I tell up. The game's up.'

Cora looked at him round-eyed. Mr Stein's idioms frightened her almost more than his German.

Stein was babbling, speaking louder and louder.

'Gone away, Burton. Bankrupt and got all the cash. . . . See? You get the sack. Starve. So do I and my vife. . . . Ach, ach, ach, ach. Mein Gott, Mein Gott, was solls. . . .'

Gertie watched from the counter with a heightened colour. Lottie and Victoria, side by side, had not moved. A curious chill had seized Victoria, stiffening her wrists and knees. Stein was talking quicker and quicker, with a voice that was not his.

'Ach, the damned scoundrel . . . the schweinehund . . . he knew the business was going to the dogs, ach, schweinehund, schweinehund. . . .' He paused. Less savage his thoughts turned to his losses. ' Two hundred shares he sold me. . . . I paid a premium . . . they vas to go to four . . . ach, ach, ach. . . . I'm in the cart.'

Gertie sniggered gently. The idiom had swamped the tragedy. Stein looked round at the sound. His face had gone leaden; his greasy plastered hair was all awry.

'Vat you laughing at, gn?' he asked savagely, suddenly resuming his managerial tone.

' Take it we're bust, ain't we?' said Gertie, stepping forward jauntily.

Stein lifted, then dropped one hand.

'Yes,' he said, ' bust.'

'Thank you for a week's wages, Mr Stein,' said Gertie, 'and I'll push off, if yer don't mind.'

Stein laughed harshly. With a theatrical movement he seized the cash drawer by the handle, drew it out and flung it on the floor. It was empty.

'Oh, that's 'ow it is,' said Gertie. 'You're a fine

gentleman, I don't think. Bloomin' lot of skunks.
What price that, mate?' she screamed addressing
Bella, who still sat in her chair, her cheeks rising and
falling like the sides of a cuttlefish. ''Ere's a fine
go. Fellers comes along and tikes in poor girl's like
me and you and steals the bread outer their mouths.
I'll 'ave yer run in, yer bloody foreigner.' She waved
her fist in the man's face. 'For two pins,' she
screamed, 'I'd smash yer fice, I'd. . . .'

'Chuck it, Gertie,' said Lottie, suddenly taking her
by the arm, 'don't you see he's got nothing to do
with it?'

'Oh, indeed, Miss Mealymouth,' sneered Gertie,
'what I want is my money. . . .'

'Leave him alone, Gertie,' said Victoria, 'you can't
kick a man when he's down.'

Gertie looked as if she were about to explode.
Then the problem became too big for her. In her
little Cockney brain the question was insolubly
revolving: 'Can you kick a man when he's down . . .?
Can you kick. . . .?'

Mr Stein passed his hand over his forehead. He
was pulling himself together.

'Close de door, Cora,' he commanded. 'Now then,
the company's bankrupt, there's nothing in the cashbox. You get the push. . . . I get the push.' His
voice broke slightly. His face twitched. 'You can
go. Get another job.' He looked at Gertie.

'Put down your address. I give it to the police.
You get something for wages.' He slowly turned away
and sat down on a chair, his eyes fixed on the wall.

There was a repressed hubbub of talking. Then
Gertie made the first move and went up to the change
room. She came back a minute or two later in her
long coat and large hat, carrying a parcel which none
noticed as being rather large for a comb. It contained
the company's cap and apron which, thought she, she
might as well save from the wreck.

Gertie shook hands with Cora. 'See yer ter-night,' she said airily, 'same old place; 'bye Miss Prodgitt, 'ope "Force" 'll lift you out of this.' She shook hands with Victoria, a trifle coldly, kissed Lottie, threw one last malevolent look at Stein's back. The door closed behind her. She had passed out of the backwater into the main stream.

Lottie, a little self consciously, pulled down the pink blinds, in token of mourning. The 'Rosebud' hung broken on its stalk. Then, silently, she went up into the change room, followed by Cora; a pace behind came Victoria, all heavy with gloom. They dressed silently. Cora, without a word, kissed them both, collected her small possessions into a reticule, then shook hands with both and kissed them again. The door closed behind her. When Lottie and Victoria went down into the shop, Cora also had passed into the main stream. Gladys had gone with her.

The two girls hesitated for a moment as to whether they should speak to Stein. It was almost dark, for the October light was too weak to filter through the thick pink blinds. Lottie went up to the dark figure.

'Cheer up,' she said kindly, 'it's a long lane that has no turning.'

Stein looked up uncomprehendingly, then sank his head into his hands.

As Lottie and Victoria turned once more, the front door open behind them, all they saw was Bella Prodgitt, lymphatic as ever, motionless on her chair, like a watcher over the figure of the man silently mourning his last hopes.

As they passed into the street the fresh air quickened by the coming cold of winter, stung their blood to action. The autumn sunlight, pale like the faded gold of hair that age has silvered, threw faint shadows on the dry white pavements where little whirlwinds of dust chased and figured like swallows on the wing.

Lottie and Victoria walked quickly down the city streets. It was half-past eleven, a time when, the rush of the morning over, comparative emptiness awaits the coming of the midday crowds; every minute they were stopped by the blocks of drays and carriages which come in greater numbers in the road as men grow fewer on the pavements. The unaccustomed liberty of the hour did not strike them; for depression, a sense of impotence before fatality, was upon them. Indeed, they did not pause until they reached on the Embankment the spot where the two beautiful youths prepare to fasten on one another their grip of bronze. They sat down upon a seat and for a while remained silent.

'What are you going to do, Lottie?' asked Victoria.

'Look out for another job, of course,' said Lottie.

'In the same line?' said Victoria.

'I'll try that first,' replied Lottie, 'but you know I'm not particular. There's all sorts of shops. Nice soft little jobs at photographers, and manicuring showrooms, I don't mind.'

Victoria, with the leaden weight of former days pressing on her, envied Lottie's calm optimism. She seemed so capable. But so far as she herself was concerned, she did not feel sure that the 'other job' would so easily be found. Indeed the memory of her desperate hunt for work wrapped itself round her, cold as a shroud.

'But what if you can't get one,' she faltered.

'Oh, that'll be all right,' said Lottie, airily. 'I can live with my married sister for a bit, but I'll find a job somehow. That doesn't worry me. What are you thinking of?'

'I don't know,' said Victoria slowly, 'I must look out I suppose.'

'Hard up?' asked Lottie.

'No, not exactly,' said Victoria. 'I'm not rolling in wealth, you know, but I can manage.'

'Well, don't you go and get stranded or anything,' said Lottie. 'It doesn't do to be proud. It's not much I can do, but anyhow you let me know if—' She paused. Victoria put her hand on hers.

'You're a bit of all right, Lottie,' she said softly, her feelings forming naturally into the language of her adopted class. For a few minutes the girls sat hand in hand.

'Well, I'd better be going,' said Lottie. 'I'm going to my married sister at Highgate first. Time enough to look about this afternoon.'

The two girls exchanged addresses. Victoria watched her friend's slim figure grow smaller and slimmer under her crown of pale hair, then almost fade away, merge into men and women and suddenly vanish at a turn, swallowed up. With a little shiver she got up and walked away quickly towards the west. She was lonely suddenly, horribly so. One by one, all the links of her worldly chain had snapped. Burton, the sensual brute, was gone; Stein was perhaps sitting still numb and silent in the darkened shop; Gertie, flippant and sharp, had sailed forth on life's ocean, there to be tossed like a cork and like a cork to swim; now Lottie was gone, cool and confident, to dangers underrated and unknown. She stood alone.

As she reached Westminster Bridge a strange sense of familiarity overwhelmed her. A well-known figure was there and it was horribly symbolical. It was the old vagrant of bygone days, sitting propped up against the parapet, clad in his filthy rags. From his short clay pipe, at long intervals, he puffed wreaths of smoke into the blue air.

CHAPTER XIX

THE russet of October had turned into the bleak
darkness of December. The threat of winter was in
the air; it hissed and sizzled in the bare branches as
they bent in the cold wind, shaking quivering drops
of water broadcast as if sowing the seeds of pain.
Victoria stopped for a moment on the threshold of the
house in Star Street, looked up and down the road.
It was black and sodden with wet; the pavement
was greasy and glistening, flecked with cabbage
stalks and orange peel. Then she looked across at
the small shop where, though it was Sunday, a tailor
sat cross-legged almost on a level with the street,
painfully collecting with weary eyes the avaricious
light. His back was bowed with habit; that and his
bandy legs told of his life and revealed his being.
In the street, when he had time to walk there, boys
mocked his shuffling gate, thus paying popular tribute
to the marks of honest toil.

. Victoria stepped down to the pavement. A dragging
sensation made her look at her right boot. The sole
was parting from the upper, stitch by stitch. With
something that was hardly a sigh Victoria put her
foot down again and slowly walked away. She turned
into Edgware Road, followed it northwards for a
while, then doubled sharply back into Praed Street
where she lingered awhile before an old curiosity
shop. She looked between two prints into the shop
where, in the darkness, she could see nothing. Yet
she looked at nothingness for quite a long while.

K   145

Then, listlessly, she followed the street, turned back through a square and stopped before a tiny chapel almost at the end of Star Street. The deity that follows with passionless eyes the wanderer in mean streets knew from her course that this woman had no errand; without emotion the Being snipped a few minutes from her earthly span.

By the side of the chapel sat an aged woman smothered in rags so many and so thick that she was passing well clad. She was hunched up on a camp stool, all string and bits of firewood. A small stove carrying an iron tray told that her trade was selling roasted chestnuts; nothing moved in the group; the old woman's face was brown and cracked as her own chesnuts and there was less life in her than in the warm scent of the roasting fruits which gratefully filled Victoria's nostrils.

The eight weeks which now separated Victoria from the old days at the 'Rosebud' had driven deeper yet into her soul her unimportance. She was powerless before the world; indeed, when she thought of it at all, she no longer likened herself to a cork tossed in the storm, but to a pebble sunken and motionless in the bed of a flowing river.

Upon the day which followed her sudden uprooting Victoria had bent her back to the task of finding work. She had known once more the despairing search through the advertisement columns of the *Daily Telegraph*, the skilful winnowing of chaff from wheat, sudden and then baffled hopes. Her new professional sense had taken her to the shops where young women are wanted to enhance the attraction of coffee and cigarettes. But the bankruptcy of the 'Rosebud' was not an isolated case. The dishonesty of Burton was not its cause but its consequence; the ship was sinking under his feet when he deserted it after loading himself with such booty as he could carry. Victoria had discovered grimly that the first result of a commercial crisis is the submerging of those whose labours create a commercial boom. Within a week of the 'Rosebud' disaster the eleven City cafés of the 'Lethe, Ltd.' had closed their doors. Two small failures in the West End were followed by a greater crash. The 'People's Restaurants, Ltd.', eaten out by the thousand depots of the 'Refreshment Rendezvous, Ltd.,' had filed a voluntary petition for liquidation; the official liquidator had at once inaugurated a policy of 'retrenchment and sound business management,' and, as a beginning, closed two hundred shops in the City and West End. He proposed to exploit the suburbs, and, after a triumphant amalgamation with the victorious 'Refreshment Rendezvous,' to retire from law into peaceful directorships and there collect innumerable guineas.

Victoria had followed the convulsion with passionate interest. For a week the restaurant slump had been the fashion. The manager of every surviving café in London had given it as his deliberate opinion that trade would be all the better for it. The financial papers published grave warnings as to the dangers of the restaurant business, to which the Stock Exchange promptly responded by marking up the prices of the survivors' shares. The Socialist papers had eloquently pleaded for government assistance for the two thousand odd displaced girls; a Cabinet Minister had marred his parliamentary reputation by endeavouring to satisfy one wing of his party that the tearoom at South Kensington Museum was not a Socialistic venture and the other wing that it was an institution leading up to State ownership of the trade. A girl discharged from the 'Lethe' had earned five guineas by writing a thousand words in a hated but largely read daily paper. The interest had been kept up by the rescue of a P.R. girl who had jumped off Waterloo Bridge. Another P.R. girl, fired by example, had been more successful in the Lea. This valuable advertisement enabled the Relief Fund to distribute five shillings a head to many young persons who had been waitresses at some time or another; there were rumours of a knighthood for its energetic promoter.

It was in the midst of this welter that Victoria had found herself cast, with her newly acquired experience a drug in the market, and all the world inclined to look upon her as a kind of adventuress. Her employer's failure was in a sense her failure, and she was handy to blame. For three weeks she had doggedly continued her search for work, applying first of all in the smart tea-rooms of the West, and every day she became more accustomed to being turned away. Her soul hardened to rebuffs as that of a beggar who learns to bear stoically the denial of alms. After vainly trying the best Victoria had tried the worst, but everywhere the story was the same. Every small restaurant keeper was drawing his horns in, feverishly casting up trial balances; some of them in their panic had damaged their credit by trying to arrange with their banks for overdrafts they would never need. The slump was such that they did not believe that the public would continue to eat and drink; they retrenched employees instead of trying to carve success out of other men's disasters.

Victoria, her teeth set, had faced the storm. She now explored districts and streets systematically, almost house by house. And when her spirit broke at the end of the week, as her perpetual walks, the buffeting of rain and wind soiled her clothing, broke breaches into her boots, chapped her hands as glove seams gave way, the only thing that could brace her up was the shrinkage of her hoard by a sovereign. She placed the coin on the mantlepiece after counting the remainder. Monday morning saw it reduced to eleven shillings and sixpence. When the crisis came she had taken in sail by exchanging into the second floor back, then fortunately vacant, thus saving three shillings in rent.

The sight of her melting capital was a horror which she faced only once a week, for at other times she thrust the thought away, but it intruded every time with greater insistence. Untrained still in economy she found it impossible to reduce her expenditure below a pound. After paying off the mortgage of eight and sixpence for her room and breakfast, she had to set aside three shillings for fares, for she dared not wade overmuch in the December mud. The manageress of a cafe lost in Marylebone had heard her kindly, but had looked at her boots plastered with mud, then at the dirty fringes of her petticoats and said, regretfully almost, that she would not do. That day had cost Victoria a pound almost wrenched out of the money drawer. But this wardrobe though an asset, was an incubus, and Victoria at times often hated it, for it cost so much in omnibus fares that she paid for it every day in food stolen from her body.

By the end of the seventh week Victoria had reduced her hoard to four pounds. She now applied for work like an automaton, often going twice to the same shop without realising it, at other times sitting for hours on a park seat until the drizzle oozed from her hair into her neck. At the end of the seventh week she had so lost consciousness of the world that she walked all through the Sunday gloom without food. Then, at eight o'clock, awakening suddenly to her need, she gorged herself with suet pudding at an eating house in the Edgware Road, came back to Star Street and fell into a heavy sleep.

About four she was aroused by horrible sickness which left her weak, every muscle relaxed and every nerve strained to breaking point. Shapes blacker than the night floated before her eyes ; every passing milk cart rattled savagely through her beating temples; twitchings at her ankles and wrists, and the hurried beat of her heart shook the whole of her body. She almost writhed on her bed, up and down, as if forcibly thrown or goaded.

As the December dawn struggled through her window, diffusing over the white wall the light of the condemned cell, she could bear it no more. She got up, washed horrible bitterness from her mouth, clots from her eyes. Then, swaying with weariness and all her pulses beating, she strayed into the street, unseeing, her boots unbuttoned, into the daily struggle.

As the blind man unguided, or the poor on the march, she went into the East, now palely glowing over the chimney pots. She did not feel her weariness. Her feet did not belong to her; she felt as if her whole body were one gigantic wound vaguely aching under the chloroform. She walked without intention, and as towards no goal. At Oxford Circus she stopped. Her eye had unconsciously been arrested by the posters which the newsvendor was deftly glueing down on the pavement. The crude colours of the posters, red, green, yellow, shocked her sluggish mind into action. One spoke of a great reverse in Nubia; another repeated the information and added a football cup draw. A third poster, blazing red, struck such a blow at Victoria that, for a wild moment, her heart seemed to stop. It merely bore the words:

P. R.

REOPENS

Victoria read the two lines five or six times, first dully, then in a whirl of emotion. Her blood seemed to go hot and tingle; the twitchings of her wrists and ankles grew insistent. With her heart pounding with excitement she asked for the paper in a choked voice, refusing the halfpenny change. Backing a step or two she opened the paper. A sheet dropped into the mud.

The newsvendor, grizzled and sunburnt right into the wrinkles, picked up the sheet and looked at her wonderingly. From the other side a corpulent policeman watched her with faint interest, reading her like a book. He did not need to be told that Victoria was out of work; her face showed that hope had come into her life.

Victoria read every detail greedily. The enterprising liquidator had carried through the amalgamation of the People's Restaurants and the Refreshment Rendezvous, and created the People's Refreshment Rendezvous. He had done this so quietly and suddenly that the effect was a thunderbolt. He had forestalled the decision of the Court, so that agreements had been ready and signed on the Saturday evening, while leave had obscurely been granted on the Friday. Being master of the situation the liquidator was re-opening fifty-five of the two hundred closed shops. The paper announced his boast that 'by ten o'clock on Monday morning fifty-five P. R. R.'s would be flying the flag of the scone and cross buns.' The paper also hailed this pronouncement as Napoleonic.

Victoria feverishly read the list of the rescued depots. They were mainly in Oxford Street and Bloomsbury. Indeed, one of them was in Princes Street. A flood of clarity seemed to come over Victoria's brain. It was impossible for the P. R. or P. R. R. or whatever it had become, to have secured a staff on the Sunday. No doubt they proposed to engage it on the spot and to rush the organisation into working order so as to capture at the outset the *succés de curiosité* which every London daily was beating up in the breast of a million idle men and women. Clutching the paper in her hand she ran across Oxford Street almost under the wheels of a motor lorry. She turned into Princes Street, and hurled herself against the familiar door, clutching at the handle.

There was another girl leaning against the door. She was tall and slim. Her fair hair went to sandiness. Her black coat was dusty and stained. Her large blue eyes started from her colourless face, pale lipped, hollow under the cheekbones. Victoria recovered her breath and put her hair straight feverishly. A short dark girl joined the group, pressing her body close against them. Then two more. Then, one by one, half a dozen. Victoria discovered that her boots were undone, and bent down to do them up with a hairpin. As she struggled with numb fingers her rivals pressed upon her with silent hostility. As she straightened herself, the throng suddenly thrust her away from the door. Victoria recovered herself and drove against them gritting her teeth. The fair girl was ground against her; but Victoria, full of her pain and bread lust, thrust her elbow twice into the girl's breast. She felt something like the rage of battle upon her and its joy as the bone entered the soft flesh like a weapon.

'Now then, steady girls,' said the voice of the policeman, faint like a dream voice.

'Blime, ain't they a 'ot lot!' said another dream voice, a loafer's.

The crowd once more became orderly. Though quite a hundred girls had now collected hardly any spoke. In every face there was tenseness, though the front ranks showed most ferocity in their eyes and the late-comers most weariness.

'Where you shovin'?' asked a sulky voice.

There was a mutter that might have been a curse. Then silence once more ; and the girls fiercely watched for their bread, looking right and left like suspicious dogs. A spruce young warehouseman slowly reviewed the girls and allowed his eyes to linger approvingly on one or two. He winked approvingly at the fair girl but she did not respond. She stood flat against the door, every inch of her body spread so as to occupy as much space as she could.

Then, half-past seven, a young man and a middle-aged woman shouldering through the wedged mass, the fierce rush into the shop and there the gasp behind closed doors among the other winners, hatless, their clothes torn, their bodices ripped open to the stays, one with her hair down and her neck marked here and there by bleeding scratches. Then, after the turmoil of the day among the strangeness, without rest or food, to make holiday for the Londoners, a night heavy as lead and a week every day more mechanical. Victoria had returned to the treadmill and, within a week, knew it.

· · · · The clock struck five. Victoria awoke from her dream epic. She had won her battle and sailed into harbour. Its waters were already as horribly still as those of a stagnant pool. The old chestnut vendor sat motionless on her seat of firewood and string. Not a thought chased over her gnarled brown face. From the stove came the faint pungent smell of the charring peel.

CHAPTER XX

A FORTNIGHT later Victoria had returned to the City. Most of the old P.R's had reopened, after passing under the yoke. A coat of paint had transformed them into P.R.R's. In fact their extinction was complete ; nothing was left of them but the P. and the chairmanship of the amalgamated company, for their chairman was an earl and part of the goodwill. The P.R. had apparently been bought up at a fair rate. Its shares having fallen to sixpence, most of the shareholders had lost large sums ; whereas the directors and their friends, displaying the acumen that is sometimes found among directors, had quietly bought the shares up by the thousand and by putting them into the new company had realised large profits. As the failure had happened during the old year and most of the shops had been reopened in the new, it was quite clear that the catering trade was expanding. It was a startling instance of commercial progress.

Within a week the P.R.R. decided to start once more in the City. Victoria, by her own request, was transferred to Moorgate Street. She did not like the neighbourhood of Oxford Circus ; it was unfamiliar without being stimulating. She objected too to serving women. If she must serve at all she preferred serving men. She did not worship men ; indeed the impression they had left on her was rather unpleasant. The subalterns at the mess were dull, Mr Parker a stick, Bobby was Bobby, Burton a cur, Stein a lout, Beauty, well perhaps Beauty was

a little better and Cairns worthy of a kind thought;
but all the others, boys and half men with their futile
talk, their slang cribbed from the music halls, their
affectations, their loud ties, were nothing but the
ballast on which the world has founded its permanent
way. Yet a mysterious sex instinct made Victoria
prefer even them to the young ladies who frequented
Princes Street. It is better to be made love to
insolently than to be ordered about.

The Moorgate P.R.R. was one of the curious crosses
between the ice cream shop and the chop house where
thirty bob a week snatches a sixpenny lunch. It was
full of magnificent indifference. You could bang your
twopence for a small coffee, or luxuriate in steak and
kidney pie, boiled (*i.e.* potatoes), stewed prunes and
cream, and be served with the difference of interest
that the recording angel may make between
No. 1,000,000 and 1,000,001. You were seldom
looked at, and, if looked at, forgotten. It was as
blatant as the ' Rosebud ' had been discreet. Painted
pale blue, it flaunted a plate glass window full of
cakes, packets of tea, pounds of chocolate, jars of
sweets ; some imitation chops garnished with imitation parsley, and a chafing dish full of stage eggs
and bacon held out the promise of strong meats.
Enormous urns, polished like silver, could be seen
from the outside emitting clouds of steam ; under
the chafing dish too came up vaporous jets.

Inside, the P.R.R. recalled the wilderness and the
animation of a bank. To the blue and red tesselated
floor were fastened many marble-topped tables
squeezed so close together that when a customer rose
to leave he created an eddy among his disturbed
fellows. The floor was swamped with chairs which,
during the lunch hour, dismally grated on the tiled
floor. It was clean ; for, after every burst of feeding,
the appointed scavenger swept the fallen crusts,
fragments of pudding, cigarette ends and banana

skins into a large bin. This bin was periodically emptied and the contents sent to the East End, whether to be destroyed or to be used for philanthropic purposes is not known.

The girls were trained to quick service here. Victoria found no difficulty in acquiring the P.R.R. swing, for she had not to memorise the variety of dishes which the more fastidious Rosebudders demanded. Her mental load seldom went beyond small teas, a coffee or two, half a veal and ham pie, sandwiches and porridge. There was no considering the bill of fare. It stood on every table, immutable as a constitution and as dull. At the P.R.R., a man absorbed a maximum of stodgy food, paid his minimum of cash and vanished into an office to pour out the resultant energy for thirty bob a week. As there were no tips Victoria soon learned that courtesy was wasted, so wasted none.

The P.R.R. did not treat its girls badly—in this sense, that it treated them no worse than its rivals did theirs; it practised commercial morality. Victoria received eight shillings a week, to which good Samaritans added an average of fourteen pence, dropped anonymously into the unobtrusive box near the cash desk. At the 'Rosebud' tips averaged fourteen shillings a week, but then they were given publicly.

Besides her wages she was given all her meals, on a scale suited to girls who waited on Mr Thirty Bob a Week. Her breakfast was tea, bread and margarine; her dinner, cold pudding or pie, according to the unpopularity of the dishes among the customers, washed down once more with tea and sometimes followed by stewed fruit if the quantity that remained made it clear that some would be left over. The day ended with supper, tea, bread and cheese—a variety of Cheddar which the company bought by the ton on account of its peculiar capacity for swelling and producing a very tolerable substitute for repletion.

As Victoria was now paid less than half her former wages she was expected to work longer hours. The P. R. R. demanded faithful service from half-past eight in the morning to nine in the evening, except on one day when freedom was earned at six. Victoria was driven to generalise a little about this; it struck her as peculiar that an increase of work should synchronise with a decrease of pay, but the early steps in any education always fill the pupil with wonderment.

Yet she did not repine, for she remembered too well the black days of the old year when the wolf slunk round the house, coming every day nearer to her door. She had beaten him off and there still was joy in the thought of that victory. Her frame of mind was quiescent, tempered still with a feeling of relief. This she shared with her companions, for every one of them had known such straits as hers and worse. They had come back to the P. R. R. filled with exceeding joy; craving bread they had been given buns.

The Moorgate P. R. R. was a big depot. It boasted, in addition to the ground floor, two smoking rooms, one on the first floor and one underground, as well as a ladies' dining-room on the second floor. It had a staff of twenty waitresses, six of whom were stationed in the underground smoking-room; Victoria was one of these. A virile manageress dominated them and drove with splendid efficiency a concealed kitchen team of four who sweated in the midst of steam in an underground stokehole.

Victoria's companions were all old P. R's except Betty. They all had anything between two and five years' service behind them. Nelly, a big raw boned country girl, was still assertive and loud; she had good looks of the kind that last up to thirty, made up of fine coarse healthy flesh lines, tending to redden at the nostrils and at the ears; her hands were shapely still, though reddened and thickened by swabbing floors and tables. Maud was a poor little thing, small boned with a flaccid covering of white flesh, inclined to quiver a little when she felt unhappy; her eyes were undecidedly green, her hair carroty in the extreme. She had a trick of drawing down the corners of her mouth which made her look pathetic. Amy and Jenny were both short and darkish, inclined to be thin, always a little tired, always willing, always in a state neither happy nor unhappy. Both had nearly five years' experience and could look forward to another fifteen or so. They had no assertiveness, so could not aspire to a managerial position, such as might eventually fall to the share of Nelly.

Betty was an exception. She had not acquired the P. R. R. manner and probably never would. The daughter of a small draper at Horley, she had lived through a happy childhood, played in the fields, been to a little private school. Her father had strained every nerve to face on the one hand the competition of the London stores extending octopus like into the far suburbs, on the other that of the pedlars. Caught between the aristrocracy and the democracy of commerce he had slowly been ground down. When Betty was seventeen he collapsed through worry and overwork. His wife attempted to carry on the business after his death, bravely facing the enemy, discharging assistants, keeping the books, impressing Betty to dress the window, then to clean the shop. But the pressure had become too great, and on the day when the mortgagees foreclosed she died. Nothing was left for Betty except the clothes she stood in. Some poor relatives in London induced her to join the 'Lethe.' That was three years ago and now she was twenty.

Betty was the tall slim girl into whose breast Victoria had thrust her elbow when they were fighting for bread among the crowd which surged round the door of the Princes Street depot. She was pretty, perhaps a little too delicately so. Her sandy hair and wide open china blue eyes made one think of a doll; but the impression disappeared when one looked at her long limbs, her slightly sunken cheeks. She had a sweet disposition, so gentle that, though she was a favourite, her fellows despised her a little and were inclined to call her 'poor Betty.' She was nearly always tired; when she was well she was full of simple and honest merriment. She would laugh then if a motor bus skidded or if she saw a Highlander in a kilt. She had just been shifted to the Moorgate Street P.R.R. From the first the two girls had made friends and Victoria was deeply glad to meet her again. The depth of that gladness is only known to those who have lived alone in a hostile world.

'Betty,' said Victoria the first morning, 'there's something I want to say. I've had it on my mind. Do you remember the first time we met outside the old P.R. in Princes Street?'

'Don't I?' said Betty. 'We had a rough time, didn't we?'

'We had. And, Betty, perhaps you remember . . . I hit you in the chest. I've thought of it so often . . . and you don't know how sorry I am when I think of it.'

'Oh, I didn't mind,' said Betty, a blush rising to her forehead, 'I understand. I was about starving, you know, I thought you were the same,'

'No, not starving exactly,' said Victoria, 'mad rather, terrified, like a sheep which the dog's driving. But I beg your pardon, Betty, I oughtn't to have done it.'

Betty put her hand gently on her companion's.

'I understand, Vic,' she said, 'it's all over now; we're friends, aren't we?'

Victoria returned the pressure. That day established a tender link between these two. Sometimes, in the slack of three o'clock, they would sit side by side for a moment, their shoulders touching. When they met between the tables, running, their foreheads beaded with sweat, they exchanged a smile.

The customers at the P.R.R. were so many that Victoria could hardly retain an impression of them. A few were curious though, in the sense that they were typical. One corner of the room was occupied during the lunch hour by a small group of chess players; five of the six boards were regularly captured by them. They sat there in couples, their eyes glued to the board, allowing the grease to cake slowly on their food; from time to time one would swallow a mouthful, sometimes dropping morsels on the table. These he would brush away dreamily, his thoughts far away, two or three moves ahead. Round each table sat a little group of spectators who now and then shifted their plates and cups from table to table and watched the games. At times, when a game ended, a table was involved in a fierce discussion: gambits, Morphy's classical games, were thrown about. On the other side of the room the young domino-players noisily played matador, fives and threes, or plain matching, would look round and mutter a gibe at the enthusiasts.

Others were more personal. One, a repulsive individual, Greek or Levantine, patronised one of Betty's tables every day. He was fat, yellow and loud; over his invariably dirty hands drooped invariably dirty cuffs; on one finger he wore a large diamond ring.

'It makes me sick sometimes,' said Betty to Victoria, 'you know he eats with both hands and drops his food; he snuffles too, as he eats, like a pig.'

Another was an old man with a beautiful thin brown face and white hair. He sat at a very small

table, so small that he was usually alone. Every
day he ordered dry toast, a glass of milk and some
stewed fruit. He never read or smoked, nor did he
raise his eyes from the table. An ancient bookkeeper
perhaps, he lived on some principle.

Most of the P. R. R. types were scheduled however.
They were mainly young men or boys between fifteen
and twenty. All were clad in blue or dark suits,
wore flannel shirts, dickeys and no cuffs. They would
congregate in noisy groups, talk with furious energy,
and smoke Virginia cigarettes with an air of dare-
devilry. Now and then one of these would be sitting
alone, reading unexpected papers such as the *Times*,
borrowed from the office. Spasmodically, too, one
would be seen improving his mind. Victoria, within
six months, noticed three starts on the part of one
of the boys; French, bookkeeping and electrical
engineering.

Many were older than these. There were little
groups of young men rather rakishly but shabbily
dressed; often they wore a flower in their buttonhole.
The old men were more pathetic; their faces were
expressionless; they came to eat, not to feast.

Victoria and Betty had many conversations about
the customers. Every day Victoria felt her faculty
of wonder increase; she was vaguely conscious
already that men had a tendency to revert to types,
but she did not realise the influence the conditions of
their lives had upon them.

'It's curious,' she once said to Betty, as they left
the depôt together, 'they're so much alike.'

'I suppose they are,' said Betty. 'I wonder why?'

'I'm not sure,' said Victoria, 'but it seems to me
somehow that they must be born different but that
they become alike because they do the same kind
of work.'

'It's rather awful, isn't it?' said Betty.

'Awful? Well, I suppose it is. Think of it,

L

Betty. There's old Dry Toast, for instance. I'm
sure he's been doing whatever he does do for thirty
or forty years.'

'And'll go on doing it till he dies,' murmured
Betty.

'Or goes into the workhouse,' added Victoria. A
sudden and horrible lucidity had come over her.
'Yes, Betty, that's what it means. The boys are
going to be like the old man; we see them every day
becoming like him. First they're in the twenties
and are smart and read the sporting news; then they
seem to get fat and don't shave every day, because
they feel it's getting late and it doesn't matter what
they look like; their hair grows grey, they take up
chess or German, or something equally ridiculous.
They don't get a chance. They're born and as soon
as they can kick they're thrust in an office to do the
same thing every day. Nobody cares; all their
employers want them to do is to be punctual and do
what they're paid thirty bob a week for. Soon they
don't try; they die, and the employers fill the billet.'

'How do you know all this, Vic?' said Betty,
eyeing her fearfully. 'It seems so true.'

'Oh, I just felt it suddenly, besides . . .' Victoria
hesitated.

'But is it right that they should get thirty bob a
week all their lives while their employers are getting
thousands?' asked Betty, full of excitement.

'I don't know,' said Victoria slowly. Betty's voice
had broken the charm. She could no longer see
the vision.

CHAPTER XXI

THE days passed away horribly long. Victoria was now an automaton ; she no longer felt much of sorrow or of joy. Her home life had been reduced to a minimum, for she could no longer afford the luxury of 'chambers in the West End' as Betty put it. She had moved to Finsbury ; where she had found a large attic for three shillings a week, in a house which had fallen from the state of mansion for a City merchant to that of tenement dwelling. For the first time since she returned to London she had furnished her own room. She had bought out the former tenant for one pound. For this sum she had entered into possession of an iron bedstead with a straw mattress, a thick horse cloth, an iron washstand supplied with a blue basin and a white mug, an old armchair and red curtains. She had no sheets, which meant dis-comfort but saved washing. A chair had cost her two shillings ; she needed no cupboard as there was one in the wall ; in lieu of a chest of drawers she had her trunk ; her few books were stacked on a shelf made out of the side of a packing case and erected by herself. She got water from the landing every morning except when the taps were frozen. There was no fireplace in the attic, but in the present state of Victoria's income this did not matter much.

Every morning she rose at seven, washed, dressed. As time went on she ceased to dust and sweep every morning. First she postponed the work to the evening, then to the week end. On Sundays she breakfasted off a stale loaf bought among the roar of Farrington Street the previous evening. A little later she introduced a spirit lamp for tea; it was a revolution, even though she could never muster enough energy to bring in milk.

After the first flush of possession, the horrible gloom of winter had engulfed her. Sometimes she sat and froze in the attic, and, in despair, went to bed after vainly trying to read Shakespeare by the light of a candle: he did not interest her much. At other times the roaring streets, the flares in the brown fog, the trams hurtling through the air, their headlights blazing, had frightened her back to her home. On Sundays, after luxuriating in bed until ten, she usually went to meet Betty who lived in a club in Soho. Together they would walk in the parks, or the squares, wherever grass grew. At one o'clock Betty would introduce her as a guest at her club and feast her for eightpence on roast beef and pudding, tea, and bread and butter. Then they would start out once more towards the fields, sometimes towards Hampstead Heath, or if it rained seek refuge in a museum or a picture gallery. When they parted in the evening, Victoria kissed her affectionately. Betty would then hold the elder woman in her arms, hungrily almost, and softly kiss her again.

The only thing that parted these two at all was the mystery which Betty guessed at. She knew that Victoria was not like the other girls; she felt that there was behind her friend's present condition a past of another kind, but when she tried to question Victoria, she found that her friend froze up. And as she loved her this was a daily grief; she looked at Victoria with a question in her eyes. But Victoria would not yield to the temptation of confiding in her; she had adopted a new class and was not going back on it.

Besides Betty there was no one in her life. None

of the other girls were able to meet her on congenial ground ; Beauty had not got her address ; and, though she had his, she was too afraid of complicating her life to write to him. She had sent her address to Edward as a matter of form, but he had not written ; apparently her desire for freedom had convinced him that his sister was mad. None of the men at the P.R.R. had made any decided advances to her. She could still catch every day a glitter in the eye of some youth, but her maturity discouraged the boys, and the older men were mostly too deeply sunk in their feeding and smoking to attempt gallantry. Besides : Victoria was no longer the cream-coloured flower of olden days ; she was thinner ; her hands too were becoming coarse owing to her having to swab tables and floors ; much standing and the fetid air of the smoking-room were making her sallow.

Soon after Victoria entered into possession of her 'station' she knew most of her customers, knew them, that is, as much as continual rushes from table to counter, from floor to floor, permits. The casuals, mostly young, left no impression ; lacking money but craving variety these youths would patronise every day a different P.R.R., for they hoped to find in a novel arrangement of the counter, a new waitress, larger or smaller quarters, the element of variety which the bill of fare relentlessly denied them. The older men were more faithful if no more grateful. One of them was a short thin man, looking about forty, who for some hidden reason had aroused Victoria's faded interest. His appearance was somewhat peculiar. His shortness, combined with his thinness and breadth, was enough to attract attention. Standing hardly any more than five foot five, he had disproportionately broad shoulders, and yet they were so thin that the bones showed bowed at the back. Better fed, he would have been a bulky man. His hair was dark, streaked with grey ; and, as it was getting very thin and beginning to recede, he gave the impression of having a very high forehead. His eyes were grey, set rather deep under thick eyebrows drawn close together into a permanent frown. Under his rather coarse and irregular nose his mouth showed closely compressed, almost lipless; a curious muscular distortion had tortured into it a faint sneer. His hands were broad, a little coarse and very hairy.

Victoria could not say why she was interested in this man. He had no outward graces, dressed poorly and obviously brushed his coat but seldom; his linen, too, was not often quite clean. Immediately on sitting down at his usual table he would open a book, prop it up against the sugar bowl, and begin to read. His books did not tell Victoria much; in two months she noted a few books she did not know, *News from Nowhere, Fabian Essays, The Odyssey,* and a book with a long title the biggest printed word of which was *Niestze* or *Niesche.* Victoria could never remember this word, even though her customer read the book every day for over a month. *The Odyssey* she had heard of, but that did not tell her anything.

She had found out his name accidentally. One day he had brought down three books and had put two under his seat while he read the third. Soon after he had left, reading still while he went up the stairs. Victoria found the books under the chair. One was a *Life of William Morris,* the other the *Vindication of the Rights of Women.* On the flyleaf of each was written in bold letters ' Thomas Farwell.'

Victoria could not resist glancing at the books during her half hour for lunch. The *Life of William Morris* she did not attempt, remembering her experiences at school with ' Lives ' of any kind: they were all dull. Marie Wollstonecraft's book seemed more interesting, but she seemed to have to wade through so much that she had never heard of and to have to face a style so crabbed and congested that she hardly understood it. Yet, something in the book interested her, and it was regretfully that she handed the volumes back to Farwell when he called for them at half-past six. He thanked her in half a dozen words and left.

Farwell continued regular in his attendance. He came in on the stroke of one, left at half-past one exactly, lighting his pipe as he got up. He never spoke to anyone; when Victoria stood before his table he looked at her for a moment, gave his order and cast his eyes down to his book.

It was about three weeks after the incident of the books that he spoke to Victoria. As he took up the bill of fare he said suddenly:

'Did you read the *Vindication*?'

'I did glance through it,' said Victoria, feeling, she did not know why, acutely uncomfortable.

'Ah? interesting, isn't it? Pity it's so badly written. What do you think of it?'

'Well, I hardly know,' said Victoria reflectively; 'I didn't have time to read much; what I read seemed true.'

'You think that a recommendation, eh?' said Farwell, his lips parting slightly. 'I'd have thought you saw enough truth about life here to like lies.'

'No,' said Victoria, 'I don't care for lies. The nastier a thing is, the better everybody should know it; then one day people will be ashamed.'

'Oh, an optimist!' sniggered Farwell. 'Bless you, my child. Give me fillets of plaice, small white and cut.'

For several days after this Farwell took no notice of Victoria. He gave his order and opened his book as before. Victoria made no advances. She had talked him over with Betty, who had advised her to await events.

'You never know,' she had remarked, as a clinching argument.

A day or two later Victoria was startled by Farwell's arrival at half-past six. This had never happened before. The smoking-room was almost empty, as it was too late for teas and a little too early for suppers. Farwell sat down at his usual table and ordered a small tea. As Victoria returned with the cup he took out a book from under two others and held it out.

'Look here,' he said a little nervously, 'I don't know whether you're busy after hours, but perhaps you might like to read this.' The wrinkles in his forehead expanded and dilated a little.

'Oh, thank you so much. I would like to read it,' said Victoria with the ring of earnestness in her voice. She took the book; it was a battered copy of *No. 5 John Street*.

'No. 5? What a queer title,' she said.

'Queer? not at all,' said Farwell. 'It only seems queer to you because it is natural and you're not used to that. You're a number in the P.R.R. aren't you? Just like the house you live in. And you're just number so and so; so am I. When we die fate shoves up the next number and it all begins over again.'

'That doesn't sound very cheerful, does it?' said Victoria.

'It isn't cheerful. It's merely a fact.'

'I suppose it is,' said Victoria. 'Nobody is ever missed.'

Farwell looked at her critically. The platitude worried him a little; it was unexpected.

'Yes, exactly,' he stammered. 'Anyhow, you read it and let me know what you think of it.' Thereupon he took up another book and began to read.

When he had gone Victoria showed her prize to Betty.

'You're getting on,' said Betty with a smile. 'You'll be Mrs Farwell one of these days, I suppose.'

'Don't be ridiculous, Betty,' snapped Victoria, ' why, I'd have to wash him.'

'You might as well wash a husband as a dish,' said Betty smoothly. 'Anyhow, the other girls are talking.'

'Let them talk,' said Victoria rather savagely, ' so long as they don't talk to me.'

Betty took her hand gently.

'Sorry, Vic dear,' she said. 'You're not angry with me, are you?'

'No, of course not, you silly,' said Victoria laughing. 'There run away, or that old gent at the end'll take a fit.'

Farwell did not engage her in conversation for a few days, nor did she make any advances to him. She read through *No. 5 John Street* within three evenings; it held her with a horrible fascination. Her first plunge into realistic literature left her shocked as by a cold bath. In the early days, at Lympton, she had subsisted mainly on Charlotte Young aud Rhoda Broughton. In India, the mess having a subscription at Mudie's, she had had good opportunities of reading; but, for no particular reason, except perhaps that she was newly married and busy with regimental nothings, she had ceased to read anything beyond the *Sketch* and the *Sporting and Dramatic.* Thus she had never heard of the 'common people' except as persons born to minister to the needs of the rich. She had never felt any interest in them, for they spoke a language that was not hers. *No. 5 John Street*, coming to her a long time after the old happy days, when she herself was struggling in the mire, was a horrible revelation; it showed her herself, and herself not as 'Tilda towering over fate but as Nancy withering in the india-rubber works for the benefit of the Ridler system.

She read feverishly by the light of a candle. At times she was repelled by the vulgarity of Low

Covey, by the grossness which seemed to revel in
poverty and dirt. But when she cast her eyes round
her own bare walls, looked at her sheetless bed,
a shiver ran over her.

'These are my people,' she said aloud. The candle,
clamouring for the snuffers, guttered, sank low, nearly
went out.

Shivering again before the omen, she trimmed the
wick. She returned the book to Farwell by slipping
it on the table next day. He took it without a word
but returned at half past six as before.

'Well?' he asked with a faint smile.

'Thank you so much,' said Victoria. 'It's
wonderful.'

'Wonderful indeed? Most commonplace, don't
you think?'

'Oh, no,' said Victoria. 'Its extraordinary, it's like
. . . like light.'

Farwell's eyes suddenly glittered.

'Ah,' he said dreamily, 'light! light in this, the
outer darkness.'

Victoria looked at him, a question in her eyes.

'If only we could all see,' he went on. 'Then, as
by a touch of a magician's wand, flowers would crowd
out the thistles, the thistles that the asses eat and
thank their God for. It is in our hands to make this
the Happy Valley and we make it the Valley of the
Shadow of Death.'

He paused for a moment. Victoria felt her pulse
quicken.

'Yes,' she said, 'I think I understand. It's because
we don't understand that we suffer. We're not cruel,
are we? we're stupid.'

' 'Stupid?' A ferocious intonation had come into
Farwell's voice. 'I should say so! Forty million
men, women and children sweat their lives out day
by day so that four million may live idly and become
too heavy even to think. I could forgive them if

they thought, but the world contains only two types :
Lazarus with poor man's gout and Dives with fatty
degeneration of the brain.'

Victoria felt nervous. Passion shook the man's
hands as he clutched the marble top of the table.

'Mr Farwell,' she faltered, 'I don't want to be
stupid. I want to understand things. I want to
know why we slave twelve hours a day when others
do nothing and, oh, can it be altered?'

Farwell had started at the mention of his name.
His passion had suddenly fallen.

'Altered? oh, yes,' he stammered, 'that's if the
race lasts long enough. Sometimes I think, as I see
men struggling to get on top of one another, like
crabs in a bucket . . . Like crabs in a bucket,' he
repeated dreamily, visualising the simile. 'But I
cannot draw men from stones,' he said smiling; 'it
is not yet time for Deucalion. I'll bring you another
book to-morrow.'

Farwell rose abruptly and left Victoria singularly
stirred. He was a personality, she felt; something
quite unusual. He was less a man than a figment, for
he seemed top heavy almost. He concentrated the
hearer's attention so much on his spoken thought
that his body passed unperceived, receded into the
distance.

While Victoria was changing to go, the staff room
somehow seemed darker and dirtier than ever. It was
seldom swept and never cleaned out. The management had thoughtfully provided nothing but p gs and
wooden benches, so as to discourage lounging. eictoria
was rather late, so that she found herself alone with
Lizzie, the cashier. Lizzie was red-haired, very curly,
plump, pink and white. A regular little spark. She
was very popular; her green eyes and full curved
figure often caused a small block at the desk.

'You look tired,' she said good-naturedly.

'I suppose I am?' said Victoria. 'Aren't you?'

'So so. Don't mind my job.'

'Mm, I suppose it isn't so bad sitting at the desk.'

'No,' said Lizzie, 'pays too.'

'Pays?'

Lizzie flushed and hesitated. Then the desire to boast burst its bonds. She must tell, she must. It didn't matter after all. A craving for admiration was on her.

'Tell you what,' she whispered. 'I get quite two and a kick a week out of that job.'

Victoria's eyebrows went up.

'You know,' went on Lizzie, 'the boys look at me a bit.' She simpered slightly. 'Well, once one of them gave me half a bar with a bob check. He was looking at me in the eye, well! that mashed, I can tell you he looked like a boiled fish. Sort of inspiration came over me.' She stopped.

'Well?' asked Victoria, feeling a little nervous.

'Well . . . I . . . I gave him one half crown and three two bob pieces. Smiled at him. He boned the money quick enough, wanted to touch my hand you see. Never saw it.'

Victoria thought for a moment. 'Then you gave him eight and six instead of nine shillings?'

'You've hit it. Bless you, *he* never knew. Mashed, I can tell *you*.'

'Then you did him out of sixpence?'

'Right. Comes off once in three. Say "sorry" when I'm caught and smile and it's all right. Never try it twice on the same man.'

'I call that stealing,' said Victoria coldly.

'You can call it what you like,' snarled Lizzie. 'Everything's stealing. What's business? getting a quid for what costs you a tanner. I'm putting a bit extra on my wages.'

Victoria shrugged her shoulders. She might have argued with Lizzie as she had once argued with Gertie, but the vague truth that lurked in Lizzie's economics had deprived her of argument. Could theft sometimes be something else than theft? Were all things theft? And above all, did the acceptance of a woman's hand as bait justify the hooking of a sixpence?

As Victoria left for home that night she felt restless. She could not go to bed so soon. She walked through the silent city lanes; meeting nothing, save now and then a cat on the prowl, or a policeman trying doors and flashing his bull's eye through the gratings of banks. The crossing at Mansion House was still busy with the procession of omnibuses converging at the feet of the Duke of Wellington. Drays, too heavily loaded, rumbled slowly past towards Liverpool Street. She turned northwards, walked quickly through the desert. At Liverpool Street station she stopped in the blaze of light. A few doors away stood a shouting butcher praying the passers-by to buy his pretty meat. Further: a fishmonger's stall, an array of glistening black shapes on white marble, a tobacconist, a jeweller—all aglow with coruscating light. And over all, the blazing light of arc lamps, under which an unending stream of motor cabs, lorries, omnibuses passed in kaleidoscopic colours. In the full glare of a lamp post stood a woman, her feet in the gutter. She was short, stunted, dirty and thin of face and body. Round her wretched frame a filthy black coat was tightly buttoned; her muddy skirt seemed almost falling from her shrunken hips. Crushed on her sallow face, hiding all but a few wisps of hair, was a battered black straw hat. With one arm she carried a child, thin of face too, and golded-haired. On its upper lip a crusted sore gleamed red and brown. In her other hand she held out a tin lid, in which were five boxes of matches.

Victoria looked at the silent watcher and passed on. A few minutes later she remembered her and a fearful flood of insight rushed upon her. The child? Then

this, this creature had known love? A man had
kissed those shrivelled lips. Something like a thrill
of disgust ran through her. That such things as
these could love and mate and bear children was
unspeakable; the very touch of them was loathsome,
their love akin to unnatural vice.

As she walked further into Shoreditch the impression of horror grew on her. It was not that the
lanes and little streets abutting into the High Street
were full of terrors when pitch dark, or more sinister
still in the pale yellow light of a single gas lamp; the
High Street itself, filled with men and women, most
of them shabby, some loudly dressed in crude colours,
shouting, laughing, jostling one another off the foot-
path was more terrible, for its joy of life was brutal as
the joy of the pugilist who feels his opponent's teeth
crunch under his fist.

At a corner, near a public house blazing with lights,
a small crowd watched two women who were about
to fight. They had not come to blows yet; their duel
was purely Homeric. Victoria listened with greedy
horror to the terrible recurrence of half a dozen words.

A child squirmed through the crowd, crying, and
caught one of the fighters by her skirt.

'Leave go . . . I'll rive the guts out 'o yer.'

With a swing of the body the woman sent the child
flying into the gutter. Victoria hurried from the
spot. She made towards the West now, between the
gin shops, the barrows under their blazing naphtha
lamps. She was afraid, horribly afraid.

Sitting alone in her attic, her hands crossed before
her, questions intruded upon her. Why all this pain,
this violence, by the side of life's graces? Could it
be that one went with the other, indissolubly? And
could it be altered before it was too late, before the
earth was flooded, overwhelmed with pain?

She slipped into bed and drew the horsecloth over
her ears. The world was best shut out.

CHAPTER XXII

THOMAS FARWELL collected three volumes from his desk, two pamphlets and a banana. It was six o'clock and, the partners having left, he was his own master half an hour earlier than usual.

'You off?' said the junior from the other end of the desk.

'Yes. Half an hour to the good.'

'What's the good of half an hour?' said the youth superciliously.

'No good unless you think it is, like everything else,' said Farwell. 'Besides, I may be run over by half past six.'

'Cheerful as ever,' remarked the junior, bending his head down to the petty cash balance.

Farwell took no notice of him. Ten times a day he cursed himself for wasting words upon this troglodyte. He was a youth long as a day's starvation, with a bulbous forehead, stooping narrow shoulders and narrow lips; his shape resembled that of an old potato. He peered through his glasses with watery eyes hardly darker than his grey face.

'Good night,' said Farwell curtly.

'Cheer, oh!' said the junior.

Farwell slammed the door behind him. He felt inclined to skip down the stairs, not that anything particularly pleasant had happened but because the bells of St Botolph's were pealing out a chime of freedom. It was six. He had nothing to do. The best thing was to go to Moorgate Street and take the books to Victoria. On second thoughts, no, he would wait. Six o'clock might still be a busy time.

Farwell walked down the narrow lane from Bishopsgate into St Botolph's churchyard. It was a dank and dreary evening, dark already. The wind swept over the paths in little whirlwinds. Dejected sparrows sought scraps of food among the ancient graves where office boys munch buns and read of woodcarving and desperate adventure. He sat down on a seat by the side of a shape that slept, and opened one of the books, though it was too dark to read. The shape lifted an eyelid and looked at him.

Farwell turned over the pages listlessly. It was a history of revolutionists. For some reason he hated them to-day, all of them. Jack Cade was a boor, Cromwell a tartuffe, Bolivar a politician, Mazzini a theorist. It would bore Victoria.

Farwell brought himself up with a jerk. He was thinking of Victoria too often. As he was a man who faced facts he told himself quite plainly that he did not intend to fall in love with her. He did not feel capable of love; he hated most people, but did not believe that a good hater was a good lover.

'Clever, of course,' he muttered, 'but no woman is everlastingly clever. I won't risk finding her out.'

The shape at his side moved. It was an old man, filthy, clad in blackened rags, with a matted beard. Farwell glanced at him and turned away.

'I'd have you poisoned if I could,' he thought. Then he returned to Victoria. Was she worth educating? And supposing she was educated, what then? She would become discontented, instead of brutalised. The latter was the happier state. Or she would fall in love with him, when he would give her short shrift. What a pity. A tiny wave of sentiment flowed into Farwell's soul.

'Clever, clever,' he thought, 'a little house, babies, roses, a fox terrier.'

'Gov'nor,' croaked a hoarse voice beside him.

Farwell turned quickly. The shape was alive, then, curse it.

'Well, what d'you want?'

'Give us a copper, gov'nor, I'm an old man, can't work. S'elp me, Gawd, gov'nor, 'aven't 'ad a bite. . . .'

'That'll do, you fool,' snarled Farwell, 'why the hell don't you go and get it in gaol?'

'Yer don't mean that, gov'nor, do yer?' whined the old man, 'I always kep my self respectable ; 'ere, look at these 'ere testimonials, gov'nor, . . .' He drew from his coat a disgusting object, a bundle of papers tied together with string.

'I don't want to see them,' said Farwell. 'I wouldn't employ you if I could. Why don't you go to the workhouse?'

The old man almost bridled.

'Why? Because you're a stuck up. D'you hear? You're proud of being poor. That's about as vulgar as bragging because you're rich. If you and all the likes of you went into the House, you'd reform the system in a week. Understand?'

The old man's eyes were fixed on the speaker, uncomprehending.

'Better still, go and throw any bit of dirt you pick up at a policeman,' continued Farwell. 'See he gets it in the mouth. You get locked up. Suppose a million of the likes of you do the same, what d'you think happens?'

'I dunno,' said the old man.

'Well, your penal system is bust. If you offend the law you're a criminal. But what's the law? the opinion of the majority. If the majority goes against the law, then the minority becomes criminal. The world's upside down.' Farwell smiled. 'The world's upside down,' he said softly, licking his lips.

M

'Give us a copper for a bed, guv'nor,' said the old man dully.

'What's the good of a bed to you?' exploded Farwell. 'Why don't you have a drink?'

'I'm a teetotaller, guv'nor; always kep' myself respectable.'

'Respectable! You're earning the wages of respectability, that is death,' said Farwell with a wolfish laugh. 'Why, man, can't you see you've been on the wrong tack? We don't want any more of you respectables. We want pirates, vampires. We want all this society of yours rotted by internal canker, so that we can build a new one. But we must rot it first. We aren't going to work on a sow's ear.'

'Give us a copper, guv'nor,' moaned the old man.

Farwell took out sixpence and laid it on the seat. 'Now then,' he said, 'you can have this if you'll swear to blow it in drink.'

'I will, s'elp me Gawd,' said the old man eagerly.

Farwell pushed the coin towards him.

'Take it, teetotaller,' he sneered, 'your respectable system of bribery has bought you for sixpence. Now let me see you go into that pub.'

The old man clutched the sixpence and staggered to his feet. Farwell watched the swing doors of the public bar at the end of the passage close behind him. Then he got up and walked away; it was about time to go to Moorgate Street.

As he entered the smoking-room, Victoria blushed. The man moved her, stimulated her. When she saw him she felt like a body meeting a soul. He sat down at his usual place. Victoria brought him his tea, and laid it before him without a word. Nelly, lolling in another corner, kicked the ground, looking away insolently from the elaborate wink of one of the scullions.

'Here, read these,' said Farwell, pushing two of the books across the table. Victoria picked them up.

'*Looking Backwards*?' she said. 'Oh, I don't want to do that. It's forward I want to go.'

'A laudable sentiment,' sneered Farwell, 'the theory of every Sunday School in the country, and the practice of none. However, you'll find it fairly soul-filling as an unintelligent anticipation. Personally I prefer the other. *Demos* is good stuff, for Gissing went through the fire.'

Victoria quickly walked away. Farwell looked surprised for a second, then saw the manageress on the stairs.

'Faugh,' he muttered, 'if the world's a stage I'm playing the part of a low intriguer.'

He sipped his tea meditatively. In a few minutes Victoria returned.

'Thank you,' she whispered. 'It's good of you. You're teaching me to live.'

Farwell looked at her critically.

'I don't see much good in that,' he said, 'unless you've got something to live for. One of our philosophers says you live either for experience or the race. I recommend the former to myself, and to you nothing.'

'Why shouldn't I live for anything?' she asked.

'Because life's too dear. And its pleasures are not white but piebald.'

'I understand,' said Victoria, 'but I must live.'

'*Je n'en vois pas la nécessité*,' quoted Farwell smiling. 'Never mind what that means,' he added, 'I'm only a pessimist.'

The next few weeks seemed to create in Victoria a new personality. Her reading was so carefully selected that every line told. Farwell knew the hundred best books for a working girl; he had a large library composed mostly of battered copies squeezed out of his daily bread. Victoria's was the appetite of a gorgon. In another month she had absorbed *Odd Women, An Enemy of the People, The*

Doll's House, *Alton Locke*, and a translation of
Germinal. Every night she read with an intensity
which made her forget that March chilled her to the
bone; poring over the book, her eyes a few inches
from the candle, she soaked in rebellion. When the
cold nipped too close into her she would get up and
wrap herself in the horsecloth and read with savage
application, rushing to the core of the thought. She
was no student, so she would skip a hard word.
Besides, in those moods, when the spirit bounds in
the body like a caged bird, words are felt, not
understood.

Betty was still hovering round her, a gentle
presence. She knew what was going on and was
frightened. A new Victoria was rising before her,
a woman very charming still, but extraordinary,
incomprehensible. Often Victoria would snub her
savagely, then take her hand as they stood together
at the counter bawling for food and drink. And as
Victoria grew hard and strong Betty worshipped her
more as she would have worshipped a strong man.

Yet Betty was not happy. Victoria lived now in
a state of excitement and hunger for solitude. She
took no interest in things that Betty could understand.
Their Sunday walks had been ruthlessly cut now and
then, for the fury was upon Victoria when eating the
fruits of the tree. When they were together now
Victoria was preoccupied; she no longer listened to
the club gossip, nor did she ask to be told once more
the story of Betty's early days.

'Do you know you're sweated?' she said suddenly
one day.

Betty's eyes opened round and blue.

'Sweated?' she said. 'I thought only people in
the East End were sweated.'

'The world's one big East End,' snapped Victoria.

Betty shivered. Farwell might have said that.

'You're sweated if you get two pounds a week,

continued Victoria. 'You're sweated when you buy a loaf, sweated when you ride in a bus, sweated when they cremate you.'

'I don't understand,' said Betty.

'All profits are sweated,' quoted Victoria from a pamphlet.

'But people must make profits,' protested Betty.

'What for?' asked Victoria.

'How are people to live unless they make profits?' said Betty. 'Aren't our wages profits?'

Victoria was nonplussed for a moment and became involved. 'No, our wages are only wages; profit is the excess over our wages.'

'I don't understand,' said Betty.

'Never mind,' said Victoria, 'I'll ask Mr Farwell; he'll make it clear.'

Betty shot a dark blue glance at her.

'Vic,' she said softly, 'I think Mr Farwell. . . .' Then she changed her mind. 'I can't, I can't,' she thought. She crushed the jealous words down and plunged.

'Vic, darling,' she faltered, 'I'm afraid you're not well. No, and not happy. I've been thinking of something; why shouldn't I leave the Club and come and live with you.'

Victoria looked at her critically for a moment. She thought of her independence, of this affection hovering round her, sweet, dangerously clinging. But Betty's blue eyes were wet.

'You're too good a pal for me, Betty,' she said in a low voice. 'I'd make you miserable.'

'No, no,' cried Betty impulsively. 'I'd love it, Vic dear, and you would go on reading and do what you like. Only let me be with you.'

Victoria's hand tightened on her friend's arm.

'Let me think, Betty dear,' she said.

Ten days later, Betty having won her point, the great move was to take place at seven o'clock. It

certainly lacked solemnity. For three days preceding
the great change Betty had hurried away from the
P.R.R. on the stroke of nine, quickly kissing Victoria
and saying she couldn't wait as she must pack.
Clearly her wardrobe could not be disposed of in a
twinkling. Yet, on moving day, at seven o'clock
sharp (the carrier having been thoughtfully commanded to deliver at five) a tin trunk kept together
by a rope, a tiny bath muzzled with a curtain, and a
hat box loudly advertising somebody's tea, were
dumped on the doorstep. The cart drove off leaving
the two girls to make terms with a loafer. The
latter compromised for fourpence, slammed their
door behind him and lurched down the creaking
stairs. Betty threw herself into Victoria's arms.

Those first days were sweet. Betty rejoiced like a
lover in possession of a long-desired mistress ; stripping off her blouse and looking very pretty, showing
her white neck and slim arms, she strutted about the
attic with a hammer in her hand and her mouth full
of nails. It took an evening to hang the curtain
which had muzzled the bath ; Betty's art treasures,
an oleograph of ' Bubbles' and another of ' I'se
Biggest,' were cunningly hung by Victoria so that
she could not see them on waking up.

Betty was active now as a will o' the wisp. She
invented little feasts, expensive Sunday suppers of
fried fish and chips, produced a basket of oranges at
three a penny ; thanks to her there was now milk
with the tea. In a moment of enthusiasm Victoria
heard her murmur something about keeping a cat.
In fact the only thing that marred her life at all was
Victoria's absorption in her reading. Often Betty
would go to bed and stay awake, watching Victoria
at the table, her fingers ravelling her hair, reading
with an intentness that frightened her. She would
watch Victoria and see her face grow paler, except
at the cheeks where a flush would rise. A wild look

would come into her eyes. Sometimes she would get up suddenly and, thrusting her hair out of her eyes, walk up and down muttering things Betty could not understand.

One night Betty woke up suddenly, and saw Victoria standing in the moonlight clad only in her nightgown. Words were surging from her lips.

'It's no good. . . . I can't go on. . . . I can't go on until I die or somebody marries me. . . . I won't marry: I won't do it. . . . Why should I sell myself? . . . at any rate why should I sell myself cheaply?'

There was a pause. Betty sat up and looked at her friend's wild face.

'What's it all mean after all? I'm only being used. Sucked dry like an orange. By and by they'll throw the peel away. Talk of brotherhood! . . . It's war, war . . . It's climbing and fighting to get on top . . . like crabs in a bucket, like crabs . . .'

'Vic,' screamed Betty.

Victoria started like a somnambulist aroused and looked at her vaguely.

'Come back to bed at once,' cried Betty with inspired firmness. Victoria obeyed. Betty drew her down beside her under the horsecloth and threw her arms round her; Victoria's body was cold as ice. Suddenly she burst into tears; and Betty, torn as if she saw a strong man weep, wept too. Closely locked in one another's arms they sobbed themselves to sleep.

CHAPTER XXIII

EVERY day now Victoria's brain grew clearer and her body weaker. A sullen spirit of revolt blended with horrible depression was upon her, but she was getting thinner, paler; dark rings were forming round her eyes. She knew pain now; perpetual weariness, twitchings in the ankles, stabs just above the knee. In horrible listlessness she dragged her weary feet over the tiled floor, responding to commands like the old cab horse which can hardly feel the whip. In this mood, growing churlish, she repulsed Betty, avoided Farwell and tried to seclude herself. She no longer walked Holborn or the Strand where life went by, but sought the mean and silent streets, where none could see her shamble or where none would care.

One night, when she had left at six, she painfully crawled home and up into the attic. At half-past nine the door opened and Betty came in; the room was in darkness, but something oppressed her; she went to the mantlepiece to look for the matches, her fingers trembling. For an eternity she seemed to fumble, the oppression growing; she felt that Victoria was in the room, and could only hope that she was asleep. With a great effort of her will she lit the candle before turning round. Then she gave a short sharp scream.

Victoria was lying across the bed dressed in her bodice and petticoat. She had tucked this up to her knees and taken off her stockings; her legs hung dead white over the edge. At her feet was the tin bath full of water. Betty ran to the bed, choking almost, and clasped her friend round the neck. It was some seconds before she thought of wetting her face. After some minutes Victoria returned to consciousness and opened her eyes; she groaned slightly as Betty lifted up her legs and straightened her on the bed.

It was then that Betty noticed the singular appearance of Victoria's legs. They were covered with a network of veins, some narrow and pale blue in colour, others darker, protruding and swollen; on the left calf one of the veins stood out like a rope. The unaccustomed sight filled her with the horror bred of a mysterious disease. She was delicate, but had never been seriously ill; this sight filled her with physical repulsion. For her the ugliness of it meant foulness. For a moment she almost hated Victoria, but the sight of the tin bath full of water cut her to the heart; it told her that Victoria, maddened by mysterious pain, had tried to assuage it by bathing her legs in the cold water.

Little by little Victoria came round; she smiled at Betty.

'Did I faint, Betty dear?' she asked.

'Yes, dear. Are you better now?'

'Yes, I'm better; it doesn't hurt now.'

Betty could not repress a question.

'Vic,' she said, 'what is it?'

'I don't know,' said Victoria fearfully, then more cheerfully,

'I'm tired I suppose. I shall be all right to-morrow.'

Then Betty refused to let her talk any more, and soon Victoria slept by her side the sleep of exhaustion.

The next morning Victoria insisted upon going to the P. R. R. in spite of Betty suggesting a doctor.

'Can't risk losing my job,' she said laughing. 'Besides it doesn't hurt at all now. Look.'

Victoria lifted up her nightshirt. Her calves were again perfectly white and smooth; the thin network

of veins had sunk in again and showed blue under
the skin.   Alone one vein on the left leg seemed dark
and angry.   Victoria felt so well, however, that she
agreed to meet Farwell at a quarter-past nine.   This
was their second expedition, and the idea of it was a
stimulant.   He went with her up to Finsbury Pavement
and stopped at a small Italian restaurant.

'Come in here and have some coffee,' he said, 'they
have waiters here; that'll be a change.'

Victoria followed him in.   They sat at a marble
topped table, flooded with light by incandescent gas.
In the glare the waiters seemed blacker, smaller and
more stunted than by the light of day.   Their faces
were pallid, with a touch of green : their hair and
moustaches were almost blue black.   Their energy
was that of automata.   Victoria looked at them,
melting with pity.

'There's a life for you,' said Farwell interpreting
her look.   'Sixteen hours' work a day in an atmosphere
of stale food.   For meals, plate scourings.   For sleep
and time to get to it, eight hours.   For living, the rest
of the day.'

'It's awful, awful,' said Victoria.   'They might as
well be dead.'

'They will be soon,' said Farwell, 'but what does
that matter?   There are plenty of waiters.   In the
shadow of the olive groves to-night in far off Calabria,
at the base of the vine-clad hills, couples are walking
hand in hand, with passion flashing in their eyes.
Brown peasant boys are clasping to their breast young
girls with dark hair, white teeth, red lips, hearts that
beat and quiver with ecstasy.   They tell a tale of love
and hope.   So we shall not be short of waiters.'

'Why do you sneer at everything, Mr Farwell?'
said Victoria.   'Can't you see anything in life to
make it worth while?'

'No, I cannot say I do.   The pursuit of a living
debars me from the enjoyments that make living

worth while. But never mind me : I am over without
having bloomed. I brought you here to talk of you,
not of me.'

'Of me, Mr Farwell?' asked Victoria. 'What do
you want to know?'

Farwell leant over the table, toyed with the sugar
and helped himself to a piece. Then without looking
at her :

'What's the matter with you, Victoria?' he asked.

'Matter with me? What do you mean?' said
Victoria, too disturbed to notice the use of her
Christian name.

The man scrutinised her carefully. 'You're ill,'
he said. 'Don't protest. You're thin; there are
purple pockets under your eyes; your underlip is
twisted with pain, and you limp.'

Victoria felt a spasm of anger. There was still in
her the ghost of vanity. But she looked at Farwell
before answering; there was gentleness in his eyes.

' Well,' she said slowly, 'if you must know, perhaps
there is something wrong. Pains.'

' Where?' he asked.

'In the legs,' she said after a pause.

'Ah, swellings?'

Victoria bridled a little. This man was laying
bare something, tearing at a secret.

'Are you a doctor, Mr Farwell?' she asked coldly.

'That's all right,' he said roughly, 'it doesn't need
much learniug to know what's the matter with a girl
who stands for eleven hours a day. Are the veins of
your legs swollen?'

'Yes,' said Victoria with an effort. She was
frightened; she forgot to resent this wrenching at
the privacy of her body.

'Ah; when do they hurt?'

'At night. They're all right in the morning.'

'You've got varicose veins, Victoria. You must
give up your job.'

'I can't,' whispered the girl hoarsely. 'I've got nothing else.'

'Exactly. Either you go on and are a cripple for life or you stop and starve. Yours is a disease of occupation, purely a natural consequence of your work. Perfectly normal, perfectly. It is undesirable to encourage laziness; there are girls starving to-day for lack of work, but it would never do to reduce your hours to eight. It would interfere with the P. R. R. dividends.'

Victoria looked at him without feeling.

'What am I to do?' she asked at length.

'Go to a hospital,' said Farwell. 'These institutions are run by the wealthy who pay two guineas a year ransom for a thousand pounds of profits and get in the bargain a fine sense of civic duty done. No doubt the directors of the P.R.R. contribute most generously.'

'I can't give up my job,' said Victoria dully.

'Perhaps they'll give you a stocking,' said Farwell, 'or sell it you, letting you pay in instalments so that you be not pauperised. This is called training in responsibility, also self-help.'

Victoria got up. She could bear it no longer. Farwell saw her home and made her promise to apply for leave to see the doctor. As the door closed behind her he stood still for some minutes on the doorstep, filling his pipe.

'Well, well,' he said at length, 'the Government might think of that lethal chamber—but no, that would never do, it would deplete the labour market and hamper the commercial development of the Empire.'

He walked away, a crackling little laugh floating behind him. The faint light of a lamp fell on his bowed head and shoulders, making him look like a Titan born a dwarf.

Two days later Victoria went to the Carew. She

had never before set foot in a hospital. Such intercourse as she had had with doctors was figured by discreet interviews in dark studies filled with unspeakably ugly and reassuringly solid furniture. Those doctors had patted her hand, said she needed a little change or may be a tonic. At the Carew, fed as it is by the misery of two square miles of North East London, the revelation of pain was dazzling, apocalyptic. The sight of the benches crowded with women and children—some pale as corpses, others flushed with fever, some with faces bandaged or disfigured by sores—almost made her sick. They were packed in serried rows; the children almost all cried persistently, except here and there a baby, who looked with frightful fixity at the glazed roof. From all this chattering crowd of the condemned rose a stench of iodoform, perspiration, unwashed bodies, the acrid smell of poverty.

The little red-haired Scotch doctor dismissed Victoria's case in less than one minute.

'Varicose veins. Always wear a stocking. Here's your form. Settle terms at the truss office. Don't stand on your feet. Oh, what's your occupation?'

'Waitress at the P.R.R., Sir.'

'Ah, hum. You must give it up.'

'I can't, Sir.'

'It's your risk. Come again in a month.'

Victoria pulled up her stockings. Walking in a dream she went to the truss office where a man measured her calves. She felt numb and indifferent as to the exposure of her body. The man looked enquiringly at the left calf.

'V.H. for the left,' he called over his shoulder to the clerk.

At twelve o'clock she was in the P.R.R., revived by the familiar atmosphere. She even rallied one of the old chess players on a stroke of ill-luck. Towards four o'clock her ankles began to twitch.

CHAPTER XXIV

THROUGH all these anxious times, Betty watched over Victoria with the devotion that is born of love. There was in the girl a reserve of maternal sweetness equalled only by the courage she showed every day. Slim and delicate as she seemed, there was in Betty's thin body a strength all nervous but enduring. She did not complain, though driven eleven or twelve hours a day by the eyes of the manageress; those eyes were sharp as a goad, but she went cheerfully.

In a sense Betty was happy. The work did not weigh too heavily upon her; there was so much humility in her that she did not resent the roughness of her companions. Nelly could snub her, trample at times on her like the cart horse she was; the manageress too could freeze her with a look, the kitchen staff disregard her humble requests for teas and procure for her the savage bullying of the customers, yet she remained placid enough.

'It's a hard life,' she once said to Victoria, 'but I suppose it's got to be.' This was her philosophy.

'But don't you want to get out of it?' cried Victoria the militant.

'I don't know,' said Betty. 'I might marry.'

'Marry,' sniffed Victoria. 'You seem to think marriage is the only way out for women.'

'Well, isn't it?' asked Betty. 'What else is there?'

And for the life of her Victoria could not find another occupation for an unskilled girl. Milliners, dressmakers, clerks, typists, were all frightfully underpaid and overworked; true there were women doctors, but who cared to employ them? And teachers, but they earned the wages of virtue neglect. Besides it was too late; both Victoria and Betty were unskilled, condemned by their sex to low pay and hard work.

'It's frightful, frightful,' cried Victoria. 'The only use we are is to do the dirty work. Men don't char. Of course we may marry, if we can, to any of those gods if they'll share with us their thirty bob a week. Talk of slaves! They're better off than we.'

Betty looked upon all this as rather wild, as a consequence of Victoria's illness. Her view was that it didn't do to complain, and that the only thing to do was to make the best of it. But she loved Victoria, and it was almost a voluptous joy for her to help her friend to undress every night, to tempt her with little offerings of fruit and flowers. When they woke up, Betty would draw her friend into her arms and cover her face with gentle kisses.

But as Victoria grew worse, stiffer, and slower, responding ever more reluctantly to the demands made upon her all day at the P. R. R., Betty was conscious of horrible anxiety. Sometimes her imagination would conjure up a Victoria helpless, wasted, bedridden, and her heart seemed to stop. But her devotion was proof against egoism. Whatever happened, Victoria should not starve if she had to pay the rent and feed herself on nine shillings or so a week until she was well again and beautiful as she had been. Her anxiety increasing, she mustered up courage to interview Farwell, whom she hated jealously. He had ruined Victoria, she thought —made her wild, discontented, rebellious against the incurable. Yet he knew her, and at any rate she must talk about it to somebody. So she mustered up courage to ask him to meet her at nine.

'Well?' said Farwell. He did not like Betty much. He included her among the poor creatures, the rubble.

'Oh, Mr Farwell, what's going to happen to Victoria?' cried Betty, with tears in her voice. Then she put her hand against the railings of Finsbury Circus. She had prepared a dignified little speech, and her suffering had burst from her. The indignity of it.

'Happen? The usual thing in these cases. She'll get worse; the veins will burst and she'll be crippled for life.'

Betty looked at him, her eyes blazing with rage.

'How dare you, how dare you?' she growled.

Farwell laughed.

'My dear young lady,' he said smoothly, 'it needs no doctor to tell you what is wanted. Victoria must stop work, lie up, be well fed, live in the country perhaps and her spirits must be raised. To this effect I would suggest a pretty house, flowers, books, some music, say a hundred-guinea grand piano, some pretty pictures. So that she may improve in health it is desirable that she should have servants. These may gain varicose veins by waiting on her, but that is by the way.'

Betty was weeping now. Tear after tear rolled down her cheeks.

'But all this costs money,' continued Farwell, 'and, as you are aware, bread is very dear and flesh and blood very cheap. Humanity finds the extraction of gold a toilsome process, whilst the production of children is a normal recreation which eclipses even the charms of alcohol. There, my child, you have the problem; and there is only one radical solution to it.'

Betty looked at him, intuitively guessing the horrible suggestion.

'The solution,' said Farwell, 'is to complain to the doctor of insomnia, get him to prescribe laudanum

and sink your capital in the purchase of half a pint.
One's last investment is generally one's best.'

'Oh, I can't bear it, I can't bear it,' wailed Betty.
'She's so beautiful, so clever.'

'Ah, yes,' said Farwell in his dreamy manner, 'but
then you see when a woman doesn't marry. . . .'
He broke off, his eyes fixed on the grey pavement.
'The time will come, Betty, when the earth will be
not only our eternal bed, but the fairy land where
joyful flowers will grow. Ah! it will be joyful,
joyful, this crop of flowers born from seas of blood.'

'But, now, now, what can we do with her?'
cried Betty.

'I have no other suggestion if she will not fight,'
growled Farwell in his old manner. 'She must sink
or swim. If she sinks she's to blame, I suppose. In
a world of pirates and cut-throats she will have elected
to be a saint, and the martyr's crown will be hers. If
suicide is not to her taste, I would recommend her
to resort to what is called criminal practices. Being
ill, she has magnificent advantages if she wishes to start
business as a begging-letter writer; burglary is not
suitable for women, but there are splendid openings
for confidence tricksters and shoplifting would be
a fine profession if it were not overcrowded by the
upper middle classes.'

Betty dabbed her eyes vigorously. Her mouth
tightened. She looked despairingly at the desolate
half circle of London Wall Buildings and Salisbury
House. Then she gave Farwell her hand for a
moment and hurriedly walked away. As she entered
the attic the candle was still burning. Victoria was
in bed and had forgotten it; she had already fallen
into stertorous sleep.

Next morning Victoria got up and dressed silently.
She did not seem any worse; and with this Betty was
content, though she only got short answers to her
questions. All that day Victoria seemed well enough.

N

She walked springily ; at times she exchanged a quick joke with a customer. She laughed even when a young man, carried away for a moment beyond the spirit of food which reigned supreme in the P.R.R., touched her hand and looked into her eyes.

As the afternoon wore Victoria felt creeping over her the desperate weariness of the hour.

At a quarter to six she made up her checks. There was a shortfall of one and a penny.

'How do you account for it?' asked the manageress.

'Sure I don't know, Miss,' said Victoria helplessly. 'I aways give checks. Somebody must have slipped out without paying.'

'Possibly. The manageress grew more tense faced than ever. Her bust expanded. 'I don't care. Of course you know the rule. You pay half and the desk pays half.'

'I couldn't help it, Miss,' said Victoria miserably. Sixpence halfpenny was a serious loss.

'No more could I. I think I can tell you how it happened, though,' said the manageress with a vague smile. 'I'm an old hand. A customer of yours had a tuck out for one and a penny. You gave him a check. Look at the foil and you'll see.'

'Yes, Miss, here it is,' said Victoria anxiously.

'Very well. Then he went upstairs on the Q.T. and had a cup of coffee. Follow !'

'Yes, Miss.'

'One of the girls gave him a twopenny check. Then he went out and handed in the twopenny check. He kept the other one in his pocket.'

'Oh, Miss. . . . it's stealing,' Victoria gasped.

'It is. But there it is, you see.'

'But it's not my fault, Miss ; if you had a pay box at the top of the stairs, I don't say . . .'

'Oh, we can't do that,' said the manageress icily, 'they would cost a lot to build and extra staff and

we must keep down expenses, you know. Competition
is very keen in this trade.'

Victoria felt stunned. The incident was as full of
revelations as Lizzie's practices at the desk. The
girls cheated the customers, the customers the girls.
And the P.R.R. sitting olympian on its pillar of
cloud, exacted from all its dividends. The P.R.R.
suddenly loomed up before Victoria's eyes as a big
swollen monster in whose veins ran China tea. And
from its nostrils poured forth torrents of coffee-
scented steam. It grew and grew, and fed men and
women, every now and then extending a talon and
seizing a few young girls with sore legs, a rival café
or two. Then it vanished. Victoria was looking at
one of the large plated urns.

'All right,' she said sullenly, 'I'll pay.'

As it was her day off, at six o'clock Victoria went
up to the change room, saying good-night to Betty,
telling her she was going out to get some fresh air.
She thought it would do her good, so rode on a bus
to the Green Park. Round her, in Piccadilly, a tide
of rich life seemed to rise redolent with scent, soft
tobacco, moist furs, all those odours that herald and
follow wealth. A savagery was upon her as she
passed along the club windows, now full of young
men telling tales that made their teeth shine in the
night, of old men, red, pink, brown, healthy in colour
and in security, reading, sleeping, eking out life.

The picture was familiar ; for it was the picture she
had so often seen when, as a girl, she came up to
town from Lympton for a week to shop in Oxford
Street and see, from the upper boxes, the three or four
plays recommended by *Hearth and Home*. Piccadilly
had been her Mecca. It had represented mysterious
delights, restaurants, little teashops, jewellers, makers
of cunning cases for everything. She had never been
well-off enough to shop there, but had gazed into its
windows and bought the nearest imitations in Oxford

Street. Then the clubs had been, if not familiar, at any rate friendly. She had once with her mother called at the In and Out to ask for a general. He was dead now, and so was Piccadilly.

Victoria remembered without joy : a sign of total flatness, for the mind that does not glow at the thought of the glamorous past is dulled indeed. Piccadilly struck her now rather as a show and a poor one, a show of the inefficients basking, of the wretched shuffling by. And the savagery that was upon her waxed fat. Without ideals of ultimate brotherhood or love she could not help thinking, half amused, of the dismay that would come over London if a bomb were suddenly to raze to the ground one of these shrines of men.

The bus stopped in a block just opposite one of the clubs ; and Victoria, from the off-side seat, could see across the road into one of the rooms. There were in it a dozen men of all ages, most of them standing in small groups, some already in evening-dress ; some lolled on enormous padded chairs reading, and, against the mantlepiece where a fire burned brightly, a youth was telling an obviously successful story to a group of oldsters. Their ease, their conviviality and facile friendship stung Victoria ; she felt an outcast. What had she now to do with these men ? They would not know her. Their sphere was their father's sphere, by right of birth and wealth, not hers who had not the right of wealth. Besides, perhaps some were share-holders in the P.R.R. Painfully shambling down the steps, Victoria got off the bus and entered the Green Park. She sat down on a seat under a tree just bursting into bud.

For many minutes she looked at the young grass, at the windows where lights were appearing, at a man seated near by and puffing rich blue smoke from his cigar. A loafer lay face down on the grass, like a bundle. Her moods altered between rage, as she

looked at the two men, and misery as she realised that
her lot was cast with the wretch grovelling on the
cold earth.

She noticed that the man with the cigar was watching her, but hardly looked at him. He was fat, that
was all she knew. Her eyes once more fastened on
the loafer. He had not fought the world; would
she? and how? Now and then he turned a little in
his sleep, dreaming perhaps of feasts in Cockayne,
perhaps of the skilly he had tasted in gaol, of love
perhaps, bright-eyed, master of the gates. It was
cold, for the snap of winter was in the spring air; in
the pale western sky the roofs loomed black. Already
the dull glow of London light rose like a halo over
the town. Victoria did not seem to feel the wind;
she was a little numb, her legs felt heavy as lead. A
gust of wind carried into her face a few drops of rain.

The man with the cigar got up, slowly passed her;
there was something familiar in his walk. He turned
so as to see her face in the light of a gas-lamp. Then
he took three quick steps towards her. Her heart
was already throbbing; she felt and yet did not know.

'Victoria,' said the man in a faint, far away voice.

Victoria gasped, put her hand on her heart, swaying
on the seat. The man sat down by her side and took
her hand.

'Victoria,' he said again. There was in his voice
a rich quality.

'Oh, Major Cairns, Major Cairns,' she burst out.
And clasping his hand between hers, she laid her face
upon it. He felt all her body throb; there were tears
on his hands. A man of the world, he very gently
lifted up her chin and raised her to a sitting posture.

'There,' he said softly, still retaining her hands,
'don't cry, dear, all is well. Don't speak. I have
found you.'

With all the gentleness of a heavy man he softly
stroked her hands.

CHAPTER XXV

Two days later Victoria was floating in the curious
ether of the unusual. It was Sunday night. She
was before a little table at one of those concealed
restaurants in Soho where blows fragrant the wind of
France. She was sitting in a softly cushioned arm
chair, grateful to arms and back, her feet propped up
on a footstool. Before her lay the little table, with
its rough cloth, imperfectly clean and shining dully
with brittania ware. There were flowers in a small
mug of Bruges pottery; there was little light save
from candles discreetly veiled by pink shades. The
bill of fare, rigid on its metal stem, bore the two
shilling table d'hôte and the more pretentious à la
carte. An immense feeling of restfulness, so complete
as to be positive was upon her. She felt luxurious
and at large, at one with the other couples who sat
near by, smiling, with possessive hands.

On the other side of the table sat Major Cairns.
He had not altered very much except that he was
stouter. His grey eyes still shone kindly from his
rather gross face. Victoria could not make up her
mind whether she liked him or not. When she met
him in the park he had seemed beautiful as an arch-
angel; he had been gentle too as big men mostly are
to women, but now she could feel him examining her
critically, noting her points, speculating on the change
in her, wondering whether her ravaged beauty was
greater and her neck softer than when he last held
her in his arms off the coast of Araby.

Victoria had compacted for a quiet place. She could not, she felt, face the Pall Mall or Jermyn' Street restaurants, their lights, wealth of silver and glass, their soft carpets, their silent waiters. The Major had agreed, for he knew women well and was not over-anxious to expose to the eyes of the town Victoria's paltry clothes. Now he had her before him he began to regret that he had not risked it. For Victoria had gained as much as she had lost in looks. Her figure had shrunk, but her neck was still beautifully moulded, broad as a pillar; her colour had gone down almost to dead white; the superfluous flesh had wasted away and had left bare the splendid line of the strong chin and jaw. Her eyes, however, were the magnet that held Cairns fast. They were as grey as ever, but dilated and thrown into contrast with the pale skin by the purple zone which surrounded them. They stared before them with a novel boldness, a strange lucidity.

'Victoria,' whispered Cairns leaning forward, 'you are very beautiful.'

Victoria laughed and a faint flush rose into her cheeks. There was still something grateful in the admiration of this man, gross and limited as he might be, centred round his pleasures, sceptical of good and evil alike. Without a word she took up a spoon and began to eat her ice. Cairns watched every movement of her hand and wrist.

'Don't,' said Victoria after a pause. She dropped her spoon and put her hands under the table.

'Don't what?' said Cairns.

'Look at my hands. They're . . . Oh, they're not what they were. It makes me feel ashamed.'

'Nonsense,' said Cairns with a laugh. 'Your hands are still as fine as ever and, when we've had them manicured. . . .'

He stopped abruptly as if he had said too much.

'Manicured?' said Victoria warily, though the 'we'

had given her a little shock. 'Oh, they're not worth manicuring now for the sort of work I've got to do.'

'Look here, Victoria,' said Cairns rather roughly. 'This can't go on. You're not made to be one of the drabs. You say your work is telling on you : well, you must give it up.'

'Oh, I can't do that,' said Victoria, 'I've got to earn my living and I'm no good for anything else.'

Cairns looked at her for a moment and meditatively sipped his port.

'Drink the port,' he commanded, 'it'll do you good.'

Victoria obeyed willingly enough. There was already in her blood the glow of Burgundy ; but the port, mellow, exquisite, and curling round the tongue, coloured like burnt almonds, fragrant too, concealed a deeper joy. The smoke from Cairns' cigar, half hiding his face, floating in wreaths between them, entered her nostrils, aromatic, narcotic.

'What are you thinking of doing now?' she asked.

'I don't know quite,' said Cairns. 'You see I broke my good resolution. After my job at Perim, they offered me some surveying work near Ormuz ; they call it surveying, but it's spying really or it would be if there were anything to spy. I took it and rather enjoyed it.'

'Did you have any adventures?' asked Victoria.

'Nothing to speak of except expeditions into the hinterland trying to get fresh meat. The East is overrated, I assure you. A butr landed off our station once, probably intending to turn us into able-bodied slaves. There were only seven of us to their thirty but we killed ten with two volleys and they made off, parting with their anchor in their hurry.'

Cairns looked at Victoria. The flush had not died from her cheeks. She was good to look upon.

'No,' he went on more slowly, 'I don't quite know what I shall do. I meant to retire anyhow, you know, and the sudden death of my uncle, old Marmaduke Cairns, settled it. I never expected to get a look in, but there was hardly anybody else to leave anything to, except his sisters whom he hated like poison, so I'm the heir. I don't yet know what I'm worth quite, but the old man always seemed to do himself pretty well.'

'I'm glad,' said Victoria. She was not. The monstrous stupidity of a system which suddenly places a man in a position enabling him to live on the labour of a thousand was obvious to her.

'I'm rather at a loose end,' said Cairns musing, 'you see I've had enough knocking about. But it's rather dull here, you know. I'm not a marrying man either.'

Victoria was disturbed. She looked at Cairns and met his eyes. There was forming in them a question. As she looked at him the expression faded and he signed to the waiter to bring the coffee.

As they sipped it they spoke little but inspected one another narrowly. Victoria told herself that if Cairns offered her marriage she would accept him. She was not sure that ideal happiness would be hers if she did; his limitations were more apparent to her than they had been when she first knew him. Yet the alternative was the P.R.R. and all that must follow.

Cairns was turning over in his mind the question Victoria had surprised. Though he was by no means cautious or shy, being a bold and good liver, he felt that Victoria's present position made it difficult to be sentimental. So they talked of indifferent things. But when they left the restaurant and drove towards Finsbury Victoria came closer to him; and, unconsciously almost, Cairns took her hand, which she did not withdraw. He leant towards her. His hand grew more insistent on her arm. She was passive, though her heart beat and fear was upon her.

'Victoria,' said Cairns, his voice strained and metallic.

She turned her face towards him. There was in it complete acquiescence. He passed one arm round her waist and drew her towards him. She could feel his chest crush her as he bent her back. His lips fastened on her neck greedily.

'Victoria,' said Cairns again, 'I want you. Come away from all this labour and pain; let me make you happy.'

She looked at him, a question in her eyes.

'As free man and woman,' he stammered. Then more firmly:

'I'll make you happy. You'll want nothing. Perhaps you'll even learn to like me.'

Victoria said nothing for a minute. The proposal did not offend her; she was too broken, too stupefied for her inherent prejudices to assert themselves. Morals, belief, reputation, what figments all these things. What was this freedom of hers that she should set so high a price on it? And here was comfort, wealth, peace—oh, peace. Yet she hesitated to plunge into the cold stream; she stood shivering on the edge.

'Let me think,' she said.

Cairns pressed her closer to him. A little of the flame that warmed his body passed into hers.

'Don't hurry me. Please. I don't know what to say. . . .'

He bent over with hungry lips.

'Yes, you may kiss me.'

Submissive, if frightened and repelled, yet with a heart where hope fluttered, she surrendered him her lips.

CHAPTER XXVI

'I DON'T approve and I don't disapprove,' snarled Farwell. 'I'm not my sister's keeper. I don't pretend to think it noble of you to live with a man you don't care for, but I don't say you're wrong to do it.'

'But really,' said Victoria, 'if you don't think it right to do a thing, you must think it wrong.'

'Not at all. I am neutral, or rather my reason supports what my principles reject. Thus my principles may seem unreasonable and my reasoning devoid of principle, but I cannot help that.'

Victoria thought for a moment. She was about to take a great step and she longed for approval.

'Mr Farwell,' she said deliberately, 'I've come to the conclusion that you are right. We are crabs in a bucket and those at the bottom are no nobler than those on the top, for they would gladly be on the top. I'm going on the top.'

'Sophist,' said Farwell smiling.

'I don't know what that means,' Victoria went on; 'I suppose you think that I'm trying to cheat myself as to what is right. Possibly, but I don't profess to know what is right.'

'Oh, no more do I,' interrupted Farwell, 'please don't set me up as a judge. I haven't got any ethical standards for you. I don't believe there are any; the ethics of the Renaissance are not those of the twentieth century, nor are those of London the same as those of Constantinople. Time and space work moral revolutions; and, even on stereotyped lines, nobody can say present ethics are the best. From a conventional point of view the hundred and fifty years that separate us from Fielding mark an improvement, but I have still to learn that the morals of to-day compare favourably with those of Sparta. You must decide that for yourself.'

'I am doing so,' said Victoria quietly, 'but I don't think you quite understand a woman's position and I want you to. I find a world where the harder a woman works, the worse she is paid, where her mind is despised and her body courted. Oh, I know, you haven't done that, but you don't employ women. Nobody but you has ever cared a scrap about such brains as I may have; the subs courted me in my husband's regiment . . .' She stopped abruptly, having spoken too freely.

'Go on,' said Farwell tactfully.

'And in London what have I found? Nothing but men bent on one pursuit. They have followed me in the streets and tubes, tried to sit by me in the parks. They have tried to touch me—yes me! the dependent who could not resent it, when I served them with their food. Their talk is the inane, under which they cloak desire. Their words are covert appeals. I hear round me the everlasting cry: yield, yield, for that is all we want from young women.'

'True,' said Farwell, 'I have never denied this.'

'And yet,' answered Victoria angrily, 'you almost blame me. I tell you that I have never seen the world as I do now. Men have no use for us save as mistresses, whether legal or not. Perhaps they will have us as breeders or housekeepers, but the mistress is the root of it all. And if they can gain us without pledges, without risks, by promises, by force or by deceit, they will.'

Farwell said nothing. His eyes were full of sorrow.

'My husband drank himself to death,' pursued

Victoria in low tones. 'The proprietor of the Rosebud tried to force me to become his toy . . . perhaps
he would have thrown me on the streets if he had had
time to pursue me longer and if I refused myself still
. . . because he was my employer and all is fair in
what they call love . . . The customers bought every
day for twopence the right to stare through my openwork blouse, to touch my hand, to brush my knees
with theirs. One, who seemed above them, tried to
break my body into obedience by force . . . Here,
at the P.R.R. I am a toy still, though more of a servant
. . . Soon I shall be a cripple and good neither for
servant nor mistress, what will you do with me?'

Farwell made a despairing gesture with his hand.

'I tell you,' said Victoria with ferocious intensity.
You're right, life's a fight and I'm going to win,
for my eyes are clear. I have done with sentiment
and sympathy. A man may command respect as a
wage earner; a woman commands nothing but what
she can cheat out of men's senses. She must be rich,
she must be economically independent. Then men
will crawl where they hectored, worship that which
they burned. And if I must be dependent to become
independent, that is a stage I am ready for.'

'What are you going to do?' asked Farwell.

'I'm going to live with this man,' said Victoria in
a frozen voice. 'I neither love nor hate him. I am
going to exploit him, to extort from him as much
of the joy of life as I can, but above all I am going
to draw from him, from others too if I can, as much
wealth as I can. I will store it, hive it bee-like, and
when my treasure is great enough I will consume it.
And the world will stand by and shout: hallelujah,
a rich woman cometh into her kingdom.'

Farwell remained silent for a minute.

'You are right,' he said, 'if you must choose, then
be strong and carve your way into freedom. I have
not done this, and the world has sucked me dry.

You can still be free, so do not shrink from the means.
You are a woman, your body is your fortune, your
only fortune, so transmute it into gold. You will
succeed, you will be rich; and the swine, instead of
trampling on you, will herd round the trough where
you scatter pearls.'

He stopped for a moment, slowly puffing at his
pipe.

'Women's profession,' he muttered. 'The time
will come . . . but to-day. . . .'

Victoria looked at him, a faint figure in the night,
He was the spectral prophet, a David in fear of
Goliath.

'Yes,' she said, 'woman's profession.'

Together they walked away. Farwell was almost
soliloquising. 'If she is brave, life is easier for a
woman than a man. She can play on him; but her
head must be cool, her heart silent. Hear this,
Victoria. Remember yours is a trade and needs
your application. To win this fight you must be well
equipped. Let your touch be soft as velvet, your
grip as hard as steel. Shrink from nothing, rise to
treachery, let the worldly nadir be your zenith.'

He stopped before a public house and opened the
door of the bar a little.

'Look in here,' he said.

Victoria looked. There were five men, half hidden
in smoke; among them sat one woman clad in vivid
colours, her face painted, her hands dirty and covered
with rings. Her yellow hair made a vivid patch
against the brown wall. A yard away, alone at a
small table, sat another woman, covered too with
cheap finery, with weary eyes and a smiling mouth,
her figure abandoned on a sofa, lost to the scene, her
look fixed on the side door through which men slink in.

'Remember,' said Farwell, 'give no quarter in the
struggle, for you will get none.'

Victoria shuddered. But the fury was upon her.

'Don't be afraid,' she hissed, 'I'll spare nobody. They've already given me a taste of the whip. I know, I understand; those girls don't. I see the goal before me and therefore I will reach it.'

Farwell looked at her again, his eyes full of melancholy.

'Go then, Victoria,' he said, 'and work out your fate.'

PART II

CHAPTER I

VICTORIA turned uneasily on the sofa and stretched her arms. She yawned, then sat up abruptly. Sudermann's *Katzensteg* fell to the ground off her lap. She was in a tiny back room, so overcrowded by the sofa and easy-chair that she could almost touch a small rosewood bureau opposite. She looked round the room lazily, then relapsed on the sofa, hugging a cushion. She snuggled her face into it, voluptuously breathing in its compactness laden with scent and tobacco smoke. Then, looking up, she reflected that she was very comfortable.

Victoria's boudoir was the back extension of the dining-room. Shut off by the folding doors, it contained within its tiny space the comfort which is only found in small rooms. It was papered red with a flowered pattern, which she thought ugly, but which had just been imported from France and was quite the thing. The sofa and easy-chair were covered with obtrusively new red and white chintz; a little pile of cushions had fallen on the indeterminate Persian pattern of the carpet. Long coffee coloured curtains, banded with chintz, shut out part of the high window, through which a little of the garden and the bare branches of a tree could be seen. Victoria took all this in for the hundredth time. She had been sleeping for an hour; she felt smooth, stroked; she could have hugged all these pretty things, the little brass fender, the books, the Delft inkpot on the little bureau. Everything in the room was already intimate. Her eyes dwelt on the clean chintzes, on the half blinds surmounted by insertion, the brass ashtrays, the massive silver cigarette box.

Victoria stood up, the movement changing the direction of her contemplative mood. The Gothic rosewood clock told her it was a little after three. She went to the cigarette box and lit a cigarette. While slowly inhaling the smoke, she rang the bell. On her right forefinger there was a faint yellow tinge of nicotine which had reached the nail.

'I shall have to be manicured again,' she soliloquised. 'What a nuisance. Better have it done to-day while I get my hair done too.'

'Yes, mum.' A neat dark maid stood at the door. Victoria did not answer for a second. The girl's black dress was perfectly brushed, her cap, collar, cuffs, apron, immaculate white.

'I'm going out now, Mary,' said Victoria. 'You'd better get my brown velvet out.'

'Yes, mum,' said the maid. 'Will you be back for dinner, mum?'

'No, I'm dining with the Major. Oh, don't get the velvet out. It's muddy out, isn't it?'

'Yes, mum. It's been raining in the morning, mum.'

'Ah, well, perhaps I'd better wear the grey coat and skirt. And my furs and toque.'

'The beaver, mum?'

'No, of course not, the white fox. And, oh, Mary, I've lost my little bag somewhere. And tell Charlotte to send me up a cup of tea at half-past three.'

Mary left the room silently. She seldom asked questions, and never expressed pleasure, displeasure or surprise.

Victoria walked up to her bedroom; the staircase was papered with a pretty blue and white pattern over a dado of white lincrusta. A few French engravings stood out in their old gold frames. Victoria stopped

O

at the first landing to look at her favourite, after
Lancret ; it represented lovers surprised in a barn by
an irate husband.

The bedroom occupied the entire first floor. On
taking possession of the little house she had realised
that, as she would have no callers, a drawing-room
would be absurd, so had suppressed the folding doors
and made the two rooms into one large one. In the
front, between the two windows, stood her dressing-
table, now covered with small bottles, some in cut
glass and full of scent, others more workmanlike,
marked vaseline, glycerine, skin food, bay rum.
Scattered about them on the lace toilet cover, were
boxes of powder, white, sepia, bluish, puffs, little
sticks of cosmetics, some silver-backed brushes, some
squat and short-bristled, others with long handles,
with long soft bristles, one studded with short wires,
another with whalebone, some clothes brushes too,
buttonhooks, silver trays, a handglass with a massive
silver handle. Right and left, two little electric lamps
and above the swinging mirror, a shaded bulb shed-
ing a candid glow.

One wall was blotted out by two inlaid mahogany
wardrobes ; through the open doors of one could be
seen a pile of frilled linen, lace petticoats, chemises
threaded with coloured ribbons. On the large armchair, covered with blue and white chintz, was a
crumpled heap of white linen, a pair of café au lait
silk stockings. A light mahogany chair or two stood
about the room. Each had a blue and white cushion.
A large wash-stand stood near the mantlepiece, laden
with blue and white ware. The walls were covered
with blue silky paper, dotted here and there with
some colour prints. These were mostly English ;
their nude beauties sprawled and languished slyly
among bushes, listening to the pipes of Pan.

Victoria went into the back of the room, and, un-
hooking her cream silk dressing jacket, threw it on

the bed. This was a vast low edifice of glittering brown wood, covered now by a blue and white silk bedspread with edges smothered in lace; from the head of the bed peeped out the tips of two lace pillows. By the side of the bed, on the little night table, stood two or three books, a reading lamp and a small silver basket full of sweets. An ivory bell-pull hung by the side of a swinging switch just between the pillows.

Victoria walked past the bed and looked at herself in the high looking-glass set into the wall which rose from the floor to well above her head. The mirror threw back a pleasing reflection. It showed her a woman of twenty-six, neither short nor tall, dressed in a white petticoat and mauve silk corsets. The corsets fitted well into the figure which was round and inclined to be full. Her arms and neck, framed with white frillings, were uniformly cream coloured, shadowed a little darker at the elbows, near the rounded shoulders and under the jaw; all her skin had a glow, half vigorous, half delicate. But the woman's face interested Victoria more. Her hair was piled high and black over a broad low white forehead; the cream of the skin turned faintly into colour at the cheeks, into crimson at the lips; her eyes were large, steel grey, long lashed and thrown into relief by a faintly mauve aura. There was strength in the jaw, square, hard, fine cut; there was strength too in the steadiness of the eyes, in the slightly compressed red lips.

'Yes,' said Victoria to the picture, 'you mean business.' She reflected that she was fatter than she had ever been. Two months of rest had worked a revolution in her. The sudden change from toil to idleness had caused a reaction. There was something almost matronly about the soft curves of her breast. But the change was to the good. She was less interesting than the day when the Major sat face to face with her in Soho, his pulse beating quicker and quicker as her ravished beauty stimulated him by its novelty; but she was a finer animal. Indeed she realised to the full that she had never been so beautiful, that she had never been beautiful before, as men understand beauty.

The past two months had been busy as well as idle, busy that is as an idle woman's time. She had felt weary now and then, like those unfortunates who are bound to the wheel of pleasure and are compelled to 'do too much.' Major Cairns had launched out into his first experiment in pseudo-married life with an almost boyish zest. It was he who had practically compelled her to take the little house in Elm Tree Place.

'Think of it, Vic,' he had said, 'your own little den. With no prying neighbours. And your own little garden. And dogs.'

He had waxed quite sentimental over it and Victoria full of the gratitude that makes a woman cling to the fireman when he has rescued her, had helped him to build a home for the idyll. Within a feverish month he had produced the house as it stood. He had hardly allowed Victoria any choice in the matter, for he would not let her do anything. He practically compelled her to keep to her suite at the hotel, so that she might get well. He struggled alone with the decoration, plumbing, furniture and linoleum, linen and garden. Now and then he would ring up to know whether she preferred salmon pink to *fraise écrasée* cushions, or he would come up to the hotel rent in twain by conflicting rugs. At last he had pronounced the house ready, and, after supplying it with Mary and Charlotte, had triumphantly installed his new queen in her palace.

Victoria's first revelation was one of immense joy; unquestioning, and for one moment quite disinterested. It was not until a few hours had elapsed that she regained mastery over herself. She went

from room to room punching cushions, pressing her
hands over the polished wood, at times feeling
voluptuously on hands and knees the pile of the
carpets. She almost loved Cairns at the moment.
It was quite honestly that she drew him down by
her side on the red and white sofa and softly kissed
his cheek and drove his ragged moustache into rebellion. It was quite willingly too that she felt his
grasp tighten on her and that she yielded to him.
Her lips did not abhor his kisses.

Some hours later she became herself again. Cairns
was good to her, but good as the grazier is to the
heifer from whom he hopes to breed ; she was his
creature, and must be well housed, well fed, well
clothed, so that his eyes might feast on her, scented
so that his desire for her might be whipped into
action. In her moments of cold horror in the past
she had realised herself as a commodity, as a beast
of burden ; now she realised herself as a beast of
pleasure. The only thing to remember then was to
coin into gold her condescension.

Victoria looked at herself again in the glass. Yes,
it was condescension. As a free woman, that is, a
woman of means, she would never have surrendered
to Cairns the tips of her fingers. Off the coast of
Araby she had yielded to him a little, so badly did
she need human sympathy, a little warmth in the
cold of the lonely night. When he appeared again as
the rescuer she had flung herself into his arms with an
appalling fetterless joy. She had plunged her life
into his as into Nirvana.

Now her head was cooler. Indeed it had been
cool for a month. She saw Cairns as an average
man, neither good nor evil, a son of his father and
the seed thereof, bound by a strict code of honour
and a lax code of morals. She saw him as a dull
man with the superficial polish that even the roughest
pebble acquires in the stream of life. He had found

her at low water mark, stranded and gasping on the
sands; he had picked her up and imprisoned her
in this vivarium to which he alone had access, where
he could enjoy his capture to the full.

'And the capture's business is to get as much out
of the captor as possible, so as to buy its freedom
back.' This was Victoria's new philosophy. She
had dexterously induced Cairns to give her a thousand
a year. She knew perfectly well that she could live
on seven hundred, perhaps on six. Besides, she
played on his pride. Cairns was after all only a
big middle-aged boy; it made him swell to accom-
pany Victoria to Sloane Street to buy a hat, to the
Leicester Gallery to see the latest one-man show.
She was a credit to a fellow. Thus she found no
difficulty in making him buy her sables, gold purses,
Whistler etchings. They would come in handy, she
reflected, 'when the big bust-up came.' For Victoria
was not rocking herself in the transitory, but from
the very first making ready for the storm which
follows on the longest stretch of fair weather.

'Yes,' said Victoria again to the mirror, 'you mean
business.' The door opened and almost noiselessly
closed. Mary brought in a tray covered with a clean
set of silver-backed brushes, and piled up the other
ready to take away. She put a water can on the
washstand and parsimoniously measured into it some
attar of roses. Victoria stepped out into the middle
of the room and stood there braced and stiff as the
maid unlaced and then tightened her stays.

'What will you wear this evening, mum?' asked
Mary, as Victoria sat down in the low dressing chair
opposite the swinging glass.

'This evening?' mused Victoria. 'Let me see,
there's the *gris perle*.'

'No, mum, I've sent it to the cleaner's,' said Mary.
Her fingers were deftly removing the sham curls from
Victoria's back hair.

'You've worn it four times, mum,' she added reproachfully.

'Oh, have I? I don't think. . . . oh, that's all right, Mary.'

Victoria reflected that she would never have a well-trained maid if she finished sentences such as this. Four times! Well, she must give the Major his money's worth.

'You might wear your red Directoire, mum,' suggested Mary in the unemotional tones of one who is paid not to hear slips.

'I might. Yes. Perhaps it's a little loud for the Carlton.'

'Yes, mum,' said Mary without committing herself.

'After all, I don't think it is so loud.'

'No, mum,' said Mary in even tones. She deftly rolled her mistress' plaits round the crown.

Victoria felt vaguely annoyed. The woman's words were anonymous.

'But what *do* you think, Mary?' she asked.

'Oh, I think you're quite right, mum,' said Mary.

Victoria watched her face in the glass. Not a wave of opinion rippled over it.

Victoria got up. She stretched out her arms for Mary to slip the skirt over her head. The maid closed the lace blouse, quickly clipped the fasteners together, then closed the placket hole completely. Without a word she fetched the light grey coat, slipped it on Victoria's shoulders. She found the grey skin bag, while Victoria put on her white fox toque. She then encased Victoria's head in a grey silk veil and sprayed her with scent. Victoria looked at herself in the glass. She was very lovely, she thought.

'Anything else, mum?' said Mary's quiet voice.

'No, Mary, nothing else.'

'Thank you, mum.'

As Victoria turned, she found the maid had disappeared, but her watchful presence was by the front door to open it for her. Victoria saw her from the stairs, a short erect figure, with a pale face framed in dark hair. She stood with one hand on the latch, the other holding a cab whistle; her eyes were fixed upon the ground. As Victoria passed out she looked at Mary. The girl's eyes were averted still, her face without a question. Upon her left hand she wore a thin gold ring with a single red stone. The ring fastened on Victoria's imagination as she stepped into a hansom which was loafing near the door. It was not the custom, she knew, for a maid to wear a ring; and this alone was enough to amaze her. Was it possible that Mary's armour was not perfect in every point of servility? No doubt she had just put it on as it was her evening out and she would be leaving the house in another half hour. And then? Would another and a stronger hand take hers, hold it, twine its fingers among her fingers. Victoria wondered, for the vision of love and Mary were incongruous ideas. It was almost inconceivable that with her cap and apron she doffed the mantle of her reserve; she surely could not vibrate; her heart could not beat in unison with another. Yet, there was the ring, the promise of passion. Victoria nursed for a moment the vision of the two spectral figures, walking in a dusky park, arms round waists, then of shapes blended on a seat, faces hidden, lip to lip.

Victoria threw herself back in the cab. What did it all matter after all? Mary was the beast of burden which she had captured by piracy. She had been her equal once when abiding by the law; she had shared her toil and her slender meed of thanks. Now she was a buccaneer, outside the social code, and as such earned the right to command. So much did Victoria dominate that she thought she would refrain from the exercise of a bourgeois prerogative : the girl should wear her ring, even though custom forbade it, load herself with trinkets if she chose, for as a worker and a respecter of social laws surely she might well be treated as the sacrificial ox.

The horse trotted down Baker Street, then through Wigmore Street. Daylight was already waning; here and there houses were breaking into light between the shops, some of which had remembered it was Christmas eve and decked themselves out in holly. At the corner near the Bechstein Hall the cab came to a stop behind the long line of carriages waiting for the end of a concert. Victoria had time to see the old crossing sweeper, with a smile on his face and mistletoe in his battered billy-cock. The festivities would no doubt yield him his annual kind word from the world. She passed the carriages, all empty still. The cushions were rich, she could see. Here and there she could see a fur coat or a book on the seat; in one of them sat an elderly maid, watching the carriage clock under the electric light, meanwhile nursing a chocolate pom who growled as Victoria passed.

'Slaves all of them,' thought Victoria. 'A slave the good elderly maid, thankful for the crumbs that fall from the pom's table. Slaves too, the fat coachman, the slim footman despite their handsome English faces, lit up by a gas lamp. The raw material of fashion.'

The cab turned into the greater blaze of Oxford Circus, past the Princes Street P.R.R. There was a great show of Christmas cakes there. From the cab Victoria, craning out, could see a young and pretty girl behind the counter busily packing frosted biscuits. Victoria felt warmed by the sight; she was not malicious, but the contrast told her of her emancipation from the thrall of eight bob a week. Through Regent Street, all congested with traffic, little figures laden with parcels darting like frightened ants under the horse's nose, then into the immensity of Whitehall, the cab stopped at the Stores in Victoria Street.

Victoria had but recently joined. A store ticket and a telephone are the next best thing to respectability and the same thing as regards comfort. They go far to establish one's social position. Victoria struggled through the wedged crowd. Here and there boys and girls with flushed faces, who enjoyed being squashed. She could see crowds of jolly women picking from the counters things useful and things pretty; upon signal discoveries loudly proclaimed followed continual exclamations that they would not do. Family parties, excited and talkative, left her unmoved. That world, that of the rich and the free, would ultimately be hers; her past, that of the worn men and women ministering behind the counter to the whims of her future world, was dead.

She only had to buy a few Christmas presents. There was one for Betty, one for Cairns, and two for the servants. In the clothing department she selected a pretty blue merino dressing-gown and a long purple sweater for Betty. The measurements were much the same as hers, if a little slighter; besides such garments need not fit. She went downstairs and disposed of the Major by means of a small gold cigarette case with a leather cover. No doubt he had a dozen, but what could she give a man?

The Stores buzzed round her like a parliament of bees. Now and then people shouldered past her, a woman trod on her foot and neglected to apologise; parcels too, inconveniently carried, struck her as she passed. She felt the joy of the lost; for none looked at her, save now and then a man drowned in the sea of women. The atmosphere was stuffy, however, and time was precious as she had put off buying presents until so late. Followed by a porter with her parcels she left the Stores, experiencing the pleasure of credit on an overdrawn deposit order account. The man piled the goods in a cab, and in a few minutes she had transferred Betty's presents to a carrier's office,

with instructions to send them off at eight o'clock by
a messenger who was to wait at the door until the
addressee returned. This was not unnecessary fore-
sight, for Betty would not be back until nine. With
the Major's cigarette case in her white muff, Victoria
then drove to Bond Street, there to snatch a cup of
tea. On the way she stopped the cab to buy a lace
blouse for Mary and an umbrella for Charlotte, having
forgotten them in her hurry. She decided to have
tea at Miss Fortesque's, for Miss Fortesque's is one of
those tearooms where ladies serve ladies, and the
newest fashions come. It is the right place to be
seen in at five o'clock. At the door a small boy in an
Eton jacket and collar solemnly salutes with a shiny
topper. Inside, the English character of the room is
emphasized. There are no bamboo tables, no skimpy
French chairs or Japanese umbrellas ; everything is
severely plain and impeccably clean. The wood
shines, the table linen is hard and glossy, the glass is
hand cut and heavy, the plate quite plain and
obviously dear. On the white distempered walls are
colour prints after Reynolds, Romney, Gainsborough.
All conspires with the thick carpet to promote silence,
even the china and glass, which seem no more to dare
to rattle than if they were used in a men's club.

Victoria settled down in a large chintz-covered arm
chair and ordered tea from a good-looking girl in a
dark grey blouse and dress. Visibly a hockey skirt
had not long ago been more natural to her. As she
returned Victoria observed the slim straight lines of
her undeveloped figure. She was half graceful, half
gawky, like most young English girls.

'It's been very cold to-day, hasn't it?' said the
girl as she set down bread and butter, then cake and
jam sandwiches.

'Very,' Victoria looked at her narrowly. 'I suppose
it doesn't matter much in here, though.'

'Oh, no, we don't notice it.' The girl looked

weary for a second. Then she smiled at Victoria and walked away to a corner where she stood listlessly.

'Slave, slave.' The words rang through Victoria's head. 'You talk to me when you're sick of the sight of me. You talk of things you don't care about. You smile if you feel your face shows you are tired, in the hope I'll tip you silver instead of copper.'

Victoria looked round the room. It was fairly full, and as Fortesquean as it was British. The Fortesque tradition is less fluid than the constitution of the Empire. Its tables shout 'we are old wood'; its cups say 'we are real porcelain'; and its customers look at one another and say 'who the devil are you?' Nobody thinks of having tea there unless they have between one and three thousand a year. It is too quiet for ten thousand a year or for three pounds a week; it caters for ladies and gentlemen and freezes out everybody else, regardless of turnover. Thus its congregation (for its afternoon rite is almost hieratical) invariably includes a retired colonel, a dowager with a daughter about to come out, several squiresses who came to Miss Fortesque's as little girls and are handing on the torch to their own. There is a sprinkling of women who have been shopping in Bond Street, buying things good but not showy. As the customers, or rather clients, lapse with a sigh into the comfortable armchairs they look round with the covert elegance that says: 'And who the devil are you?'

Victoria was in her element. She had had tea at Miss Fortesque's some dozen years before when up for the week from Lympton; thus she felt she had the freedom of the house. She sipped her tea and dropped crumbs with unconcern. She looked at the dowager without curiosity. The dowager speculated as to the maker of her coat and skirt. Victoria's eyes fixed again on the girl who was passing her with a laden tray. The effort was bringing out the beautiful lines of the slender arms, drooping shoulders, round bust. Her fair hair clustered low over the creamy nape.

'Slave, slave,' thought Victoria again. 'What are you doing, you fool? Roughening your hands, losing flesh, growing old. And there's nothing for a girl to do but serve on, serve, always serve. Until you get too old. And then, scrapped. Or you marry . . . anything that comes along. Good luck to you, paragon, on your eight bob a week.'

Victoria went downstairs and got into the cab which had been waiting for her with the servants' presents. It was no longer cold, but foggy and warm. She undid her white fox stole, dropping on the seat her crocodile skin bag, whence escaped a swollen purse of gold mesh.

Upstairs the girl cleared away. Under the butter-smeared plate which slipped through her fingers she found half-a-crown. Her heart bounded with joy.

CHAPTER II

'Tom, you know how I hate *tournedos*,' said Victoria petulantly.

'Sorry, old girl.' Cairns turned and motioned to the waiter. While he was exchanging murmurs with the man Victoria observed him. Cairns was not bad looking, redder and stouter than ever. He was turning into the 'jolly old Major' type, short, broad, strangled in cross barred cravats and tight frockcoats. In evening dress, his face and hands emerging from his shirt and collar, he looked like an enormous dish of strawberries and cream.

'I've ordered quails for you? Will that do, Miss Dainty?'

'Yes, that's better.'

She smiled at him and he smiled back.

'By jove, Vic,' he whispered, 'you look fine. Nothing like pink shades for the complexion.'

'I think you're very rude,' said Victoria smiling.

'Honest,' said Cairns. 'And why not? No harm in looking your best is there? Now my light's yellow. Brings me down from tomato to carrot.'

'Fishing again. No good, Tommy old chap.'

'Never mind me,' said Cairns with a laugh. He paused and looked intently at Victoria, then cautiously round him. They were almost in the middle of the restaurant, but it was still only half full. Cairns had fixed dinner for seven, though they were only due for a music hall; he hated to hurry over his coffee. Thus they were in a little island of pink light surrounded by penumbra. Softly attuned, Mimi's song before the gates of Paris floated in from the balcony.

'Vic,' said Cairns gravely, 'you're lovely. I've never seen you like this before.'

'Do you like my gown?' she asked coquettishly.

'Your gown!' Cairns said with scorn. 'Your gown's like a stalk, Vic, and you're a big white flower bursting from it . . . a big white flower, pink flecked, scented. . . .'

'Sh . . . Tom, don't talk like that in here.' Victoria slid her foot forward, slipped off her shoe and gently put her foot on the Major's instep. His eyes blinked quickly twice. He reached out for his glass and gulped down the champagne.

The waiter returned, velvet footed. Every one of his gestures consecrated the quails resting on the flowered white plates, surrounded by a succulent lake of aromatic sauce.

They ate silently. There was already between them the good understanding which makes speech unnecessary. Victoria looked about her from time to time. The couples interested her, for they were nearly all couples. Most of them comprised a man between thirty and forty, and a woman some years his junior. Their behaviour was severely decorous, in fact a little languid. From a table near by a woman's voice floated lazily,

'I rather like this pub, Robbie.'

Indeed the acceptance of the pubbishness of the place was characteristic of its frequenters. Most of the men looked vaguely weary; some keenly interested bent over the silver laden tables, their eyes fixed on their women's arms. Here and there a foreigner with coal black hair, a soft shirt front and a fancy white waistcoat, spiced with originality the sedateness of English gaiety. An American woman was giving herself away by a semitone, but her gown was exquisite and its *décolletage* challenged gravitation.

Cairns' attitude was exasperatingly that of Gallio, save as concerned Victoria. His eyes did not leave her. She knew perfectly well that he was inspecting her, watching the rise and fall on her white breast of his Christmas gift, a diamond cross. They both refused the mousse and Victoria mischievously leant forward, her hands crossed under her chin, her arms so near Cairns' face that he could see on them the fine black shading of the down.

'Well, Tom?' she asked. 'Quite happy?'

'No,' growled Cairns, 'you know what I want.'

'Patience and shuffle the cards,' said Victoria, 'and be thankful I'm here at all. But I musn't rot you Tommy dear, after a present like that.'

She slipped her fingers under the diamond cross. Cairns watched the picture made by the rosy manicured finger nails, the sparkling stones, the white skin.

'A pity it doesn't match my rings,' she remarked.

Cairns looked at her hand.

'Oh, no more it does. I thought you had a half hoop. Never mind, dear. Give me that sapphire ring.'

'What do you want it for?' asked Victoria with a conscious smile.

'That's my business.'

She slipped it off. He took it, pressing her fingers.

'I think you ought to have a half hoop,' he said conclusively.

Victoria leant back in her chair. Her smile was triumphant. Truly, men are hard masters but docile slaves.

'You'll spoil me, Tom,' she said weakly. 'I don't want you to think that I'm fishing for things. I'm quite happy, you know. I'd rather you didn't give me another ring.'

'Nonsense,' said Cairns, 'I wouldn't give it you if I didn't like to see it on your hand.'

'I don't believe you,' she said smoothly, but the phrase rang true.

Some minutes later, as they passed down the stairs into the palm room, she was conscious of the eyes that followed her. Those of the men were mostly a little dilated; the women seemed more cynically interested, as suits those who appraise not bodies but garments. Major Cairns, walking a step behind her, was still looking well, with his close cut hair and moustache, stiff white linen and erect bearing. Victoria realised herself as a queen in a worthy kingdom. But the kingdom was not the one she wished to hold with all the force of her beauty. That beauty was transitory, or at least its subtler quality was. As Victoria lay in the brougham with Cairns's arm holding her close to him, she still remembered that the fading of her beauty might synchronise with the growth of her wealth. A memory from some book on political economy flashed through her mind : beauty was a wasting asset.

Cairns kissed her on the lips. An atmosphere of champagne, coffee, tobacco, enveloped her as her breath mixed with his. She coiled one arm round his neck and returned his kisses.

'Vic, Vic,' he murmured, 'can't you love me a little?'

She put her hand behind his neck and once more kissed his lips. He must be lulled, but not into security.

Victoria had never realised her strength and her freedom so well as that night, as she leant back in her box. Her face and breast, the Major's shirt front, were the only spots of light which emerged from the darkness of the box as if pictured by a German impressionist; down below, under the mist, the damned souls revelled in the cheap seats; they swayed, a black mass speckled with hundreds of white collars, dotted with points of fire in the bowls of pipes. By the side of the men, girls in white

P

blouses or crude colours, shrouded in the mist of
tobacco smoke. Now and then a ring coiled up from
a cigar in the stalls, swirled in the air for a moment
and then broke.

Just behind the footlights blazing over the blackness, a little fat man, with preposterous breeches, a
coat of many colours, a yellow wisp of hair clashing
with his vinous nose, sang of the Bank and his
manifold accounts. A faint salvo of applause ushered
him out, then swelled into a tempest as the next
number went up.

'Tommy Bung, you're in luck,' said the Major,
taking off Victoria's wrap.

She craned forward to see. A woman with masses
of fair hair, bowered in blue velvet, took a long
look at her from the stage box through an opera
glass.

The curtain went up. There was a roar of applause.
Tommy Bung was ready for the audience and had
already fallen into a tub of whitewash. The sorry
object extricated itself. His red nose shone, star like.
He rolled ferocious eyes at a girl. The crowd rocked
with joy. Without a word the great Tommy Bung
began to dance. At once the hall followed the
splendid metre. Up and down, up and down, twisting, curvetting, Tommy Bung held his audience
spellbound with rhymth. They swayed sharply with
the alternations.

Victoria watched the Major. His hands were
beating time. Tommy Bung brought his effort to a
conclusion by beating the floor, the soles of his feet,
the scenery, and punctuated the final thwack with
a well timed leap on the prompter's box.

Victoria was losing touch with things. Waves of
heat seemed to overwhelm her; little figures of
jugglers, gymnasts, performing dogs, passed before
her eyes like arabesques. Then again raucous voices.
The crowd was applauding hysterically. It was

Number Fourteen, whose great name she was fated
never to know.   Unsteadily poised on legs wide
apart, Number Fourteen sang.   Uncontrollable glee
radiated from him—

> Now kids is orl right
> When yer ain't got none ;
> Yer can sit at 'ome
> An' eat 'cher dam bun.
> I've just 'ad some twins ;
> Nurse says don't be coy,
> For they're just the picture
> Of the lodger's boy.
> > Tinka, Tinka, Tinka ; Tinka, Tinka, Tink
> > 'It 'im in the eye and made the lodger blink.
> > Tinga, Tinga, Tinga ; Tinga, Tinga, Teg
> > Never larfed so much since farver broke 'is leg.

A roar of applause encouraged him.   Victoria saw
Cairns carried away, clapping, laughing.   In the bar
below she could hear continuously the thud of the
levers belching beer.   Number Fourteen was still
singing, his smile wide-slit through his face—

> Now me paw-in-law
> 'E's a rum ole bloke ;
> Got a 'and as light
> As a ton o' coke.
> Came 'ome late one night
> An' what oh did 'e see ?
> Saw me ma-in-law
> On the lodger's knee.
> > Tinka, Tinka, Tinka ; Tinka, Tinka, Tink
> > 'It 'im in the eye an' made the lodger blink.
> > Tinga, Tinga, Tinga ; Tinga, Tinga, Teg,
> > Never larfed so much since farver broke 'is leg.

Enthusiasm was rising high.   Number Fourteen
braced himself for his great effort on the effects of
beer.   Then, gracious and master of the crowd, he
beat time with his hands while the chorus sounded
from a thousand throats.   Victoria happened to look

at Cairns. His head was beating time and, from his lips issued gleefully:

> Tinka, Tinka, Tinka; Tinka, Tinka, Tink
> 'It 'im in the eye—

Victoria scrutinised him narrowly. Cairns was a phenomenon.

'Never larfed so much since farver broke 'is leg,' roared Cairns. 'I say, Vic, he really *is* good.' He noticed her puzzled expression. 'I say, Vic, what's up? Don't you like him?'

Victoria did not answer for a second.

'Oh, yes, I—he's very funny—you see I've never been in a music hall before.'

'Oh, is that it?' Cairns's brow cleared. 'It's a little coarse, but so natural.'

'Is that the same thing?' asked Victoria.

'S'pose it is. With some of us anyhow. But what's the next?'

Cairns had already relapsed into the programme. He hated the abstract; a public school, Sandhurst and the army had armoured him magnificently against intrusive thought. They watched the next turn silently. A couple of cross-talk comedians, one a shocking creature in pegtop trousers, a shock yellow head and a battered opera hat, the other young, handsome and smart as a superior barber's assistant, gibbered incomprehensibly of songs they couldn't sing and lies they could tell.

The splendid irresponsibility of the music hall was wasted on Victoria. She had the mind of a school-mistress grafted on a social sense. She saw nothing before her but the gross riot of the drunken. She saw no humour in that cockney cruelty, capable though it be of absurd generosity. She resented too Cairns's boyish pleasure in it all; he revelled, she felt, as a buffalo wallows in a mud bath. He was gross, stupid, dull. It was degrading to be his instrument of pleasure. But, after all, what did it matter? He was the narrow way which would lead her to the august.

Though Cairns was not thin-skinned he perceived a little of this. Without a word he watched the cross-talk comedians, then the 'Dandy Girl of Cornucopia,' a rainbow of stiff frills with a voice like a fretsaw. As the lights went down for the , bioscope, the idea of reconciliation that springs from fat cheery hearts overwhelmed him. He put his hand out and closed it over hers. With a tremendous effort she repressed her repulsion, and in so doing won her victory. In the darkness Cairns threw his arms round her. He drew her towards him, moved, the least bit hysterical. As if fearful of losing her he crushed her against his shirt front.

Victoria did not resist him. Her eyes fixed on the blackness of the roof she submitted to the growing brutality of his kisses on her neck, her shoulders, her cheeks. Pressed close against him she did not withdraw her knees from the grasp of his.

'Kiss me,' whispered Cairns imperiously.

She cast down her eyes; she could hardly see his face in the darkness, nothing but the glitter of his eyeballs. Then, unhurried and purposeful, she pressed her lips to his. The lights went up again. Many of the crowd were stirring; Victoria stretched out her arms in a gesture of weariness.

'Let's go home, Vic,' said Cairns, 'you're tired.'

'Oh, no, I'm not tired,' she said. 'I don't mind staying.'

'Well, you're bored.'

'No, not at all, it's quite interesting,' said Victoria judicially.

'Come along, Vic,' said Cairns sharply. He got up.

She looked up at him. His face was redder, more swollen than it had been half-an-hour before. His

eyes followed every movement of her arms and
shoulders. With a faint smile of understanding and
the patience of those who play lone hands, she got
up and let him put on her wrap. As she put it on
she made him feel against his fingers the sweep
of her arm; she rested for a moment her shoulder
against his.

In the cab they did not exchange a word. Victoria's
eyes were fixed on the leaden sky; she was this man's
prey. But, after all, one man's prey or another?
The prey of those who demand bitter toil from the
charwoman, the female miner, the P.R.R. girl; or of
those who want kisses, soft flesh, pungent scents,
what did it all amount to? And, in Oxford Street,
a sky sign in the shape of a horse-shoe advertising
whisky suddenly reminded her of the half hoop, a
step towards that capital which meant freedom.
No, she was not the prey—at least not in the sense of
the bait which finally captures the salmon.

Cairns had not spoken a word. Victoria looked at
him furtively. His hands were clenched before him;
in his eyes shone an indomitable purpose. He was
going to the feast and he would foot the bill. On
arriving at Elm Tree Place he walked at once into
his dressing room, while Victoria went into her
bedroom. She knew his mood well and knew too
that he would not be long. She did not fancy overmuch the scene she could conjure up. In another
minute or two he would come in with the culture of
a thousand years ground down, smothered beneath
the lava-like flow of animalism. He would come
with his hands shaking, ready to be cruel in the
exaction of his rights. She hovered between repulsion and an anxiety which was almost anticipation;
Cairns was the known and the unknown at once.
But whatever his demands they should be met and
satisfied, for business is business and its justification
is profits. So Victoria braced herself and, with

feverish activity, twisted up her hair, sprayed herself with scent, jumped into bed and turned out the light.

As she did so the door opened. She was conscious for a fraction of a second of the bright quadrilateral of the open door where Cairns stood framed, a broad black silhouette.

CHAPTER III

'YES, I'm a lucky beggar,' soliloquised Cairns. He gave a tug to the leads at which two Pekingese spaniels were straining. 'Come along, you little brutes,' he growled. The spaniels, intent upon a piece of soiled brown paper in the gutter, refused to move.

'Obstinate, sir,' said a policeman respectfully.

'Devilish. Simply devilish. Fine day, isn't it?'

'Blowing up for rain, sir.'

'Maybe. Come along, Snoo; that'll do.'

Cairns dragged the dogs up the road. Snoo and Poo, husband and wife, had suddenly fascinated him in Villiers Street that morning. He was on his way to offer them at Victoria's shrine. Instinctively he liked the smart dog, as he liked the smart woman and the American novel. Snoo and Poo, tiny, fat, curly, khaki-coloured, with their flat Kalmuck faces, unwillingly trundled behind him. They would, thought Cairns, be in keeping with the establishment. A pleasant establishment. A nice little house, in its quiet street where nothing ever seemed to pass, except every hour or so a cab. It was better than a home, for it offered all that a home offers, soft carpets, discreet servants, nice little lunches among flowers and well-cleaned plate, and beyond, something that no home contains. It was adventurous. Cairns had knocked about the world a good deal and had collected sensations as finer natures collect thoughts. The women of the past met and caressed on steam-boats, in hotels at Cairo, Singapore and Cape Town, the tea gardens of Kobe and the stranger mysteries of Zanzibar, all this had left him weary and sighing for something like the English home. Indeed he grew more sentimental as he thought of Dover cliffs every time his tailor called the measurement of his girth. An extra quarter of an inch invariably coincided with a sentimental pang. Cairns, however, would not yet have been capable of settling down in a hunting county with a well-connected wife, a costly farming experiment and the shilling weeklies. A transition was required; he had no gift of introspection, but his relations with Victoria were expressions of this mood. Thus he was happy.

He never entered the little house in Elm Tree Place without a thrill of pleasure. Under the placid mask of its respectability and all that went with it, clean white steps, half curtains, bulbs in the window boxes, there flowed for him a swift hot stream. And in that stream flourished a beautiful white lily whose petals opened and smiled at will.

'I wonder whether I'm in love with her?' This was a frequent subject for Cairns's meditations. Victoria was so much more for him than any other woman had been that he always hesitated to answer. She charmed him sensually, but other women had done likewise; she was beautiful, but he could conceive of greater beauty. Her intellect he did not consider, for he was almost unaware of it. For him she was clever, in the sense that women are clever in men's eyes when they can give a smart answer, understand Bradshaw and order a possible combination at a restaurant. What impressed him was Victoria's coolness, the balance of her unhurried mind. Now and then he caught her reading curious books, such as *Smiles's Self-Help, Letters of a Self-Made Merchant to his Son* and *Thus Spake Zara* . . .

Something, by a man with a funny name; but this was all part of her character and of its novelty. He did not worry to scratch the surface of this brain; virgin soils did not interest him in the mental sense. Sometimes, when he enounced a political opinion or generalised on the problems of the day as stated in the morning paper, he would find, a little uneasily, her eyes fixed on him with a strangely interested look. But her eyelids would at once be lowered and her lips would part, showing a little redder and moister, causing his heart to beat quicker, and he would forget his perplexity as he took her hand and stroked her arm with gentle insistence.

Cairns dragged Snoo and Poo up the steps of the little house still grumbling, panting and protesting that, as drawing-room dogs, they objected to exercise in any form. He had a latchkey, but always refrained from using it. He liked to ring the bell, to feel like a guest. It would have been commonplace to enter *his* hall and hang up *his* hat on *his* peg. That would have been home and home only. To ask whether Mrs Ferris was in was more adventurous, for she might be out. And if she expected him, then it was an assignation; adventure again.

The unimposing Mary let him in. For a fraction of a second she looked at the Major, then at the floor.

'Mrs Ferris in?'

'Yes, sir, Mrs Ferris is in the boudoir.' Mary's voice fell on the last necessary word like a dropgate. She had been asked a question and answered it. That was the end of it. Cairns was the master of her mistress. What respect she owed was paid.

Cairns deposited his hat and coat in Mary's hands. Then, lifting Snoo under one arm and Poo under the other, both grumbling vigorously and kicking with their hind legs, he walked to the boudoir and pushed it open with his shoulder. Victoria was sitting at the little bureau writing a letter. Cairns watched her for two seconds, rejoicing in the firm white moulding of her neck, in the dark tendrils of hair clustering low, dwindling into the central line of down which tells of breeding and health. Then Victoria turned round sharply.

'Oh,' she said, with a little gasp. 'Oh, Tom, the ducks!'

Cairns laughed and, walking up to her, dropped Snoo on her lap and Poo, snuffling ferociously, on the floor. Victoria buried her hands in Snoo's thick coat; the dog gurgled joyfully and rolled over on its side. Victoria laughed, muzzling Snoo with her hand.

Cairns watched the picture for a moment. He was absurdly reminded of a girl in Java who nursed a black marmoset against her yellow breast. And as Victoria looked up at him, her chin now resting on Snoo's brown head, a soft wave of scent rose towards him. He knelt down, throwing his arms round her and the dog, gathering them both into his embrace. As his lips met hers and clung to them, her perfume and the ranker scent of the dog filled his nostrils, burning aphrodisiac into his brain.

Victoria freed herself gently and rose to her feet, still nursing Snoo, and laughingly pushed him into Cairns's face.

'Kiss him,' she said, 'no favours here.'

Cairns obeyed, then picked up Poo and sat down on the couch.

'This is sweet of you, Tom,' said Victoria. 'They *are* lovebirds.'

'I'm glad you like them; this is Poo I'm holding, yours is Snoo.'

'Odd names,' said Victoria.

'Chinese according to the dealer,' said Cairns, 'but I don't pretend to know what they mean.'

'Never mind,' said Victoria, 'they're lovebirds, and so are you, Tom.'

Cairns looked at her silently, at her full erect figure and smiling eyes. He was a lucky beggar, a damned lucky beggar.

'And what is this bribe for?' she asked.

'Oh, nothing. Knew you'd like them, beastly tempers and as game as mice. Women's dogs, you know.'

'Generalising again, Tom. Besides I hate mice.'

Cairns drew her down by his side on the couch. Everything in this woman interested and stimulated him. She was always fresh, always young. The touch of her hand, the smell of her hair, the feel of her skirts winding round his ankles, all that was magic ; every little act of hers was a taking of possession. Every time he mirrored his face in her eyes and saw the eyelids slowly veil and unveil them, something like love crept into his soul. But every passionate embrace left him weak and almost repelled. She was his property ; he had paid for her ; and, insistent thought, what would she have done if he had not been rich?

Half an hour passed away. Victoria lay passive in his arms. Snoo and Poo, piled in a heap, were snuffling drowsily. There was a ring at the front door, then a slam. They could hear voices. They started up.

'Who the deuce . . . . ?' said Cairns.

Then they heard someone in the dining-room beyond the door. There was a knock at the door of the boudoir.

'Come in,' said Victoria.

Mary entered. Her placid eyes passed over the Major's tie which had burst out of his waistcoat, Victoria's tumbled hair.

'Mr Wren, mum,' she said.

Victoria staggered. Her hands knotted themselves together convulsively.

'Good God,' she whispered.

'Who is it? What does he want? What name did you say?' asked Cairns. Victoria's excitement was infecting him.

Victoria did not answer. Mary stood before them, her eyes downcast before the drama. She was waiting for orders.

'Can't you speak?' growled Cairns. 'Who is it?'

Victoria found her voice at last.

'My brother,' she said hoarsely.

Cairns did not say a word. He walked once up and once down the room, stopped before the mirror to settle his tie. Then turned to Mary.

'Tell the gentleman Mrs Ferris can't see him?'

Mary turned to go. There was a sound of footsteps in the dining-room. The button of the door turned twice as if somebody was trying to open it. The door was locked but Cairns almost leaped towards it. Victoria stopped him.

'No,' she said, 'let me have it out. Tell Mr Wren I'm coming, Mary.'

Mary turned away. The incident was fading from her mind as a stone fades away as it falls into an abyss. Victoria clung to Cairns and whispered in his ear.

'Tom, go away, go away. Come back in an hour. I beg you.'

'No, old girl, I'm going to see you through,' said Cairns doggedly.

'No, no, don't.' There was fear in her voice. 'I must have it out. Go away, for my sake, Tom.'

She pushed him gently into the hall, forced him to pick up his hat and stick and closed the door behind him. She braced herself for the effort; for a second the staircase shivered before her eyes like a road in the heat.

'Now for it,' she said, 'I'm in for a row.'

A pleasant little tingle was in her veins. She opened the dining-room door. It was not very light.

There was a slight singing in her ears. She saw
nothing before her except a man's legs clad in worn
grey trousers where the knees jutted forward sharply.
With an effort she raised her eyes and looked Edward
in the face.

He was pale and thin as ever. A ragged wisp of
yellow hair hung over the left side of his forehead.
He peered at her through his silver-mounted glasses.
His hands were twisting at his watch chain, quickly,
nervously, like a mouse in a wheel. As she looked at
his weak mouth his insignificance was revealed to her.
Was this, this creature with the vague idealistic face,
the high shoulders, something to be afraid of? Pooh!

'Well, Edward?' she said, involuntarily aggressive.

Wren did not answer. His hands suddenly stopped
revolving.

'Well, Edward?' she repeated. 'So you've found
me?'

'Yes,' he said at length. 'I . . . . Yes, I've
found you.' The movement of his hands began again.

'Well?'

'I know. I've found out. . . . I went to Finsbury.'

'Oh? I suppose you mean you tracked me from
my old rooms. I suppose Betty told you I . . . my
new occupation.'

Wren jumped.

'Damn,' he growled. 'Damn you.'

Victoria smiled. Edward swearing. It was too
funny. What an awful thing it was to have a sense
of humour.

'You seem to know all about it,' she said smoothly.
'But what do you want?'

'How dare you?' growled Edward. 'A woman
like you. . . .'

A hard look came into Victoria's eyes.

'That will do Edward, I know my own business.'

'Yes, a dirty business.' A hot flush spread over
the man's thin cheeks.

'You little cur.' Victoria smiled ; she could feel
her lips baring her eye teeth. 'Fool.'

Edward stared at her. Passion was stifling his
words.

'It's a lot you know about life, schoolmaster,' she
sneered. 'Who are you to preach at me? Is it your
business if I choose to sell my body instead of selling
my labour?'

'You're disgraced.' His voice went down to a
hoarse whisper. 'Disgraced.'

Victoria felt a wave of heat pass over her body.

'Disgraced, you fool? Will anybody ever teach
you what disgrace is? There's no such thing as
disgrace for a woman. All women are disgraced
when they're born. We're parasites, toys. That's
all we are. You've got two kinds of uses for us, lords
and masters! One kind is honourable labour, as you
say, namely the work undertaken by what you call
the lower classes; the other's a share in the
nuptial couch, whether illegal or legal. Yes, your
holy matrimony is only another name for my
profession.'

'You've no right to say that,' cried Edward.
'You're trying to drag down marriage to your level.
When a woman marries she gives herself because she
loves ; then her sacrifice is sublime.' He stopped for
a second. Idealism, sentimentalism, other names for
ignorance of life, clashed in his self-conscious brain
without producing light. 'Oh, Victoria,' he said,
'you don't know how awful it is for me to find you
like this, my little sister . . . of course you can't
love him . . . if you'd married him it would have
been different.'

'Ah, Edward, so that's your philosophy. You say
that though I don't love him, if I'd married him it
would have been different. So you won't let me
surrender to a man unless I can trick him or goad
him into binding himself to me for life. If I don't

love him I may marry him and make his life a hell and I shall be a good woman; but I mustn't live with him illegally so that he may stick to me only so long as he cares for me.'

'I didn't say that,' stammered Edward. 'Of course, it's wrong to marry a man you don't care for . . . but marriage is different, it sanctifies.'

'Sanctifies! Nothing sanctifies anything. Our deeds are holy or unholy in themselves. Oh, understand me well, I claim no ethical revelation; I don't care whether my deeds are holy or not. I judge nothing, not even myself. All I say is that your holy bond is a farce; if women were free—that is, trained, able and allowed to earn fair wages for fair labour— then marriage might be holy. But marriage for a woman is a monetary contract. It means that she is kept, clothed, amused; she is petted like a favourite dog, indulged like a spoiled child. In exchange she gives her body.'

'No, no.'

'Yes, yes. And the difference between a married woman and me is her superior craft, her ability to secure a grip upon a man. You respect her because she is permanent, as you respect a vested interest.'

The flush rose again in Edward's cheeks. As he lost ground he fortified his obstinacy.

'You've sold yourself,' he said quickly, 'gone down into the gutter. . . . Oh!'

'The gutter!' Victoria was so full of contempt that it almost hurt her. 'Of course I'm in the gutter. I always was in the gutter. I was in the gutter when I married and my husband boarded and lodged me to be his favourite. I was in the gutter when I had to kow-tow to underbred people; to be a companion is to prostitute friendship. You don't mind that, do you? I was in the gutter in the tea shops, when I decoyed men into coming to the place because they could touch me, breathe me. I'm in the gutter now,

but I'm in the right one. I've found the one that's
going to make me free.'

Edward was shaken by her passion.

'You'll never be free,' he faltered, 'you're an
outcast.'

'An outcast from what?' sneered Victoria. 'From
society? What has society done for me? It's
kicked me, it's bled me. It's made me work ten
hours a day for eight bob a week. It'd have sucked
me dry and offered me the workhouse, or the Thames
at the end. It made me almost a cripple.'

Edward stared.

'Yes,' said Victoria savagely. 'That makes you
squirm, sentimentalist. Look at that!'

She put her foot on a chair, tucked up her skirt,
tore down the stocking. Purplish still, the veins
stood out on the firm white flesh.

Edward clenched both his hands and looked away.
A look of pain was in his eyes.

'Yes, look at that,' raged Victoria. 'That's what
your society's done for me. It's chucked me into the
water to teach me to swim, and it's gloated over every
choke. It's fine talking about chivalry, isn't it, when
you see what honest labour's done for me, isn't it?
It's fine talking about purity when you see the price
your society pays me for being what I am, isn't it?
Look at me. Look at my lace, look at my diamonds,
look at my house . . . and think of the other side:
eight bob a week, ten hours work a day, a room
with no fire, and a bed with no sheets. But
I know your society now, and as I can't kill
it I'll cheat it. I've served it and it's got two
years of my life; but I'm going to get enough out of
it to make it crawl.'

She strode towards Edward.

'So don't you come preaching to me,' she hissed.

Edward's head bent down. Slowly he walked
towards the door.

Q

'Yes,' she said, 'go. I've no use for you. I'm out for stronger meat.'

He opened the door, then, without looking up,

'Good-bye,' he said.

The door closed behind him. Victoria looked about her for some seconds, then sat down in the carving chair, her arms outstretched on the table. Her teeth were clenched now, her jaw set; with indomitable purpose she looked out into the darkening room where she saw the battle and victory of life.

CHAPTER IV

VICTORIA had never loved adventure for its own sake. The change from drudgery to leisure was grateful as was all it brought in the shape of pretty clothes, jewels and savoury dishes ; but she realised every day better that, taking it as a profession, her career was no great success. It afforded her a fair livelihood, but the wasting asset of her beauty could not be replaced; thus it behoved her to amortize its value at a rapid rate. She felt much better in health; her varicose veins had gone down a good deal, but she still preserved a dark mystery about them; after six months of intimate association, Cairns did not yet know why he had never seen Victoria without her stockings. Being man of the world enough to know that discretion is happiness, he had never pressed the point; a younger or more sensitive man would have torn away the veil, so as to achieve total intimacy at the risk of wrecking it. He was not of these, and vaguely Victoria did not thank him for a sentiment half discreet, half indifferent; such an attitude for a lover suggested disregard for essentials. As she grew stronger and healthier her brain worked more clearly, and she began to realise that even ten years of association with this man would yield no more than a pittance. And it would be difficult to hold him for ten years.

Victoria certainly went ably to work to preserve for Cairns the feeling of novelty and adventure. It was practically in deference to her suggestions that he retained his chambers; he soon realised her wisdom and entered into the spirit of their life. He still understood very well the pleasure of being her guest. Victoria found no decline in his desire; perhaps it was less fiery, but it was as coarse and as constant. Certainly she was woman for him rather than merely a woman; moreover she was a habit. Victoria saw this clearly enough and resolved to make the most of it.

In accordance with her principles she kept her expenses down. She would not even allow herself the luxury of a maid; she found it cheaper to pay Mary higher wages. When Cairns was not expected her lunch was of the simplest, and Charlotte discovered with amazement that her rakish mistress could check a grocer's book. Victoria was not even above cheating the Water Board by omitting to register her garden tap. All these, however, were petty economies; they would result in a saving of perhaps three hundred a year, a beggarly sum when pitted against the un-certainties of her profession.

She realised all this within three or four months of her new departure, and promptly decided that Cairns must be made to yield a higher revenue. She felt that she could not very well tell him that a thousand a year was not enough; on the face of it it was ample. It was necessary therefore to launch out a little. The first step was to increase her visible supply of clothes, and this was easily done by buying the cheap and effective instead of the expensive and good. Cairns knew enough about women's clothes to detect this now and then, but the changes bewildered him a little and he had some difficulty in seeing the difference between the latest thing and the cheapest. Whenever she was with him she affected the manners of a spendthrift; she would call cabs to carry her a hundred yards, give a beggar a shilling, or throw a pair of gloves out of the window because they had been worn once.

Cairns smiled tolerantly. She might as well have her fling, he thought, and a lack of discipline was as charming in a mistress as it was deplorable in a wife. He was therefore not surprised when, one morning, he found Victoria apparently nervous and worried. She owned that she was short of cash. In fact the manager of her bank had written to point out that her account was overdrawn.

'Dear me,' said Cairns with mock gravity, 'you've been going it, old girl! What's all this? "Self," "Self," why all these cheques are to "Self." You'll go broke.'

'I suppose I shall,' said Victoria wearily. 'I don't know how I do it, Tom. I'm no good at accounts. And I hate asking you for more money . . . but what am I to do?'

She crossed her hands over her knees and looked up at him with a pretty expression of appeal. Cairns laughed.

'Don't worry,' he said, curling a lock of her hair round a fat forefinger. 'I'll see you through.'

Victoria received that afternoon a cheque for two hundred and fifty pounds which she paid into her account. She did not, however, inform Cairns that the proceeds of the "Self" cheques had been paid into a separate account which she had opened with another bank. By this means, she was always able to exhibit a gloomy pass book whenever it was required.

Having discovered that Cairns was squeezable Victoria felt more hopeful as to the future. She was his only luxury and made the most of his liking for jewellery and furs. She even hit upon the more ingenious experiment of interesting Barbezan Soeurs in her little speculations. The device was not novel: for a consideration of ten per cent these bustling dressmakers were ready to provide fictitious bills and even solicitor's letters couched in frigidly menacing terms. Cairns laughed and paid solidly. He had apparently far more money than he needed. Victoria was almost an economy; without her he would have lost a fortune at bridge, kept a yacht perhaps and certainly a motor. As it was he was quite content with his poky chambers in St James', a couple of clubs which he never thought of entering, the house in Elm Tree Place and a stock of good cigars.

Cairns was happy, and Victoria labouring lightly for large profits, was contented too. Theirs were lazy lives, for Cairns was a man who could loaf. He loafed so successfully that he did not even think of interfering with Victoria's reading. She now read steadily and voraciously; she eschewed novels, fearing the influence of sentiment. 'It will be time for sentiment by and by,' she sometimes told herself. Meanwhile she armoured her heart and sharpened her wits. The earlier political opinions which had formed in her mind under the pressure of toil remained unchanged but did not develop. She recognised herself as a parasite and almost gloried in it. She evolved as a system of philosophy that one's conduct in life is a matter of alternatives. Nothing was good and nothing was evil; things were better than others or worse and there was an end of her morality. Victoria had no patience with theories. One day, much to Cairns surprise, she violently flung Ingersoll's essays into the fender.

'Steady on,' said Cairns, 'steady on, old girl.'

'Such rot,' she snarled.

'Hear, hear,' said Cairns, picking up the book and looking at its title. 'Serve you right for reading that sort of stuff. I can't make you out, Vic.'

Victoria looked at him with a faint smile, but refused to assign a cause for her anger. In fact she had suddenly been irritated by Ingersoll's definition of morality. 'Perceived obligation,' she thought.

' And I don't perceive any obligation ! ' She consoled
herself suddenly with the thought that her amorality
was a characteristic of the superman.

The superman preoccupied her now and then. He
was a good subject for speculation because imponder-
able and inexistent. The nearest approach she could
think of was a cross between an efficient colonial
governor and a latter-day prophet. She believed
quite sincerely that the day must come when children
of the light must be born, capable of ruling and of
keeping the law. She saw very well too that their production did not lie with an effete aristocracy any more
than with a dirty and drunken democracy; probably
they would be neo-plutocrats, men full of ambition,
lusting for power and yet imbued with a spirit of
icy justice. Her earliest tendency had been towards
an idealistic socialism. Burning with her own wrongs
and touched by the angelic wing of sympathy, she
had seen in the communisation of wealth the only
means of curbing the evils it had hitherto wrought.
Further observation showed her however that an
idealism of this kind would not lead the world
speedily into a peaceful haven. She saw too well
that covetousness was still lurking snakelike in the
bosom of man, ready to rear its ugly head and strike
at any hand. Thus she was not surprised to see the
chaos which reigned among socialists, their intriguing,
their jealousies, their unending dissensions, their
apostacies. This did not throw her back into the
stereotyped philosophy of individualism; for she could
not help seeing that the system of modern life was
absurd, stupidly wasteful above all of time, labour
and wealth. To apply Nietzscheism to socialism
was, however, beyond her; to reconcile the two
doctrines which apparently conflict and really only
overlap was a task too difficult for a brain which had
lain fallow for twenty-five years. But she dimly felt
that Nietzscheism did not mean a glorified im-

perialism, but a worship of intellectual efficiency and the stringent morality of *noblesse oblige*.

Where Victoria began to part issue with her own thoughts was when she considered the position of women. Their outlook was one of unrelieved gloom ; and it one day came upon her as a revelation that Nietzsche and Schopenhauer, following in a degree on Rousseau, had forgotten women in the scheme of life. There might be supermen, but there would be no superwomen : if the supermen were true to their type they would have to crush and to dominate the women. As the latter fared so hard at the hands of the pigmies of to-day, what would they do if they could not develop in time to resist the sons of Anak ? Victoria saw that the world was entering upon a sex war. Hitherto a shameful state of peace had left women in the hands of men, turning over the other cheek to the smiter. The sex war, however, held forth no hopes to her ; in the dim future, sex equality might perhaps prevail ; but she saw nothing to indicate that women had sown the seeds of their victory. She had no wish to enrol herself in the ranks of those who were waging an almost hopeless battle, armed with untrained intellects and unathletic bodies. She could not get away from the fact that the best women athletes cannot compete with ordinary men, that even women with high intellectual qualifications had not ousted from commanding positions men of inferior ability.

All this, she thought, was unjust ; but why hope for a change ? There was nothing to show that men grew much better as a sex ; then why pin faith to the coming of better times ? Women were parasites, working only under constraint, badly and at uncongenial tasks ; their right to live was based on their capacity to please. This brought her to her own situation. The future lay before her in the shape of two roads. One was the road which led to the struggle for life ; ending, she felt it too well, in a crawl to death on crippled limbs. The other was the road along which grew roses, roses which she could pluck and sell to men ; at the end of that was the heaven of independence. It had golden gates ; it was guarded by an angel in white garments with a palm leaf in his hands and beyond lay the pleasant places where she had a right of way. And as she looked again the heaven with the golden gates turned into a bank with a commissionaire at the door.

Her choice being made, she did not regret it. For the time being her life was pleasant enough, and if it could be made a little more profitable it would soon be well worth living, and her freedom would be earned. Meanwhile she took pleasure in small things. The little house was almost a show place, so delicate and refined were its inner and outer details. Victoria saw to it that frequently changed flowers decorated the beds in the front garden ; Japanese trees, dwarfed and gnarled, stood right and left of the steps, scowling like tiny Titans ; all the blinds in the house were a mass of insertion. These blinds were a feature for her ; they implied secrecy. Behind the half blinds were thick curtains of decorated muslin ; behind these again, heavy curtains which could be drawn at will. They were the impenetrable veil which closed off from the world and its brutalities this oasis of forbidden joys.

In the house also she was ever elaborating sybaritising her life. She had a branch telephone fixed at the head of her bed ; the first time that Cairns used it to tell his man to bring up his morning coat she had the peculiar sensation that her bed was in touch with the world. She could call up anybody, the Archbishop of Canterbury, the Governor of the Bank of England or the headquarters of the Salvation Army. Her bed was the centre of the world. She fitted the doors of her bedroom and her boudoir with curious little locks which acted on the pressure of a fin ger

for her mind was turned on delicacies and the sharp
click of a bolt, the grating of a key savoured of the
definite, therefore of the coarse. A twist of the knob
between two fingers and the world was silently shut
out.

Now too that she was beautiful once more she
revelled in mirrors. The existing ones in her bedroom and in the boudoir were not enough ; they were
public, unintimate. She had a high mirror fixed in
the bathroom, so that she could see herself in her
freshness, covered with pearly beads like a naiad.
She rejoiced in her beauty, in her renewed strength ;
she often stood for many minutes in the dim steamy
light of the room, analysing her body, its grace and
youth, with a growing consciousness of latent power.
Then, suddenly, the faint violet streaks of the varicose
veins would intrude upon the rite and she would
wrap herself up jealously in her bath robe so that not
even the mirror should be a confidant of the past.

CHAPTER V

WEEK after week passed on, and now monotony drew her stifling cloak over Victoria. Cairns was still in a state of beatitude which made him an unexciting companion; satisfied in his egoism, it never came into his mind that Victoria could tire of her life. He spent many afternoons in the back garden under a rose-covered pergola. By his side was a little table with a syphon, a decanter of whisky, and a box of cigars; he read desultorily, sometimes the latest motor novel, at other times the improving memoirs of eighteenth century noblewomen. Now and then he would look approvingly at Victoria in plain white drill, delightfully mischievous under a sun-bonnet, and relapse into his book. Once he quoted 'A flask of wine, a book of verse . . . .' and Victoria went into sudden fits of laughter when she remembered Neville Brown. The single hackneyed line seemed to link malekind together.

Cairns was already talking of going away. June was oppressively hot and he was hankering after some quiet place where he might do some sea-fishing and get some golf. He was becoming dangerously fat; and Victoria, foreseeing a long and very cheap holiday, favoured the idea in every way. They could go up to Scotland later too; but Cairns rather hesitated about this, for he neither cared to show off Victoria before the people he knew on the moors, nor to leave her for a fortnight. He was paying the penalty of Capua. His plans were set back, however, by serious trouble

which had taken place on his Irish estate, his though
still in the hands of Marmaduke Cairns's executors.
There had been nightriding, cattle driving, some
boycotting. The situation grew so tense that the
executors advised Cairns to sell the estate to the
tenants but the latter declined the terms; matters
came to a deadlock and it was quite on the cards that
an application might be made under the Irish Land
Act. It was clear that in this case the terms would
be bad, and Cairns was called to Limerick by telegram
as a last chance. He left Victoria, grumbling and
cursing Ireland and all things Irish.

Left to herself, Victoria felt rather at a loose end.
The cheerful if uninteresting personality of Major
Cairns had a way of filling the house. He had an
expansive mind; it was almost chubby. For two
days she rather enjoyed her freedom. The summer
was gorgeous; St John's Wood was bursting everywhere into flower; the trees were growing opaque in
the parks. At every street corner little whirlwinds of
dry grit swayed in the hot air. One afternoon
Victoria indulged in the luxury of a hired private
carriage, and flaunted it with the best in the long line
on the south side of the Park. Wedged for a quarter
of an hour in the mass she felt a glow come over her.
The horses all round her shone like polished wood,
the carriage panels were lustrous, the harness was
glittering, the brass burnished; all the world seemed
to radiate warmth and light. Gaily enough, because
not jaded by repetition, she caused the carriage to do
the Ring, twice. She felt for a moment that she was
free, that she could vie with those women whose lazy
detachment she stirred for a moment into curiosity
by her deep eyes, dark piled hair and the audacity
of her diaphanous *crèpe de chine*.

Cairns was still in Ireland, struggling conscientiously to pile up unearned increment; and Victoria,
thoroughly aimless, suddenly bethought herself of

Farwell. She had been remiss in what was almost
a duty. Surely she ought to report progress to the
man who had helped to open her eyes to the realities
of life. She had misapplied his teaching perhaps,
or rather remoulded it, but still it was his teaching.
Or rather it was what a woman should know, as
opposed to what Thomas Farwell preached; if men
were to practise that, then she should revise her
philosophy.

At ten minutes to one she entered the Moorgate
Street P.R.R. with a little thrill. Everything
breathed familiarity; it was like coming home, but
better, for it is sweeter to revisit the place where one
has suffered, when one has emerged, than to brood
with gentle sorrow on the spot, where there once was
joy. She knew every landmark, the tobacconist, the
picture shop, still full of 'Mother's Helps' and of
'artistic' studies in the nude; there was the red-
coated bootlack too, as dirty and as keenly solicitous
as ever. The P.R.R. itself did not chill her. In the
crude June sunlight its nickel shone gaily enough.
Everything was as before; the cakes had been
moulded in the old moulds, and here was the old
bill of fare, unchanged no doubt; even the marble-
topped tables and the half cleaned cruets looked
kindly upon her; but the tesselated red and blue
floor aroused the hateful memory of another Victoria
on her hands and knees, an old sack round her waist,
painfully swaying from right to left, swabbing the
tiles. Little rivulets of water and dirt flowed slowly
across the spectre's hand.

As she went down the steps into the smoking-room
she crossed with the manageress, still buxom and
erect; but she passed unnoticed, for this was the busy
hour when the chief tried to be simultaneously on
three floors. The room was not so full as it had once
been. She sat down at a little table and watched
the familiar scene for some minutes. She told the

girl she would wait a minute, for she did not want to miss Farwell. The world had gone round, but apparently the P.R.R. was the axis. There in the corner were the chess players; to-day they only ran four boards, but at one of them a fierce discussion was going on as to a variation of the queen's pawn opening. On the other side of the room were the young domino players, laughing and smoking cigarettes. The fat and yellow Levantine was missing. Victoria regretted him, for the apocalyptic figure was an essential part of the ugly past. But there was ' old dry toast ' all alone at his little table. He had not changed; his white hair still framed thickly his beautiful old brown face. There he sat, still silent and desolate, waiting for the end. Victoria felt a pang of sorrow. She was not quite hardened yet and she realised it angrily. There must be no sympathy and no quarter in her game of life. It was too late or too soon for that. Victoria let her eyes stray round the room. There were the young men and boys or some of the same breed, in their dark suits, brilliant ties, talking noisily, chaffing one another, gulping down their small teas and toasted scones. A conversation between two older men was wafted in to her ears.

' Awful. Have you tried annelicide ? '

At that moment a short broad figure walked smartly down the steps. It was Thomas Farwell, a thin red book under his arm. He went straight through to the old table, propped his book against the cruet and began to read. Victoria surveyed him critically. He was thinner than ever; his hair was more plentifully sprinkled with grey but had receded no further. He was quite near her, so she could see his unbrushed collar and his frayed cuffs. After a moment the girl came and stood before him; it was Nelly, big and raw-boned as ever, handsome still like the fine beast of burden she was. She wore no apron

now in proud token of her new position as head
waitress. Now the voices by her side were talking
holidays.

'No, Ramsgit's good enough for me. Broadstairs
and all these little places, they're so tony—'

Maud passed quickly before Victoria. The poor
little girl was as white as ever; her flaccid cheeks
danced up and down as she ran. The other voice
was relating at length how its owner had taken his
good lady to Deal. Nelly had left Farwell, walking
more slowly than the other girls, as befitted her
station. Victoria felt herself pluck up a little
courage, crossed the room followed by many admiring
glances, and quickly sat down at Farwell's table.
He looked up quickly. The book dropped suddenly
from the cruet.

'Victoria,' he gasped.

'Yes,' she said smiling.

'Well . . .' His eyes ran over her close fitting
tussore dress, her white kid gloves.

'Is that all you've got to say to me?' she asked.
'Won't you shake hands?'

Farwell put out his hand and held hers for a
second. He was smiling now, with just a touch of
wistfulness in his eyes.

'I'm very glad to see you,' he said at length.

'So am I,' said Victoria. 'I hope you don't mind
my coming here, but I only thought of it this
morning.'

'Mind,' snapped Farwell. 'People who understand
everything never mind anything.'

Victoria smiled again. The bumptious aphorism
was a sign that Farwell was still himself. For a
minute or so they looked at one another. Victoria
wondered at this man; so powerful intellectually
and physically; and yet content to live in his ideals
on a pittance, to do dull work, to be a subordinate.
Truly a caged lion. Farwell, on the other hand, was

looking in vain for some physical ravishes to justify Victoria's profession, for some gross development at least. He looked in vain. Instead of the pale dark girl with large grey eyes whom he had known, he now saw a healthy and beautiful woman with a clear white skin, thick hair, red lips.

'Well,' he said with a laugh, 'can I invite you to lunch with me?'

'You may,' she said. 'I'll have a small coffee and . . . a sunny side up.'

Farwell laughed and signed to Nelly. After a minute he attracted her attention and gave the order without Nelly taking any interest in Farwell's guest. It might be rather extraordinary, but her supervisory duties were all-absorbent. When she returned, however, she stole a curious look at Victoria while placing before her the poached egg on toast. She looked at her again, and her eyes dilated.

'Law,' she said, 'Vic!'

'Yes, Nelly, how are you?' Victoria put out her gloved hand. Nelly took it wonderingly.

'I'm all right,' she answered slowly. 'Just been made head waitress,' she added with some unction. Her eyes were roving over Victoria's clothes, valuing them like an expert.

'Congratulations,' said Victoria. 'Glad you're getting on.'

'I see *you're* getting on,' said Nelly, with a touch of sarcasm.

'So, so, things aren't too bad.' Victoria looked up. The women's eyes crossed like rapiers; Nelly's were full of suspicion. The conversation stopped then, for Nelly was already in request in half a dozen quarters.

'She knows,' said Victoria smoothly.

'Of course,' said Farwell. 'Trust a woman to know the worst about another and to show it up. Every little helps in a contest such as life.'

Farwell then questioned her as to her situation,
but she refused him all details.

'No,' she said, 'not here. There's Nelly watching
us, and Maud has just been told. Betty's been
shifted, I know, and I suppose Mary and Jennie are
gone, but there's the manageress and some of the
girls upstairs. I've nearly done. Let me return the
invitation. Dine with me to-night . . .' She was
going to say 'at home,' but changed her mind to the
prudent course. . . . 'at, well, anywhere you like.
Whereabouts do you live, Mr Farwell?'

'I live in the Waterloo Road,' said Farwell, 'an
artery named after the playing fields of Eton.'

'I don't know it well,' said Victoria, 'but I seem
to remember an Italian place near Waterloo Station.
Suppose you meet me at the south end of Waterloo
Bridge at seven?'

'It will do admirably,' said the man. 'I suppose
you want to go now? Well, you've put out my
habits, but I'll come too.'

They went out; the last Victoria saw of the P.R.R.
was the face of the cook through the hole in the
partition, red, sweating, wrinkled by the heat and
hurry of the day. They parted in the churchyard.
Victoria watched him walk away with his firm swing,
his head erect.

'A man,' she thought, 'too clever to succeed.'

Being now again at a loose end and still feeling
fairly hungry, she drove down to Frascati's to lunch.
She was a healthy young animal, and scanty fare was
now a novelty. At three o'clock she decided to look
up Betty at her depot in Holborn; and by great good
luck found that Betty was free at half past five, as
the Holborn depôt for unknown reasons kept
shorter hours than Moorgate Street. She whiled
away the intervening time easily enough by shop-
gazing and writing a long letter to Cairns on
the hospitable paper of the Grand Hotel. At

R

half-past five she picked up Betty at the door of
the P.R.R.

'Thank you again so very, very much for the
sweater and the dressing gown,' said Betty as she
slipped her arm through that of her friend.

'Don't be silly, Betty, I like giving you things.'
Victoria smiled and pressed the girl's arm. 'You're
not looking well, Betty.'

'Oh, I'm all right,' said Betty wearily.

Victoria looked at her again. Under the pretty
waved sandy hair Betty's forehead looked waxen;
her cheeks were too red. Her arm felt thinner than
ever. What was one to do? Betty was a weakling
and must go to the wall. But there was a sweetness
in her which no one could resist.

'Look here, Betty,' said Victoria, 'I've got very
little time; I've got to meet Mr Farwell at Waterloo
Bridge at seven. It's beautifully fine, let's drive
down to Embankment Gardens and talk.'

Betty's face clouded for a moment at the mention
of Farwell's name. She hated him with the ferocity
of the weak; he had ruined her friend. But it was
good to have her back. The cab drove down
Chancery Lane at a spanking rate, then across the
Strand and through a lane. The unaccustomed
pleasure and the rush of air brought all her face
into pink unison with her cheeks.

The two women sat side by side for a moment.
This was the second time they had met since Victoria
had entered her new life. There had been a few
letters, the last to thank Victoria for her Christmas
present, but Betty did not say much in them.
Her tradition of virtue had erected a barrier between
them.

'Well, Betty,' said Victoria suddenly, 'do you still
think me very bad?'

'Oh, Vic, how can you? I never, never said
that.'

'No, you thought it,' answered Victoria a little cruelly. 'But never mind, perhaps you're right.'

'I never said so, never thought so,' persisted Betty. 'You can't go wrong, Vic, you're . . . you're different.'

'Perhaps I am,' said Victoria. 'Perhaps there are different laws for different people. At any rate I've made my choice and must abide by it?'

'And are you happy, Vic?' Anxiety was in the girl's face.

'Happy? Oh, happy enough. He's a good sort.'

'I'm so glad. And . . . Vic . . . do you think he'll marry you?'

'Marry me?' said Victoria laughing. 'You little goose, of course not. Why should he marry me now he's got me?'

This was a new idea for Betty.

'But doesn't he love you very, very much?' she asked, her blue eyes growing rounder and rounder.

'I suppose he does in a way,' said Victoria. 'But it doesn't matter. He's very kind to me but he won't marry me; and, honestly, I wouldn't marry him.'

Betty looked at her amazed and a little shocked.

'But, dear,' she faltered, 'think of what it would mean; you . . . he and you, you see . . . you're living like that . . . if he married you . . .'

'Yes, I see,' said Victoria with a slight sneer, 'you mean that I should be an honest woman and all that? My dear child, you don't understand. Whether he marries me or not it's all the same. So long as a woman is economically dependent on a man she's a slave, a plaything. Legally or illegally joined it's exactly the same thing; the legal bond has its advantages and its disadvantages and there's an end of the matter.'

Betty looked away over the Thames; she did not

understand. The tradition was too strong. Time went quickly. Betty had no tale to unfold; the months had passed leaving her doing the same work for the same wage, living in the same room. Before her was the horizon on which were outlined two ships; 'ten hours a day' and 'eight bob a week.' And the skyline?

As they parted, Victoria made Betty promise to come and see her. Then they kissed twice, gently and silently, and Victoria watched her friend's slim figure fade out of sight as she walked away. She had the same impression as when she parted with Lottie, who had gone so bravely into the dark. A wave of melancholy was upon her. Poor girls, they were without hope; she at least was viewing life with her eyes open. She would wrench something out of it yet. She shook herself; it was a quarter to seven.

An hour later she was sitting opposite Farwell. They were getting to the end of dinner. Conversation had flagged while they disposed of the earlier courses. Now they were at the ice and coffee stage. The waiters grew less attentive; indeed there was nobody to observe them save the olive-skinned boy with the mournful eyes who looked at the harbour of Palermo through the Waterloo Road door. Farwell lit the cigar which Victoria forced upon him, and leant back, puffing contentedly.

'Well,' he said at length, 'how do you like the life?'

'It is better than the old one,' she said.

'Oh, so you've come to that. You have given up the absolutes.'

'Yes, I've given them up. A woman like me has to.'

'Yes, I suppose you've got to,' pondered Farwell. 'But apart from that, is it a success? Are you attaining your end? That's the only thing that matters, you know.'

'I am, in a sense ; I'm saving money. You see, he's generous.'

'Excellent, excellent,' sneered Farwell. 'I like to see you making out of what the bourgeois call vice that which will enable you to command bourgeois respect. By-and-by I suppose you'll have made a fortune ? '

'Well, no ; a competency perhaps, with luck.'

'With luck, as you say. Do you know, Victoria, this luck business is grand ! My firm goes in for mines : they went prospecting in America twenty years ago and they happened to strike copper. That was good. Other men struck granite only. That was bad. But my boss is a City Sheriff now. Frightfully rich. There used to be four of them, but one died of copper poisoning, and another was found shot in a gulch. Nobody knows how it happened, but the other two got the mines.'

Victoria smiled. She liked this piratical tit-bit.

'Yes,' she said, ' luck's the thing. And merit . . . well, I suppose the surviving partners had merit.'

'Anyhow, I wish you luck,' said Farwell. 'But tell me more. Do you find you've paid too high a price for what you've got ? '

'Too high a price ? '

'Yes. Do you have any of that remorse we read about ; would you like to be what you were ? Unattached, you know . . . eligible for Young Women's Christian Associations ? '

'Oh, no,' Victoria laughed. 'I can't pay too high a price for what I think I'll get. I don't mean these jewels or these clothes, that's only my professional uniform. When I've served my time I shall get that for which no woman can pay too much : I shall be economically independent, free.'

'Free.' Farwell looked towards the ceiling through a cloudlet of smoke. 'Yes, you're right. With the world as it is it's the only way. To be independent you must acquire the right to be dependent on the world's labour, to be a drone . . . and the biggest drone is queen of the hive. Yet I wish it had been otherwise with you.' He looked at her regretfully.

Victoria toyed with a dessert knife.

' Why ? ' she asked.

' Oh, you had possibilities . . . but after all, we all have. And most of them turn out to be impossibilities. At any rate, you're not disgusted with you're life, with any detail ? '

' No, I don't think so. I don't say I'll go on any longer than I need, but it's bearable. But even if it were repulsive in every way I'd go on if I saw freedom ahead. If I fight at all I fight to a finish.'

' You're strong,' said Farwell looking at her. ' I wish I had your strength. You've got that force which makes explorers, founders of new faiths, prophets, company promoters.' He sighed.

' Let's go,' he added, ' we can talk in the warm night.'

For an hour they talked, agreeing always in the end. Farwell was cruelly conscious of two wasted lives : his, because his principles and his capacity for thought had no counterweight in a capacity for action ; Victoria's, because of her splendid gifts ignobly wasted and misused by a world which had asked her for the least of them.

Victoria felt a peculiar pleasure in this man's society. He was elderly, ugly, ill-clad ; sometimes he was boorish, but a halo of thought surrounded him, and the least of his words seemed precious. All this devirilised him, deprived him of physical attractiveness. She could not imagine herself receiving and returning his caresses. They parted on Waterloo Bridge.

' Good-bye,' said Farwell, ' you're on the right track. The time hasn't come for us to keep the law,

for we don't know what the law is. All we have is
the edict of the powerful, the prejudice of the fool;
the last especially, for these goaled souls have their
traditions, and their convictions are prisons all.'

Victoria pressed his hand and turned away. She
did not look back. If she had she would have seen
Farwell looking into the Thames, his face lit up by a
gas lamp, curiously speculative in expression. His
emotions were not warring, but the chaos in his
brain was such that he was fighting the logical case
for and against an attempt to find enlightenment on
the other slope of the valley.

CHAPTER VI

VICTORIA stretched herself lazily in bed. Her eyes took in a picture of Cairns on the mantelpiece framed between a bottle of eau-de-cologne and the carriage clock; then, little by little, she analysed details, small objects, powderpuffs, a Chelsea candlestick, an open letter, the wall paper. She closed her eyes again and buried her face in the pillow. The lace edge tickled her ear pleasantly. She snuggled like a stroked cat. Then she awoke again, for Mary had just placed her early cup of tea on the night table. The tray seemed to come down with a crash, a spoon fell on the carpet. Victoria felt daylight rolling back sleep from her brain while Mary pulled up the blinds. As light flooded the room and her senses became keener she heard the blinds clash.

'You're very noisy, Mary,' she said, lifting herself on one elbow.

The girl came back to the bed her hands folded together.

'I'm sorry, mum . . . I . . . I've . . .'

'Yes? what's the matter?'

Mary did not answer, but Victoria could see she was disturbed. Her cap was disarranged; it inclined perhaps five degrees from the vertical. There was a faint flush on her cheeks.

'What's the matter?' said Victoria sharply. 'Is there anything wrong?'

'No, mum. . . . Yes mum. . . . They say in the paper . . . . There's been trouble in Ireland, mum. . . .'

'In Ireland?' Victoria sat bolt upright. Her heart gave a great bang and then began to go with a whirr.

'At Rossbantry, mum . . . last night . . . he's shot. . . .'

'Shot? Who? can't you speak?'

'The Major, mum.'

Mary unfolded her hands suddenly and drew them up and down her apron as if trying to dry them. Victoria sat as if frozen, looking at her wide-eyed. Then she relapsed on the pillow. Everything swam for a second, then she felt Mary raising her head.

'Go away,' whispered Victoria. 'Leave me for a minute. I'm all right.'

Mary hesitated for a moment, then obeyed, softly closing the door. Victoria lay staring at the ceiling. Cairns was dead, shot. Awful. A week ago his heavy frame was outlined under these very blankets. She shuddered. But why, how? It wasn't true, it couldn't be true. She sat up as if impelled by a spring, and rang the bell violently. The broken rope fell on her face in a coil. With both hands she seized her chin as if to stop a scream.

'The paper! get me the paper!' she gasped as Mary came in. The girl hesitated. Victoria's face frightened her. Victoria looked at her straight, and she ran out of the room. In another minute she had laid the open paper before her mistress.

Victoria clutched at it with both hands. It was true. True. It was true. The headlines were all she could see. She tried to read the text, but the letters danced. She returned to the headlines.

SHOCKING OUTRAGE IN IRELAND

LANDLORD SHOT

In the next column :—

M. C. C.'S HARD TASK

Her heart's action was less violent now. She understood; every second increased her lucidity. Shot. Cairns was shot. Oh, she knew, he had carried strife with him and some tenant had had his revenge. She took up the paper and could read it now. Cairns had refused to make terms, and on the morning of his death had served notices of eviction on eigheen cottagers. The same night he was sitting at a window of his bailiff's house. Then two shots from the other side of the road, another from lower down. Cairns was wounded twice, in the lung and throat, and died within twenty minutes. A man was under arrest.

Victoria put down the paper. Her mind was quite clear again. Poor old Tom! She felt sorry but above all disturbed; every nerve in her body seemed raw. Poor old Tom, a good fellow! He had been kind to her; and now, there he was. Dead when he was thinking of coming back to her. He would never see her again, the little house and things he loved. Yes, he had been kind; he had saved her from that awful life . . . . Victoria's thoughts turned into another channel. What was going to become of her.

'Old girl,' she said aloud, 'you're in the cart.'

She realised that she was again adrift, alone, face to face with the terrible world. Cairns was gone; there was nobody to protect her against the buffeting waves. A milkman's cart rattled by; she could hear the distant rumble of the Underground, a snatch carried by the wind from a German band. Well, the time had come; it had to come. She could not have held Cairns for ever; and now she had to prove her mettle, to show whether she had learned enough of the world, whether she had grit. The thought struck cold at her, but an intimate counseller in her brain was already awake and crying out:

'Yes, yes, go on! you can do it yet.'

Victoria threw down the paper and jumped out

of bed. She dressed feverishly in the clothes and
linen she had thrown in a heap on a chair the night
before, twisting her hair up into a rough coil. Just
before leaving the room she remembered she had
not even washed her hands. She did so hurriedly;
then, seeing the cold cup of tea, drank it off at a
gulp; her throat felt parched.

She pushed back the untasted dish on the breakfast
table. Her head between her hands, she tried to
think. At intervals she poured out cups of tea and
drank them off quickly.

Snoo and Poo, after vainly trying to induce her to
play with them, lay in a heap in an armchair snuffling
as they slept.

The better she realised her position the greater
grew her fears. Once more she was the cork tossed
in the storm; and yet, rudderless, she must navigate
into the harbour of liberty. If Cairns had lived and
she had seen her power over him wane, she would have
taken steps; she did not know what steps, but felt she
surely would have done something. But Cairns was
dead; in twenty minutes she had passed from comparative security into the region where thorns are
many and roses few.

Poor old Tom! She felt a tiny pang; surely this
concern with herself when his body still lay unburied
was selfish, ugly. But, pooh! why make any bones
about it? As Cairns had said himself, he liked to
see her beautiful, happy, well clad. His gifts to her
were gifts to himself: she was merely his vicar.

Victoria drank some more cold tea. Good or bad,
Cairns belonged to the past and the past has no
virtues. None, at any rate, for those whose present
is a wind-swept table-land. Men must come and go,
drink to the full of the cup and pay richly for every
sip, so that she might be free, hold it no longer to
their lips. There was no time to waste, for already
she was some hours older; some of those hours which

might have been transmuted into gold, that saving gold. She must take steps.

The 'steps to be taken,' a comforting sentence, were not easy to evolve. But another comforting catchward, 'reviewing the situation,' saved her from perplexity. She went into the little boudoir and took out her two pass books. The balance seemed agreeably fat, but she did not allow herself to be deluded ; she checked off the debit side with the foils of her cheque book and found that two of the cheques had not been presented. These she deducted, but the result was not unsatisfactory ; she had exactly three hundred pounds in one bank and a few shillings over fifty pounds in the other. Three hundred and fifty pounds. Not so bad. She had done pretty well in these nine months. Of course that banker's order of Cairns would be stopped. She could hardly expect the executors to allow it to stand. Thus her capital was three hundred and fifty pounds. And there was jewellery too, worth a couple of hundred pounds, perhaps, and lace, and furs. The jewellery might come in handy ; it could be 'gophirised.' The furniture wasn't bad either.

Of course she must go on with the house. It was no great responsibility, being held on a yearly agreement. Victoria then looked through her accounts ; they did not amount to much, for Barbezan Soeurs, though willing to assist in extracting money by means of bogus invoices, made it a rule to demand cash for genuine purchases. Twenty pounds would cover all the small accounts. The rent was all right, as it would not be due until the end of September. The rates were all right too, being payable every half year ; they could be ignored until the blue notice came, just before Christmas.

Victoria felt considerably strengthened by this investigation. At a pinch she could live a year on the present footing, during which something must turn up. She tried to consider for a moment the various things that might turn up. None occurred to her. She settled the difficulty by going upstairs again to dress. When she rang for Mary to do her hair, the girl was surprised to find her mistress perfectly cool. Without a word, however, Mary restored her hair to order. It was a beautiful and elegant woman, perhaps a trifle pale and open mouthed, who, some minutes later, set out to walk to Regent's Park.

Victoria sat back in her chair. Peace was upon her soul. Perhaps she had just passed through a crisis, perhaps she was entering upon one, but what did it matter? The warmth of July was in the clear air, the canal slowly carried past her its film of dust. No sound broke through the morning; save the cries of little boys fishing for invisible fishes, and, occasionally, a raucous roar from some prisoner in the Zoo. Now that she had received the blow and was recovering she was conscious of a curious feeling of lightness; she felt freer than the day before. Then she was a man's property, tied to him by the bond of interest; now she was able to do what she chose, know whom she chose, so long as that money lasted. Ah, it would be good one day when she had enough money to be able to look the future in the face and flaunt in its forbidding countenance the fact that she was free, for ever free.

Victoria was no longer a dreamer; she was a woman of action. The natural sequence of her thoughts brought her up at once against the means to the triumphant end. Three hundred and fifty pounds, say six hundred if she realised everything, would not yield enough to feed a superannuated governess. She would need quite eight or ten thousand pounds before she could call herself free and live her dreams.

'I'll earn it,' she said aloud, 'yes, sure enough.'

A little Aberdeen terrier came bounding up to her, licked her hand and ran away after his master. A friendly omen. Six hundred pounds was a large sum in a way. She could aspire to a partnership in some business now. A vision arose before her; Victoria Ferris, milliner. The vision grew; Victoria Ferris and Co., Limited, wholesalers; then Ferris' Stores, for clothes and boots and cheese and phonographs, with a branch of Cook's agency, a Keith Prowse ticket office; Ferris' Stores as an octopus, with its body in Knightsbridge and a tentacle hovering over every draper from Richmond to Highgate.

Yes, that was all very well, but what if Victoria Ferris failed? 'No good,' she thought, 'I can't afford to take risks.' Of course the idea of seeking employment was absurd. No more ten hours a day for eight bob a week for her. Besides, no continuous references and a game leg . . . The situations crowded into and out of Victoria's brain like dissolving views. She could see herself in the little house, with another man, with other men, young men, old men; and every one of them was rocked in the lap of Delilah, who laughingly shore off their golden locks.

'By Jove,' she said aloud, bringing her gloved fist down on her knee, 'I'll do it.'

Of course the old life could not begin again just now. She did not know a man in London who was worth capturing. She must go down into the market, stand against the wall as a courtesan of Alexandria and nail a wreath of roses against the highest bid. The vision she saw was now no longer the octopus. She saw a street with its pavements wet and slithering, flares, barrows laden with greens; she could smell frying fish, rotting vegetables, burning naptha; a hand opened the door of a bar and, in the glare, she could see two women with vivid hair, tired eyes, smiling mouths, each one patiently waiting before a

little table and an empty glass. Then she saw once
more the courtesan of Alexandria, dim in the night,
not lit up by the sun of sweet Egypt, but clad in
mercerised cotton and rabbit's fur, standing, watching
like a shadow against a shop door in Regent Street.

No, she had not come to that. She belonged to the
upper stratum of the profession, and, knowing it,
could not sink. Consciousness was the thing. She
was not going into this fight soft-handed or soft-
hearted. She knew. There was high adventure in
store for her yet. If she must fish it should be for
trout not chub. Like a wise woman, she would not
love lightly, but where money is. There should be
no waiting, no hesitating. That very night she
would sup at the Hotel Vesuvius . . . all in black
. . . like an ivory Madonna set in ebony . . . with
a tea rose in her hair as a foil to her shoulders . . .
and sweeping jade earrings which would swim like
butterflies in the heavy hair. Ah, it would be high
adventure when Demetrious knelt at the feet of
Aphrodite with jewels in his sunburnt palm, when
Croesus bargained away for a smile a half of his
Lydian wealth.

She got up, a glow in her veins as if the lust of
battle was upon her. Quickly she walked out of the
park to conquer the town. A few yards beyond the
gates newspaper placards shouted the sensation of the
day ; placards pink, brown, green, all telling the tale
of murder, advertising for a penny the transitory joy
of the fact. Victoria smiled and walked on. She let
herself into the house. It was on the stroke of one.
She sat down at the table, pressing the bell down with
her foot.

'Hurry up, Mary,' she said, 'I'm as hungry as a
hunter.'

A voice floated through the window like an echo :
'Irish murder ; latest details.'

'Shut the window, Mary,' she said sharply.

CHAPTER VII

THE Hotel Vesuvius is a singular place. It stands on
the north side of Piccadilly, and for the general its
stuccoed front and severe sash windows breathe an
air of early Victorian respectability. Probably it was
once a ducal mansion, for it has all the necessary
ugliness, solidity and size ; now it is the most remarkable instance of what can be done by a proprietor
who remembers that an address in Piccadilly exempts
him from the rules which govern Bloomsbury. One
enters it through a small hall all alight with white
and gold paint. Right and left are the saloon bar
and the buffet ; this enables the customer to select
either without altering the character of his accommodation, while assuming superiority for a judicious
choice. A broad straight staircase leads up to the
big supper room on the first floor. Above are a score
of private dining-rooms.

Victoria jumped out of the cab and walked up the
steps, handing the liveried commissionaire two shillings
to pay the cabman. This was an inspiration calculated
to set her down at once with the staff as one who knew
the ropes. In the white and gold hall she halted for
a moment, puzzled and rather nervous. She had
never set foot in the Vesuvius ; she had never heard
it mentioned without a smile or a wink. Now, a little
flushed and her heart beating, she realised that she
did not know her way about.

Victoria need have had no fears. Before she had
time to take in the scene, a tall man with a perfectly

groomed head and a well fitting evening dress bowed low before her.

'Madame wishes no doubt to deposit her wrap,' he said in gentle tones. His teeth flashed white for a moment.

'Yes,' said Victoria, . . . 'Yes, where is the cloak room?'

'This way, madame. If madame will permit me. . . .' He pointed towards the end of the hall and preceded her steps. An elderly woman behind the counter received Victoria's wrap and handed her a brass token without looking at her. While she pulled up her gloves she looked round curiously. The cloak room was small; behind the counter the walls were covered by a mahogany rack with some hundred pigeon-holes. The fiercer light of an unshaded chandelier beat down upon the centre of the room. Victoria was conscious of an extraordinary atmosphere, a blend of many scents, tobacco smoke, leather; most of the pigeon-holes were bursting with coloured wraps, many of them vivid blue or red; here and there long veils, soiled white gloves hung out of them; a purple ostrich feather hung from an immense black hat over a white and silver Cingalese shawl. Victoria turned sharply. The man was inspecting her coolly with an air of intentness that showed approval.

'Where does madame wish to go?' he asked as they entered the hall. 'In the buffet perhaps?'

He opened the door. Victoria saw for a second a long counter laden with bottles, at which stood a group of men, some in evening dress, some in tweed suits; she saw a few women among them, all with smiles upon their faces. Behind the counter she had time to see the barmaid, a beautiful girl with dark eyes and vivid yellow hair.

'No, not there,' she said quickly. It reminded her of the terrible little bar of which Farwell had given

s

her a glimpse. ' You are the manager, I believe . . .
I want to go up into the supper room.'

' Certainly, madame; will madame come this
way ? '

The manager preceded her up to the first floor.
On the landing, two men in tweeds suddenly stopped
talking as she passed. A porter flung the glazed
door open. A short man in evening dress looked at
her, then at the manager. After a second's hesitation
the two men in tweeds followed her in.

The manager put his hands in his pockets,
walked up to the other man and nodded towards the
door.

' *Pas mal, hein ?* '

' *Epatante,*' said the short man. ' *Du chic. Et une
peau !* '

The manager smiled and turned to go downstairs.
' *Surveillez moi ça Anatole,*' he said.

Victoria, meanwhile, had stopped for a moment on
the threshold, a little dazed by the scene. Though
it was only half-past ten, the eighty tables of the
Vesuvius were almost every one occupied; the crowd
looked at first like a patchwork quilt. The room
was all white and gold like the hall; a soft radiance
fell from the lights hidden in the cornice; two heavy
chandeliers with faintly pink electric bulbs and a few
pink shaded lights on the table diffused a roseate
glow over the scene. Victoria felt like an intruder,
and her discomfiture was heightened by the gripping
hot perfume. But already a waiter was by her side;
she let him be her pilot. In a few seconds she found
herself sitting at a small table alone, near the middle
of the room. The waiter reappeared almost at once
carrying on a tray a liqueur glass containing some
colourless fluid. She had ordered nothing, but his
adroitness relieved her. Clearly the expert had
divined her inexperience and had resolved to smooth
her way.

She lifted the glass to her lips and sipped at it.
It was good stuff, rather strong. The burn on her
palate seemed to brace her; she looked round the
room. It was a peculiar scene; for the Vesuvius is
a luxurious place, and a provincial might well be
excused for thinking it was the Carlton or the Savoy;
indeed there was something more outwardly opulent
about it. It suggested a place where men not only
spent what they had but spent more. But for a few
men in frock-coats and tweeds it would have been
almost undistinguishable from the recognised resorts
of fashion. Victoria took stock of her surroundings;
of the shining plate and glass, the heavy red carpet,
the red and gold curtains, drawn but fluttering at
the open windows. The guests, however, interested
her more. At half the tables sat a woman and a
man, at others a woman alone before a little glass.
What struck her above all was the beauty of the
women, the wealth they carried on their bodies.
Hardly one of them seemed over thirty; most of them
had golden or vivid red hair, though a few tables off
Victoria could see a tall woman of colour with black
hair stiffened by wax and pierced with massive ivory
combs. They mostly wore low-necked dresses, many
of them white or faintly tinted with blue or pink.
She could see a dark Italian-looking girl in scarlet from
whose ears long coral earrings drooped to her slim
cream-coloured shoulders. There was an enormously
stout woman with puffy pink cheeks, strapped slightly
into a white silk costume, looking like a rose at the
height of its bloom. There were others too! short
dark women with tight hair; minxish French
faces and little shrewd dark eyes: florid Dutch and
Belgian women with massive busts and splendid
shoulders, dazzlingly white; English girls too, most
of them slim with long arms and rosy elbows and
faintly outlined collar bones. Many of these had the
aristocratic nonchalance of 'art' photographs.

Opposite Victoria, under the other chandelier, a splendid creature, white as a lily, with flashing green eyes, copper coloured hair, had thrown herself back in her armchair and was laughing at a man's joke. Her head was bent back, and as she laughed her splendid bust rose and fell and her throat filled out. An elderly man with a close clipped grey moustache, immaculate in his well-cut dress clothes, leaned towards her with a smile on his brown face.

Victoria turned her eyes away from the man, (a soldier, of course), and looked at the others. They, too, were a mixed collection. There were a good many youths, all clean shaven and mostly well-groomed; these talked loudly to their partners and seemed to fill the latter with merriment; now and then they stared at other women with the boldness of the shy. There were elderly men too; a few in frock coats in spite of the heat, some very stout and red, some bald and others half concealing their scalps under cunning hair arrangements. The elderly men sat mostly with two women, some with three, and lay back smiling like courted pachas. By far the greater number of the guests, however, were anything between thirty and forty; and seemed to cover every type from the smart young captain with the tanned face, bold blue eyes and a bristly moustache, to ponderous men in tweeds or blue reefer jackets who looked about them with a mixture of nervousness and bovine stolidity.

From every corner came a steady stream of loud talk; continually little shrieks of laughter pierced the din and then were smothered by the rattling of the plates. The waiters flitted ghostly through the room with incredible speed, balancing high their silver trays. Then Victoria became conscious that most of the women round her were looking at her; for a moment she felt her personality shrivel up under

their gaze. They were analysing her, speculating as
to the potentialities of a new rival, stripping off her
clothes too and her jewels. It was horrible, because
their look was more incisive than the merely brutal
glance by which a man takes stock of a woman's
charms.

She pulled herself together however, and forced
herself to return the stares. 'After all,' she thought,
'this is the baptism of fire.' She felt strengthened,
too, as she observed her rivals more closely. Beautiful
as most of them seemed at first sight, many of them
showed signs of wear. With joyful cruelty Victoria
noted here and there faint wrinkles near their eyes,
relaxed mouths, cheekbones on which rosacia had
already set its mark. She could not see more than
half a dozen whose beauty equalled hers; she threw
her head up and drew back her shoulders. In the
full light of the chandelier she looked down at the
firm white shapeliness of her arms.

'Well, how goes it?'

Victoria started and looked up from her contemplation. A man had sat down at her table. He seemed
about thirty, fairish, with a rather ragged moustache.
He wore a black morning coat and a grey tie. His
hands and wrists were well kept and emerged from
pale blue cuffs. There was a not unkindly smile
upon his face. His tip tilted nose gave him a cheerful, rather impertinent expression.

'Oh, I'm all right,' said Victoria vaguely. Then
with an affectation of ease. 'Hot, isn't it?'

'Ra-*ther*,' said the man. 'Had your supper?'

'No,' said Victoria, 'I don't want any.'

'Now, come, really that's too bad of you. Thought
we were going to have a nice little family party and
you're off your feed.'

'I'm sorry,' said Victoria smiling. 'I had dinner
only two hours ago.' This man was not very attractive; there was something forced in his ease.

'Well, have a drink with me,' he said.

'What's yours?' asked Victoria. That was an inspiration. The plunge braced her like a cold bath. The man laughed.

'Pop, of course. Unless you prefer a Pernot. You know '"absinthe makes the . . . "' He stopped and laughed again. Victoria did likewise without understanding him. She saw that the other women laughed when men did.

They filled their glasses. Victoria liked champagne. She watched the little bubbles rise, and drank the glass down. It was soft and warm. How strong she felt suddenly. The conversation did not flag. The man was leaning towards her across the table, talking quickly. He punctuated every joke with a high laugh.

'Oh, I say, give us a chance,' floated from the next table. Victoria looked. It was one of the English girls. She was propped up on one elbow on the table; her legs were crossed showing a long slim limb and slender ankle in a white open work stocking. A man in evening dress with a foreign looking dark face was caressing her bare arm.

'Penny for your thoughts,' said Victoria's man.

'Wasn't thinking,' she said. 'I was looking.'

'Looking? are you new here?'

'Yes, it's the first time I've come.'

By Jove! It *must* be an eye-opener.' He laughed.

'It is rather. It doesn't seem half bad.'

'You're right there. I'm an old stager.' A slightly complacent expression came over his face. He filled up the glasses. 'You don't spoil the collection, you know,' he added. 'You're a bit of all right.' He looked at her approvingly.

'Am I?' She looked at him demurely. Then, plunging once more, 'I hope you'll still think so by and by.' The man's eyes dwelled for a moment on her face and neck, his breath became audible suddenly. She felt his foot softly stroke hers. He drew his napkin across his lips.

'Well,' he said with an assumption of ease, 'shall we go?'

'I don't mind,' said Victoria getting up.

It was with a beating heart that Victoria climbed into the cab. As soon as he got in the man put his arm round her waist and drew her to him. She resisted gently but gave way as his arm grew more insistent.

'Coy little puss.' His face was very near her upturned eyes. She felt it come nearer. Then, suddenly, he kissed her on the lips. She wanted to struggle; she was a little frightened. The lights of Piccadilly filled her with shame. They spoke very little. The man held her close to him. As the cab rattled through Portland Place, he seized her once more. She fought down the repulsion with which his breath inspired : it was scented with strong cigars and champagne. Victoriously she coiled one arm round his neck and kissed him on the mouth. In her disgust there was a blend of triumph; not even her own feelings could resist her will.

As she waited on the doorstep while he paid the cabman a great fear came upon her. She did not know this man. Who was he? Perhaps a thief. She suddenly remembered that women of her kind were sometimes murdered for the sake of their jewellery. As the man turned to come up the steps she pulled herself together. 'After all,' she thought, 'it's only professional risk.'

They stood for a moment in the hall of the silent house. She felt awkward. The man looked at her and mistook her hesitation.

'It's all right,' he faltered. He looked about him, then, quickly whipping out a sovereign purse, he drew out two sovereigns with a click and laid them on the hall table.

'You see,' he said ' . . . a girl like you. . . .
three more to-morrow morning . . . . I'm square
you know.'

Victoria smiled and, after a second's hesitation,
picked up the money.

'So'm I,' she said.   Then she switched on the light
and pointed upstairs.

CHAPTER VIII

VICTORIA'S new career did not develop on unkindly
lines. Every night she went to the Vesuvius, where
she soon had her appointed place full under one of the
big chandeliers. She secured this spot without
difficulty, for most of her rivals were too wise to
affront the glare; as soon as she realised this she
rather revelled in her sense of power, for she now
lived in a world where the only form of power was
beauty. She felt sure of her beauty now she had
compared it minutely with the charms of the preferred
women. She was finer, she had more breed. Almost
every one of those women showed a trace of coarseness: a square jaw, not moulded in big bone like hers
but swathed in heavy flesh; a thick ankle or wrist;
spatulate fingertips; red ears. Her pride was in the
courage with which she welcomed the flow of the
light on her neck and shoulders; round her chandelier
the tables formed practically into circles, the nearest
being occupied by the very young and venturesome,
a few by the oldest who desperately clung to their
illusion of immortal youth; then came the undecided,
those who are between ages, who wear thick veils and
sit with their backs to the light; the outer fringe
was made up of those who remembered. Their smiles
were hard and fixed.

She was fortunate enough too. She never had to
sit long in front of the little glass which she discovered to be kummel; the waiter always brought it
unasked. Sometimes they would chat for a moment,

for Victoria was assimilating the lazy familiarity of her surroundings. He talked about the weather, the latest tips for Goodwood, the misfortune of Camille de Valenciennes who had gone off to Carlsbad with a barber who said he was a Russian prince and had left her there stranded.

Her experiences piled up, and, after a few weeks she found she had exhausted most of the types who frequented the Vesuvius. Most of them were of the gawky kind, being very young men out for the night and desperately anxious to get off on the quiet by three o'clock in the morning; of the gawky kind too were the Manchester merchants paying a brief visit to town on business and who wanted a peep into the inferno; these were easily dealt with and, if properly primed with champagne, exceedingly generous. Now and then Victoria was confronted with a racier type which tended to become rather brutal. It was recruited largely from obviously married men whose desires, dammed and sterilised by monotonous relations, seemed suddenly to burst their bonds.

In a few weeks her resources developed exceedingly. She learned the scientific look that awakes a man's interest: a droop of the eyelid followed by a slow raising of it, a dilation of the pupil, then again a demure droop and the suspicion of a smile. She learned to prime herself from the papers with the proper conversation; racing, the latest divorce news, ragging scandals, marriages of the peerage into the chorus. She learned to laugh at chestnuts and to memorise such stories as sounded fresh; a few judicious matinées put her up to date as to the latest musical comedies. On the whole it was an easy life enough. Six hours in the twenty-four seemed sufficient to afford her a good livelihood, and she did not doubt that by degrees she would make herself a connection which might be turned to greater advantage ; as it was she had two faithful admirers whom she could count on once a week.

The life itself often struck her as horrible, foul ; still she was getting inured to the inane and could listen to it with a tolerant smile ; sometimes she looked dispassionately into men's fevered eyes with a little wonder and an immense satisfaction in her power and the value of her beauty. Sometimes a thrill of hatred went through her and she loathed those whose toy she was ; then she felt tempted to drink, to drugs, to anything that would deaden the nausea ; but she would rally : the first night, when she had drunk deep of champagne after the kummel, had given her a racking headache and suggested that beauty does not thrive on mixed drinks.

Another painful moment had been the third day after her new departure. It seemed to force realisation upon her. Tacitly the early cup of tea had been stopped. Mary now never came to the door, but breakfast was laid for two in the dining-room at half past nine ; the hot course stood on a chafing dish over a tiny flame ; the teapot was stocked and a kettle boiled on its own stand. Neither of the servants ever appeared. On the third day, however, as Victoria lay in her boudoir, reading, preparatory to ringing the cook to give her orders for the day, there was a knock at the door.

'Come in,' said Victoria a little nervously. She was still in the mood of feeling awkward before her servants.

Mary came in. For a moment she tugged at her belt. There was a slight flush on her sallow face.

' Well Mary ? ' asked Victoria, still nervous.

' If you please, mum, may I speak to you ? I've been talking to cook, mum, and—'

' And ? '

' Oh, mum, I hope you won't think it's because

we're giving ourselves airs but it isn't the same as it
was here before, mum—'

'Well?'

'Well, mum, we think we'd rather go mum.
There's my young man, mum, and—and—'

'And he doesn't like your being associated with a
woman of my kind? Very right and proper.'

'Oh, mum, I don't mean that. You've always
been kind to me. Cook too, she says she feels it
very much, mum. When the major was alive, mum,
it was different. It didn't seem to matter then, mum,
but now—'

Mary stopped. For a moment the eyes behind the
glasses looked as if they were going to cry.

'Don't trouble to explain, Mary,' said her mistress
with some asperity. 'I understand. You and cook
can't afford to jeopardise your characters. From the
dizzy heights of trained domesticity, experts in your
own line, you are justified in looking down upon an
unskilled labourer. I have no doubt that you have
considered the social problem in all its aspects, that
you fully realise the possibilities of a woman wage-
earner and her future. By all means go where your
moral sense calls you : I shall give you an excellent
character and demand none in exchange. There!
I don't want to hurt your feelings, Mary, I spoke
hastily,' she added as the maid's features contracted,
'you only do this to please your young man ; that is
woman's profession, and I of all people must approve
of what you do. If you don't mind, both of you, you
will leave on Saturday. You shall have your full
month and a month's board allowance. Now send
up cook, I want to order lunch.'

She could almost have wept as she lay with her
face in the cushion. Her servants had delivered
an ultimatum from womankind, and lack of supplies
compelled her to pick up the gage of battle. Mary
and cook were links between her and all those women

who shelter behind one man only, and from that vantage ground hurl stones at their sisters beyond the gates. The significance of it was not that their services were lost to her, but that she must now be content to associate with another class. Soon, however, her will was again supreme. 'After all,' she thought, 'I have done with Society. I'm a pirate; Society 'll be keen enough when I've won.'

Within three days she had readjusted her household. She had decided to make matters easy by engaging two German girls. Laura, the cook, said at once that it was all one to her who came to the house and who didn't, so long as they left her alone in the kitchen, and provided she might bring her large tabby cat. Augusta the maid, a long lanky girl with strong peasant hands and carroty hair, declared herself willing to oblige the *herrschaft* in any way; she thereupon demanded an increase on the wages scheduled for her at the registry office. She also confided to her new mistress that she had a *kerl* in Germany, and that she would do anything to earn her dowry.

Thus the establishment settled down again. Laura cooked excellently. Augusta never flinched when bringing in the tea tray. Her big blue Saxon eyes seemed to allow everything to pass through them leaving her mind unsoiled, so armoured was her heart by the thought of that dowry. As for Snoo and Poo: they chased the tabby cat all over the house most of the day, which very soon improved their figures.

Thus the even tenour of Victoria's life continued. She was quite a popular favourite. As soon as she sat down under the chandelier half-a-dozen men were looking at her. Sometimes men followed her into the Vesuvius; but these she seldom encouraged, for her instinct told her that so beautiful a woman as she was should set a high price on herself, and high prices were not to be found in Piccadilly. Among her faithful was a bachelor of forty, whom she only knew as Charlie. This, by the way, was a characteristic of her acquaintances. She never discovered their names; some in fact were so guarded that they had apparently discarded their watches before coming out, so as to conceal even their initials. None ever showed a pocketbook. Charlie was dark and burned by the sun of the tropics; there was something bluff and good-natured about him, great strength too. He had sharp grey eyes and a dark moustache. He spoke extraordinarily fast, talked loosely of places he had been to: China, Mozambique, South America. Victoria rather liked him; he was totally dull, inclined to be coarse; but as he invariably drank far too much before and when he came to the Vesuvius, he made no demands on her patience, slept like a log and went early, leaving handsome recognition behind him.

There was Jim too, a precise top-hatted city clerk who had forced himself on her one Saturday afternoon as she crossed Piccadilly Circus. He seemed such a pattern of rectitude, was so perfectly trim and brushed that she allowed herself to be inveigled into a cab and driven to a small flat in Bayswater. He was too prudent to visit anybody else's rooms, he said; he had his flat on a weekly tenancy. Jim kept rather a hold on her. He was neither rich nor generous; in fact Victoria's social sense often stabbed her for what she considered undercutting, but Jim used to hover about the Vesuvius five minutes before closing time, and once or twice when Victoria had had no luck he succeeded like the vulture on the stricken field.

Most of the others were dream figures; she lost count of them. After a month she could not remember a face. She even forgot a big fellow whom she had called Black Beauty, who came down from somewhere in Devonshire for a monthly bust; he was

so much offended that she had the mortification of
seeing him captured by one of the outer circle who sit
beyond the lights.

In the middle of August the streets she called
London were deserted. Steamy air, dust laden,
floated over the pavements. The Vesuvius was half
empty, and she had to cut down her standards.
Just as she was contemplating moving to Folkestone
for a month, however, she received a letter from
solicitors in the Strand, Bastable, Bastable & Sons,
informing her that 're Major Cairns deceased,' they
were realising the estate on behalf of the administra-
tors, and that they would be obliged if she would say
when it would be convenient for her to convey the
furniture of Elm Tree Place into their hands. This
perturbed Victoria seriously. The furniture had a
value, and besides it was the plant of a flourishing
business.

'Pity he died suddenly,' she thought, 'he'd have
done something for me. He was a good sort, poor
old Tom.'

She dressed herself as becomingly and quietly as
she could, and, after looking up the law of intestacy in
Whitaker, concluded that Marmaduke Cairns's old
sisters must be the heirs. Then she sallied forth to
beard the solicitor in his den. The den was a magnificent suite of offices just off the Strand. She was
ushered into a waiting-room partitioned off from the
general office by glass. It was all very frowsy and
hot. There was nothing to read except the *Times*
and she was uncomfortably conscious of three clerks
and an office boy who frequently turned round and
looked through the partition. At last she was ushered
in. The solicitor was a dry-looking man of forty or
so; his parchment face, deeply wrinkled right and
left, his keen blue eyes and high forehead impressed
her as dangerous. He motioned her to an armchair
on the other side of his desk,

'Well, Mrs Ferris,' he said, 'to what do I owe the honour of this visit?' He sat back in his armchair and bit his penholder. A smile elongated his thin lips. This was his undoing, for he looked less formidable and Victoria decided on a line of action. She had come disturbed, now she was on her mettle.

'Mr Bastable,' she said, plunging at once into the subject, 'you ask me to surrender my furniture. I'm not going to.'

'Oh?' The solicitor raised his eyebrows. 'But, my dear madame, surely you must see . . .'

'I do. But I'm not going to.'

'Well,' he said, 'I hardly see . . . My duty will compel me to take steps . . .'

'Of course,' said Victoria smiling, 'but if you refuse to let me alone I shall go out of this office, have the furniture moved to-day and put up at auction to-morrow.'

A smile came over the solicitor's face. By Jove, she was a fine woman, and she had some spirit.

'Besides,' she added, 'all this would cause me a great deal of annoyance. Major Cairns's affairs are still very interesting to the public. 1 shall be compelled, if you make me sell, to write a serial, say *My Life with an Irish Martyr* for a Sunday paper.'

Mr Bastable laughed frankly.

'You want to be nasty, I see. But you know, we can stop your sale by an application to a judge in chambers this afternoon. And as for your serial, well, Major Cairns is dead, he won't mind.'

'No, but his aunts will. Their name is Cairns. As regards the sale, perhaps you and the other lawyers can stop it. Very well, either you promise or I go home and . . . perhaps there'll be a fire to-night and perhaps there won't. I'm fully insured.'

'By Jove!' Bastable looked at her critically. Cairns had been a lucky man. 'Well, Mrs Ferris,' he added, 'we're not used to troublesome customers like you,

I don't suppose the furniture is valuable, is it?'

'Oh, a couple of hundred,' said Victoria dishonestly.

'M'm. Do you absolutely want me to pledge myself?'

'Absolutely.'

'Well, Mrs Ferris, I can honestly promise you that you won't hear anything more about it. I . . . I don't think it would pay us.'

Victoria laughed. A great joy of triumph was upon her. She liked Bastable rather, now she had brought him to heel.

'All right,' she said, 'it's a bargain.' Then she saw that his mouth was smiling still and his eyes fixed on her face.

'There's no quarrel between us, is there?'

'No, of course not. All in the way of business, you know.'

He bent across the table; she heard him breathe in her perfume.

'Then,' she said slowly, getting up and pulling on her gloves, 'I'm not doing anything to-night. You know my address. Seven o'clock. You may take me out to dinner.'

T

CHAPTER IX

WITHIN a few days of her victory over Mr Bastable, Victoria found herself in an introspective mood. The solicitor was the origin of it, though unimportant in himself as the grain of sand which falls into a machine, and for a fraction of a second causes a wheel to rasp before the grain is crunched up. She reflected, as she looked out over her garden, that she was getting very hard. She had brought this man to his knees by threats; she had vulgarly bullied him by holding exposure over his head; she had behaved like a tragedy queen. Finally, with sardonic intention, she had turned the contest to good account by entangling him while he was still under the influence of her personality.

All this was not what disturbed her; for after all she had only lied to Bastable, bullied him, threatened him, bluffed as to her intentions: she had been perfectly businesslike. Thoughtfully she opened the little door at the end of the hall and stepped out on the outer landing where the garden steps ended. Snoo and Poo, asleep in a heap in the August blaze, raised heavy eyelids, and, yawning and stretching, followed her down the steps.

This was a joyful little garden. The greater part of it was a lawn, close cut, but disfigured in many places by Snoo and Poo's digging. Flower beds ran along both sides and the top of the lawn, while the bottom was occupied by the pergola, now covered with massive red blooms; an acacia tree, and an

elder tree, both leafy but refusing to flower, shaded
the bottom of the garden, which was effectively cut
off by a hedge of golden privet. It was a tidy
garden, but it showed no traces of originality.
Victoria had ordered it to be potted with geraniums,
carnations, pinks, marguerites; and was quite content
to observe that somebody had put in sweet peas,
clematis and larkspur. Hers was not the tempera-
ment which expresses itself in a garden; there was
no sense of peace in her idea of the beautiful. If
she liked the garden to look pretty at all, it was
doubtless owing to her heredity.

Victoria picked up a couple of stones and threw
them towards the end of the garden. Snoo and Poo
rushed into the privet, snuffling excitedly, while their
mistress drew down a heavy rose-laden branch from
the pergola and breathed the blossoms. Yes, she
was hard, and it was beginning to make her nervous.
In the early days she had sedulously cultivated the
spirit which was making a new woman out of the
quiet, refined, rather shy girl she had been. There
had been a time when she would have shuddered at
the idea of a quarrel with a cabman about an over-
charge; now, if it were possible, she felt coldly certain
that she would cheat him of his rightful fare. This
process she likened to the tempering of steel, and
called a development of the mental muscles. She
rather revelled in this development in the earlier
days, because it gave her a sense of power; she
benefited by it too, for she found that by cultivating
this hardness she could extort more money by stooping to wheedle, by accepting snubs, by flattery and
lies too. The consciousness of this power redeemed
the exercise of it; she often felt herself lifted above
this atmosphere of deceit by looking coldly at the
deed she was about to do, recognising its nature and
doing it with her eyes open.

A realization of another kind, however, was upon

Victoria that rich August day. In a sense she was
doing well. Her capital had not been touched; in
fact it had probably increased, and this in spite of
town being empty. She had not yet found the man
who would make her fortune; but she had no doubt
that he would appear if she continued on her even
road, selecting without passion, judging values and
possibilities. For the moment she brushed aside the
question of success; it was assured. But, after
success, what then? Say she had four or five
hundred a year at thirty and retired into the country
or went to America. What use would she be to
herself or to anybody if she had learned exclusively
to bide her time and to strike for her own advantage?
Life was a contest for the poor and for the rich alike;
but the first had to fight to win and to use any means,
fair or foul, while the latter could accept knightly
rules, be magnanimous when victorious, graceful
when defeated.

'Yes,' said Victoria, 'I must keep myself in trim.
It's all very well to win and I've got to be as hard as
nails to men, but . . .'

She stopped abruptly. The problem had solved
itself. 'Hard as nails to men,' did not include
women, for 'men' seldom means mankind when the
talk is of rights. She did not know what her mission
might be. Perhaps, after she had succeeded, she
would travel all over Europe, perhaps settle on the
English downs where the west winds blow, perhaps
even be the pioneer of a great sex revolt; but
whatever she did, if her triumph was not to be
sterile, she would need sympathy, the capacity to
love. Thus she amended her articles of war:
'Woman shall be spared, and I shall remember that,
as a member of a sex fighting another sex, I must
understand and love my sister warrior.'

It was in pursuance of her new policy that, on her
way to the Vesuvius, Victoria dawdled for a moment

at the entrance of Swallow Street, under its portico.
A few yards beyond her stood a woman whom she
knew by sight as having established practically a
proprietary right to her beat. She was a dark
girl, good-looking enough, well set up in her
close fitting white linen blouse, drawn tight to set
off her swelling bust. In the dim light Victoria
could see that her face was rather worn, and that the
ravages of time had been clumsily repaired. The
girl looked at her curiously at first; then angrily,
evidently disliking the appearance of what might be
a dangerous rival in her own preserves. Victoria
walked up and down on the pavement. The girl
watched her every footstep. Once she made as if to
speak to her. It was ghostly, for passers-by in
Regent Street came to and fro beyond the portico
like arabesques. A passing policeman gave the girl
a meaning look. She tossed her head and walked
away down Regent Street, while Victoria nervously
continued down Swallow Street to Piccadilly.

These two women were to meet, however. About
a week later, Victoria, happening to pass by at the
same hour, saw the girl and stopped under the arch.
In another second the girl was by her side.

'What are you following me about for?' she
snarled. 'If you're a grote it's no go. You won't
teach the copper anything he doesn't know.'

'Oh, I'm not following you,' said Victoria. 'Only
I saw you about and thought I'd like to talk to you.'

The girl shot a dark glance at her.

'What's your game?' she asked. 'You're not one
of those blasted sisters. Too toffish. Seen you come
out of the Vez', besides.'

'I'm in the profession,' said Victoria coolly. 'But
that doesn't mean I've got to be against the
others.'

'Doesn't it! The girl's eyes glowed. 'You don't
know your job. Of course you've got to be against

the others. We were born like that. Or got like that. What's it matter?'

'Matter? oh, a lot,' said Victoria. 'We want friends, all of us.'

'Friends. Oh, Lord! The likes of you and me don't have friends. Women, they won't know us . . . too good. Except our sort. We can't talk; we got nothing to talk of, except money and the boys. And the boys, what's the good of them? There's the sort you pick up and all you've got to do's to get what you can out of them. Haven't fallen in love with one, have you?' The girl's voice broke a little, then she went on. 'Then, there's the other sort, like my Hugo, p'raps you've heard of him?'

'No,' she said, 'I haven't. What is he like?'

'Bless you, he's a beauty.' The girl smiled; her face was full of pride.

'Does he treat you well?'

'So so. Sometimes.' The shadow had returned. 'Not like my first. Oh, it's hard you know, beginning. He left me with a baby after three months. I was in service in Pembridge Gardens—such a swell house! I had to keep baby. It died then, jolly good thing too! Couldn't go back to service. Everybody knew.'

The girl burst into tears and Victoria putting an arm round her drew her against her breast.

'Everybody knew, everybody knew!' wailed the girl.

Victoria had the vision of a thousand spectral eyes, all full of knowledge, gazing at the housemaid caught by them sinning. The girl rested her head against Victoria's shoulder for a moment, holding one of her hands. Suddenly she raised her head again and cleared her throat.

'There,' she said, 'let me go. Hugo's waiting for me at the Carcassonne. Never mind me. We've all got to live, he-he!'

She turned into Regent Street and another 'he-he' floated back. Victoria felt a heavy weight at her heart; poor girl, weak, the sport of one man, deceived, then a pirate made to disgorge her gains by another man; handsome, subtle, playing upon her affections and her fears. What did it matter? Was she not in the same position, but freer because conscious; poor slave soul. But the time had come for Victoria to make for the Vesuvius. 'It must be getting late,' she thought, putting up her hand to her little gold watch-brooch.

It was gone. She had it on when she left, but it could not have dropped out, for the lace showed two long rips; it had just been torn out. Victoria stood frozen for a moment. So this was the result of a first attempt at love. She recovered, however. She was not going to generalise from one woman. 'Besides,' she thought bitterly, 'the girl's theories are the same as mine. She merely has no reservations or hesitations. The bolder pirate, she is perhaps the better brain.'

Then she walked down Swallow Street into Piccadilly, and at once a young man in loud checks was at her side. She looked up into his face, her smile full of covert promise as they went into the Vesuvius together. Victoria was now at home in the market place, and could exchange a quip with the frequenters. Languidly she dropped her cloak into the hands of the porter and preceded the young man into the supper-room. As they sat at the little table before the liqueur, her eyes saw the garish room through a film. How deadening it all was, and how lethal the draughts sold here. An immense weariness was upon her, an immense disgust, as she smiled full-toothed on the young man in checks. He was a cheerful rattle, suggested the man who has got beyond the retail trade without reaching the professions, a house agent's clerk perhaps.

'Oh, yes, I'm a merry devil, ha! ha!' He winked

a pleasant grey eye. Victoria noticed that his
clothes were too new, his boots too new, his manners
too a recent acquisition.

'Don't worry. That's how you keep young,
ha! ha! Besides, don't have much time to mope in
my trade?'

'What's that?' asked Victoria vacuously. Men
generally lied as to their occupation, but she had
noticed that when their imagination was stimulated
their temper improved.

'Inspector of bun-punchers, ha! ha!'

'Bun-punchers?'

'Yes, bun-punchers. South Eastern Railway, you
know. Got to have them dated now. New Act of
Parliament, ha! ha!'

Victoria laughed, for his cockney joviality was
infectious. Then again the room faded and re-
materialised as his voice rose and fell.

'The wife don't know I'm out on the tiles, ha! ha!
She's in Streatham, looking after the smalls. . . .
Oh, no, none of your common or garden brass
fenders. . . .'

Victoria pulled herself together. This was what
she could not bear. Brutality, the obscene even,
were preferable to this dreary trickling of the inane
masquerading as wit. Yet she smiled at him.

'You're saucy,' she said. 'You're my fancy
to-night.'

A shadow passed over the man's face. Then again
he was rattling along.

'Talk of inventions? What'd you think of mine:
indiarubber books to read in your bath? ha! ha! . . .'

But these are only the moths that flutter round the
lamp, too far off to burn their wings. They love to
breathe perfume, to touch soft hands, gaze at bright
eyes and golden hair; then they flutter away, and the
hand that would stay their flight cannot rob them even
of a few specks of golden dust. In a few minutes

Victoria sat philosophically before her empty glass while Fascination Fledgeby was by the side of a rival, being 'an awful dog,' for the benefit of his fellow clerks on the morrow. She was in the mood when it did not matter whether she was unlucky or not. There were quite two women present for every man this hot August night. At the next table sat a woman known as 'Duckie,' fair, very fat and rosy; she was the vision bursting from a white dress which Victoria had seen the first night. On the first night she had embodied for Victoria—so large, so fat, so coarsely animal was she—the very essence of her trade; now she knew her better she found that Duckie was a good sort, careless, generous, perfectly incapable of doing anybody an ill turn. She was *bonne fille* even, so unmercenary as sometimes to accede good humouredly to the pleadings of an impecunious youth. Her one failing was a fondness for 'a wet.' She was drinking her third whisky and soda; if she was invited to supper she would add to that at least half a bottle of champagne, follow that up by a couple of liqueurs and a peg just before going to bed. She carried her liquor well; she merely grew a little vague.

'Hot,' remarked Duckie.

'Rather,' said Victoria. 'I'm going soon, can't stick it.'

'Good for you. I've got to stay. Always harder for grandmas like me when the fifth form boy's at the seaside.' Duckie laughed, without cynicism though; she had the reasoning powers of a cow.

Victoria laughed too. A foreign-looking girl in scarlet bent over from the next table, her long coral earrings sliding down over her collar-bones.

'Tight again,' said the girl.

'As a drum, Lissa, old girl!' said Duckie good temperedly.

'Nothing to what you'll be by and by,' added Lissa
with the air of a comforter.

'Nothing like, old dear! Have one with me, Lissa?
No? No offence. You, Zoé, have a *tord boyaux*?'

'No thanks.' Zoé was a good-looking short girl;
her French nationality written in every line of her
round face, plump figure, and hands. Her hair was
pulled away from the fat nape of her neck. She
looked competent and wide awake. A housewife
gone astray. Lissa, dark and Italian looking in her
red dress and coral earrings, was more languid than
the others. She was really a Greek, and all the grace
of the East was in every movement of her slim figure.
In a moment the four women had clustered together,
forgetting strife.

Lissa had had a 'Bank of Engraving' note palmed
off on her by a pseudo-South American planter, and
was rightly indignant. They were still talking of
Camille de Valenciennes and of her misfortunes with
the barber. Boys, the latest tip for Gatwick, 'what
I said to him,' the furriers' sales, boys again . . .
Victoria listened to the conversation. It still seemed
like another world and yet her world. Here they
were, she and the other atoms, hostile every one, and
a blind centripetal force was kneading them together
into a class. Yet any class was better than the isolation in which she lived. Why not go further, hear
more?

'I say, you girls,' she said suddenly, 'you've never
been to my place. Come and . . . no, not dine, it
won't work . . . come and lunch with me next week.'

Duckie smiled heavily.

'I don' min',' she said thickly.

Zoé looked suspicious for a moment.

'Can I bring Fritz?' asked Lissa.

'No, we can't have Fritz,' said Victoria smiling.
'Ladies only.'

'I'm on,' said Zoé suddenly. 'I was afraid you

were going to have a lot of swells in. Hate those
shows. Never do you any good and you get so
crumpled.'

'You might let me bring Fritz,' said Lissa
querulously.

'No men,' said Victoria firmly. 'Wednesday at
one o'clock. All square?'

'Thatawright,' remarked Duckie. 'Shut it
Lissa. Fritzawright. Tellm its biz . . . bizness.'

With some difficulty they hoisted Duckie into a
cab and sent her off to Bloomsbury. As it drove
off she popped her head out.

'Carriage paid?' she spluttered, 'or C. O. D.?'

Zoé and Lissa walked away to the circus. On her
little hall table, as Victoria went into her house, she
found a note scrawled in pencil on some of her own
notepaper. It was from Betty. It said that Farwell
had been stricken down by a sudden illness and was
sinking fast. His address followed.

CHAPTER X

IN a bed sitting-room at the top of an old house off
the Waterloo Road three women were watching by
the bedside of a man. One was dressed in rusty
black; she was pale faced, crowned with light hair;
the other, shifting uneasily from one foot to the other,
was middle-aged and very stout; her breast rolled
like a billow in her half buttoned bodice. The third
was beautiful, all in black, her sumptuous neck and
shoulders bare. None of them moved for a moment.
Then the beautiful woman threw back her cloak and
her long jade earrings tinkled. The face on the
pillow turned and opened its eyes.

'Victoria,' said a faint voice.

'Yes . . . are you better?' Victoria bent over the
bed. The face was copper coloured; every bone
seemed to start out. She could hardly recognise
Farwell's rough hewn features.

'Not yet . . . soon,' said Farwell. He closed his
eyes once more.

'What is it, Betty?' whispered Victoria.

'I don't know . . . hemorrhage they say.'

'It's all up mum,' whispered the landlady in
Victoria's ear. 'Been ill two days only. Doctor said
he wouldn't come again.'

Victoria bent over the bed once more. She could
feel the eyes of the landlady probing her personality.

'Can't you do something?' she asked savagely.

'Nothing.' Farwell opened his eyes again and
faintly smiled. 'And what's the good, Victoria?

Victoria threw herself on her knees by the side of the bed. ' Oh, you musn't ! ' she whispered. ' You . . . the world can't spare you ! '

' Oh, yes . . . it can . . . you know . . . the world is like men . . it spends everything on luxuries . . . it can't afford necessaries.'

Victoria smiled and felt as if she were going to choke. The last paradox.

' Are you in pain ? ' she asked.

' No, not just now. . . . I shall be, soon. Let me speak while I can.' His voice grew firmer suddenly.

' I have asked you to come so that you may be the last thing I see ; you, the fairest. I love you.'

Not one of the three women moved.

' I have not spoken before, because when I could speak we were slaves. Now you are free and I a slave. It is too late, so it is time for me to speak. For I cannot influence you.'

Farwell shut his eyes. But soon his voice rose again.

' You must never influence anybody. That is my legacy to you. You cannot teach men to stand by giving them a staff. Let the halt and the lame alone. The strong will win. You must be free. There is nothing worth while. . . .' A shiver passed over him, his voice became muffled.

' No, nothing at all . . . freedom only. . . .'

He spoke quicker. The words could not be distinguished. Now and then he groaned.

' Wait,' whispered Betty, ' it will be over in a minute.' For two minutes they waited.

Victoria's eyes fastened on a basin by the bedside, full of reddish water. Then Farwell's face grew lighter in tone. His voice came faint as the sound of a spinet.

'There will be better times. But before then fighting . . . the coming to the top of the leaders . . . gold will be taken from the rich . . . given to the

vile . . . pictures burnt . . . chaos . . . woman rise
as a tyrant . . . there will be fighting . . . the
coming to the top. . . .' His voice thinned down to
nothing as his wandering mind repeated his predic-
tion. Then he spoke again.

'You are a rebel . . . you will lead . . . you have
understood . . . only by understanding are you saved.
I asked you to come here to tell you to go on . . .
earn your freedom . . . at the expense of others.'

'Why at the expense of others?' asked Betty,
leaning over the bed. Farwell was hypnotising her.
His eyes wandered to her face.

'Too late . . .' he said, 'you do not see . . . you
are a slave . . . a woman has only one weapon . . .
otherwise, a slave . . . ask . . . ask Victoria.' He
closed his eyes but went on speaking.

'There is not freedom for everybody . . . capitalism
means freedom for a few . . . you must have freedom,
like food . . . food for the soul . . . you must capture
the right to respect . . . a woman may not toil . . .
make money . . .'

Then again: 'I am going into the blackness . . .
before Death . . . the Judge . . . Death will judge
me. . . .'

''E's thinking of his Maker, poor genelman,' said
the landlady hoarsely.

Victoria and Betty looked at one another. Agnostic
or indifferent in their cooler moments, the superstition
of their ancestors worked in their blood, powerfully
assisted by the spectacle of this being passing step
by step into an unknown. There must be life there,
feeling, loving. There must be Something.

The voice stopped. Betty had seized Victoria's
arm and now clutched it violently. Victoria could
feel through her own body the shudders that shook
the girl's frame. Then Farwell's voice rose again,
louder and louder, like the upward flicker of a dying
candle.

'Yes, freedom's my message, the right to live.
This world into which we are evolved by a selfish act
of joy, into which we are dragged unwilling with
pain for our usher, it is a world which has no justification save the freedom to enjoy it as we may. I have
lived a stoic, but it is a hedonist I die. Unshepherded
I go into a perhaps. But I regret nothing . . . all
the certainties of the past are not worth the possible
of the future. Behind me others tread the road that
leads up the hill.'

He paused for breath. Then again his voice arose
as a cry, proclaiming his creed.

'On the top of the hill. There I see the unknown
land, running with milk and honey. I see a new
people; beautiful young, beautiful old. Its fathers
have ground the faces of the helots ; they have fought
and lusted, they have suffered contumely and stripes.
Now they know the Law, the Law that all may keep
because they are beyond the Law. They do not
desire, for they have, they do not weigh, for they
know. They have not feared, they have dared ; they
have spared no man, nor themselves. Ah ! now they
have opened the Golden Gates. . . .'

The man's voice broke, he coughed, a thin
stream of blood trickled from the side of his mouth.
Victoria felt a film come over her eyes. She leant
over him to staunch the flow. They saw one
another then. Farwell's voice went down to a
whisper.

'Victoria . . . victorious . . . my love . . . never
more. . . .'

She looked into his glazing eyes.

'Beyond . . .' he whispered; then his head fell
to one side and his jaw dropped.

Betty turned away. She was crying. The landlady wiped her hands on her apron. Victoria hesitatingly took hold of Farwell's wrist. He was dead.
She looked at him stupidly for a moment, then drew

her cloak round her shivering shoulders. The landlady too was crying now.

'Oh, mum, sich a nice genelman,' she moaned.
'But 'e did go on so!'

Victoria smiled pitifully. What an epitaph for a
sunset! She drove away with Betty and, as the horse
trotted through the deserted streets, hugged the girl
in her arms. Betty was shuddering violently, and
nestled close up to her. They did not speak.
Everything seemed to have become loose in Victoria's
mind and to be floating on a black sea. The pillar
of her individualism was down. Her codes were in
the melting pot; a man, the finest she had known,
had confessed his love in his extremity, and before
she could respond passed into the shadow. But
Farwell had left her as a legacy the love of freedom
for which he died, for which she was going to live.

When they arrived at Elm Tree Place, Victoria
forced Betty to drink some brandy, to tell her how
Farwell had sent her a message, asking her to send
him Victoria, how she had waited for her.

'Oh, it was awful,' whispered Betty, 'the maid said
you'd be late . . . she said I mustn't wait because
you might not . . .'

'Not come home alone?' said Victoria in a frozen
voice.

'Oh, I can't bear it, I can't bear it.' Betty flung
herself into her friend's arms, wildly weeping.

Victoria soothed her, made her undress. As Betty
grew more collected she let drop a few words.

'Oh, so then you too are happy?' said Victoria
smiling faintly.

'You love?' A burning blush rose over Betty's face.

That night, as in the old Finsbury days, they lay
in one another's arms and Victoria grappled with her
sorrow. Gentle, almost motherly, she watched over
this young life; blushing, full of promise, preparing
already to replace the dead.

CHAPTER XI

THE death of Farwell seemed to leave Victoria struggling and gasping for breath, like a shipwrecked mariner who tries to secure his footing on shifting sand while waves knock him down every time he rises to his knees. Though she hardly ever saw him and though she had no precise idea that he cared for her more than does the scientist for the bacteria he observes, he had been her tower of strength. He was there, like the institutions which make up civilisation, the British Constitution, the Bank and the Established Church. Now he was gone and she saw that the temple of life was empty. He was the last link. Cairns's death had turned her out among the howling wolves; now Farwell seemed to have carried away with him her theory of life. Above all, she now knew nobody; save Betty, who counted as a charming child. It was then she began to taste more cruelly the isolation of her class.

In the early days, when she paced up and down fiercely in the room at Portsea Place, she had already realised that she was alone, but then she was not an outcast; the doors of society were, if not open, at any rate not locked against her. Then the busy hum of the Rosebud and the P.R.R., the back-breaking work, the hustle, the facile friendships with City beaus—all this had drawn a veil over her solitude. Now she was really alone because none knew and none would know her. Her beauty, her fine clothes, contributed to clear round her a circle as if she were

U 305

a leper. At times she would talk to a woman in a park, but before a few sentences had passed her lips the woman would take in every detail of her, her clean gloves, her neat shoes, her lace handkerchief, her costly veil; then the woman's face would grow rigid, and with a curt 'good morning' she would rise from her seat and go.

Victoria found herself thrust back, like the trapper in the hands of Red Indians; like him she ran in a circle, clubbed back towards the centre every time she tried to escape. She was of her class, and none but her class would associate with her. Women such as herself gladly talked to her, but their ideas sickened her, for life had taught them nothing but the ethics of the sex-trade. Their followers too—barbers, billiard markers, shady bookmakers, unemployed potmen; who sometimes dared to foist themselves on her—filled her with yet greater fear and disgust, for they were the only class of man alternative to those on whose bounty she lived. Thus she withdrew herself away from all; sometimes a craving for society would throw her into equivocal converse with Augusta, whose one idea was the dowry she must take back to Germany. Then, tiring of her, she would snatch up Snoo and Poo and pace round and round her tiny lawn like a squirrel in its wheel.

A chance meeting with Molly emphasised her isolation, like the flash of lightning which leaves the night darker. She was standing on the steps of the Sandringham Tea House in Bond Street, looking into the side window of the photographer who runs a print shop on the ground floor. Some sprawling Boucher beauties in delicate gold frames fascinated her. She delighted in the semi-crude, semi-sophisticated atmosphere, the rotundity of the well-fed bodies, their ribald rosy flesh. As she was wondering whether they would not do for the stairs the door opened suddenly and a plump little woman almost rushed into her arms. The little woman apologised, giving her a quick look. Then the two looked at one another again.

'Victoria!' cried Molly, for it was she, with her wide open blue eyes, small nose, fair frizzy hair.

A thrill of joy and fear ran through Victoria. She felt her personality criddle up like a scorched moth, then expand like a flower under gentle dew. She was found out; the terrible female instinct was going to detect her, then to proclaim her guilt. However, bravely enough, she braced herself up and held out her hand.

'Oh, Vic, why haven't you written to me for, let me see, three years, isn't it?'

'I've been away, abroad,' said Victoria slowly. She seemed to float in another world. Molly was talking vigorously; Victoria's brain, feverishly active, was making up the story which would have to be told when Molly's cheerful egotism had had its way.

'Don't let's stay here on the doorstep,' she interrupted, 'let's go upstairs and have tea. You haven't had tea yet?'

'I should love to,' said Molly, squeezing her arm. 'Then you can tell me about yourself.'

Seated at a little table Molly finished her simple story. She had married an army chaplain, but he had given up his work in India and was now rector of Pontyberis in Wales. They had two children. Molly was up in town merely to break the journey, as she was going down to stay with her aunt in Kent. Oh, yes, she was very happy, her husband was very well.

'They're talking of making him Dean of Ffwr,' she added with unction. 'But that's enough about me. How have you been getting on, Vic? I needn't ask how you are; one only has to look at you.' Molly's eyes roved over her friend's beautiful young face, her clothes which she appraised with the skill of those poor who are learned in the fashions.

'I? Oh, I'm very well,' said Victoria hysterically.

'Yes, but how have you been getting on? Weren't you talking about having to work when you came over?'

'Yes, but I've been lucky . . . a week after I got here an aunt of my mother's died of whom I never even heard before. They told me at Dick's lawyers a month later, and you wouldn't believe it, there was no will and I came in for . . . well, something quite comfortable.'

Molly put out her hand and stroked Victoria's.

'I'm so glad,' she said. . . . 'Oh, you don't know how hard it is to have to work for your living. I see something of it in Wales. Oh, if you only knew . . .'

Victoria pressed her lips together, as if about to cry or laugh.

'But what did you do then? You only wrote once. You didn't tell me?'

'No, I only heard a month after, you know. Oh, I had a lot to do. I travelled a lot. I've been in America a good deal. In fact, my home is in . . . Alabama.' She plunged for Alabama, feeling sure that New York was unsafe.

'Oh, how nice,' said Molly ingenuously. 'You might have sent me picture postcards, you know.'

Skilfully enough Victoria explained that she had lost Molly's address. Her friend blissfully accepted all she said, but a few other women less ingenuous than the clergyman's wife were casting sharp glances at her. When they parted, Victoria audaciously giving her address as 'care of Mrs. Ferris, Elm Tree Place,' she threw herself back on the cushions of the cab and told herself that she could not again go through with the ordeal of facing her own class. She almost hungered for the morrow, when she was to entertain the class she had adopted.

CHAPTER XII

THE Fulton household had always been short of money, for Dick spent too much himself to leave anything for entertaining; thus Victoria had very little experience of lunch parties. Since she had left the Holts she hardly remembered a bourgeois meal. The little affair on the Wednesday was therefore provocative of much thought. Mutton was dismissed as common, beef in any form as coarse; Laura's suggestion (for Laura and Augusta had been called in) of a savoury sauerkraut ('mit Blutwurst, Frankfurter, Leberwurst, etc.'), was also dismissed. Both servants took a keen interest in the occasion.

'But why no gentleman come?' asked Laura, who was clearly ill-disposed to do her best for her own sex.

'In the house I was . . .' began Augusta . . . then she froze up under Victoria's eye. Her mistress still had a strain of the prig in her.

Then Augusta suggested hors d'œuvres, smoked salmon, anchovies, olives, radishes; Laura forced forward fowl à la Milanaise to be preceded by baked John Dory cayenne. Then Augusta in a moment of inspiration thought of French beans and vegetable marrow . . . stuffed with chestnuts. The three women laughed, Laura clapped her hands with the sheer joy of the creative artist.

When Victoria came into the dining-room at half-past twelve she was almost dazzled by her own magnificence. Neither the Carlton nor the Savoy could equal

the blaze of her plate, the brilliant polish of her table-
cloths. The dahlias blazed dark red in cut glass by
the side of pale belated roses from the garden. On
the sideboard fat peaches were heaped in a modern
Lowestoft bowl, and amber-coloured plums lay like
portly dowagers in velvet.

A few minutes before the hour Zoé and Lissa
arrived together. They were nervous ; not on
account of Victoria's spread, for they were of the
upper stratum, but because they were in a house.
Accustomed to their small flats off Shaftesbury Avenue,
where tiny kitchens jostled with bedroom and boudoir,
they were frightened by the suggestion of a vast basement out of which floated the savoury aroma of the
John Dory baking. Victoria tried to put them at
their ease, took their parasols away and showed them
into the boudoir. There they sat in a triangle, the
hot sun blazing in upon them, stiff and starched with
the formality of those who are seldom formal.

'Have a Manhattan cocktail?' asked the hostess.

'No thanks ; very hot, isn't it?' said Lissa in her
most refined manner. She was looking very pretty,
dark, slim and snaky in her close-fitting lemon
coloured frock.

'Very hot,' chimed in Zoé. She was sitting un-
necessarily erect. Her flat French back seemed to
abhor the easy chair. Her tight hair, her trim hands,
her well boned collar, everything breathed neatness,
well laced stays, a full complement of hooks and
eyes. She might have been the sedate wife of a
prosperous French tradesman.

'Yes, it is hot, said Victoria.

Then the conversation flagged. The hostess tried
to draw out her guests. They were obviously anxious
to behave. Lissa posed for 'The Sketch,' Zoé remained
très correcte.

'Do you like my pictures?' asked Victoria pointing
to the French engravings.

'They are very pretty,' said Lissa.

'I am very interested in engravings,' said Zoé, looking at the rosewood clock. There was a longish pause.

'I must show you my little dogs,' cried Victoria. She must do something. She went out to the landing and opened the garden door. There she met Augusta carrying a trayful of finger bowls. She felt inspired to overturn it if only to break the ice. Snoo and Poo rushed in, but in the boudoir they also instinctively became very well-bred.

'I am very fond of dogs,' said Lissa. Snoo lay down on her back.

'She is very pretty,' remarked Zoé.

Victoria punched the dogs in the ribs, rolled them over. It was no good. They would do nothing but gently wag their tails. She felt she would like to swear, when suddenly the front door was slammed, a cheerful voice rang in the hall.

'Hulloa, here's Duckie,' said Lissa.

The door opened loudly and Duckie seemed to rush in as if seated on a high wind.

'Here we are again!' cried the buxom presence in white. Every one of her frills rattled like metal. 'Late as usual. Oh, Vic, what angel pups!'

Duckie was on her knees. In a moment she had stirred up the Pekingese. They forgot their manners. They barked vociferously; and Zoé's starch was taken out of her by Poo, who rushed under her skirts. Lissa laughed and jumped up.

'Here Vic,' said Duckie ponderously, 'give us a hand, old girl. Never can jump about after gin and. bitters,' she added confidentially as they helped her up.

The ice was effectually broken. They filed into the dining-room in pairs, Victoria and Lissa being slim playing the part of men. How they gobbled up the hors d'œuvres and how golden the John Dory was; the flanks of the fish shone like an old violin.

Augusta flitted about quick but noisy. There was a
smile on her face.

'Steady on, old love,' said Duckie to her as the
maid inadvertently poured her claret into a tumbler.

'Never you mind, Gussie,' cried Zoé, bursting with
familiarity, ' she'll be having it in a bucket by and by.'

Augusta laughed. What easy going *herrschaft*!

The talk was getting racier now. By the time
they got to the dessert the merriment was rather
supper than lunch-like.

'Victoria plums,' said Lissa, 'let us name them
Bonne Hotesse.'

The idea was triumphant. Duckie insisted on
drinking a toast in hock, for she never hesitated to
mix her wines. Victoria smiled at them indulgently.
The youth of all this and the jollity, the ease of it ;
all that was not of her old class.

'Confusion to the puritans,' she cried, and drained
her glass. Snoo and Poo were fighting for scraps,
for Duckie was already getting uncertain in her aim.
Lissa and Zoé, like nymphs teasing Bacchus, were
pelting her with plum stones, but she seemed quite
unconscious of their pranks. They had some difficulty
in getting her into the boudoir for coffee and liqueurs ;
once on the sofa she tried to go to sleep. Her companions roused her, however ; the scent of coffee,
acrid and stimulating, stung their nostrils ; the
liqueurs shone wickedly, green and golden in their
glass bottles ; talk became more individual, more
reminiscent. Here and there a joke shot up like a
rocket or stuck quivering in Duckie's placid flanks.

'Well Vic,' said Zoé, ' you are very well *installée.*'
She slowly emptied of cigarette smoke her expanded
cheeks and surveyed the comfortable little room.

'Did you do it yourself ? ' asked Lissa. 'It must
have cost you a lot of money.'

'Oh, I didn't pay.' Victoria was either getting
less reticent or the liqueur was playing her tricks.

'I began with a man who set me up her,' she added;
'he was . . . he died suddenly' she went on more
cautiously.
  'Oh!' Zoé's eyebrows shot up. 'That's what I
call luck. But why do you not have a flat? It is
cheaper.'
  'Yes, but more inconvenient,' said Lissa. 'Ah, Vic.
I do envy you. You don't know. We're always in
trouble. We are moving every month.'
  'But why?' asked Victoria. 'Why must you move?'
  'Turn you out. Neighbours talk and then the
landlord's conscience begins to prick him,' grumbled
Duckie from the sofa.
  'Oh, I see,' said Victoria. 'But when they turn
you out what do you do?'
  'Go somewhere else, softy,' said Duckie.
  'But then what good does it do?'
  All the women laughed.
  'Law, who cares?' said Duckie. 'I dunno.'
  'It is perfectly simple,' began Zoé in her precise
foreign English. 'You see the landlord he will not
let flats to ladies. When the police began to watch
it would cause him *des ennuis*. So he lets to a
gentleman who sublets the flats, you see? When the
trouble begins, he doesn't know.'
  'But what about the man who sublets?' asked the
novice.
  'Him? Oh, he's gone when it begins,' said Lissa.
'But they arrest the hall porter.'
  'Justice must have its way, I see,' said Victoria.
  'What you call justice,' grumbled Duckie, 'I call
it damned hard lines.'
  For some minutes Victoria discussed the housing
problem with the fat jolly woman. Duckie was in a
cheerful mood. One could hardly believe, when one
looked at her puffy pink face, that she had seen
fifteen years of trouble.
  'Landladies,' she soliloquised, 'it's worse. You

take my tip Vic, you steer clear of them. You pay as much for a pigsty as a man pays for a palace. If you do badly they chuck you out and stick to your traps and what can you do? You don't call a policeman. If you do well, they raise the rent, steal your clothes, charge you key money, and don't give 'em any lip if you don't want a man set at you. Oh, Lor!'

Duckie went on, and as she spoke her bluntness caused Victoria to visualise scene after scene, one more horrible than another: a tall dingy house in Bloomsbury with unlit staircases leading up to black landings suggestive of robbery and murder; bedrooms with blinded windows, reeking with patchouli, with carpets soiled by a myriad ignoble stains. The house Duckie pictured was like a warren in every corner of which soft-handed, rosy-lipped harpies sucked men's life-blood; there was drinking in it, and a piano played light airs; below in the ground floor, through the half open door, she could see two or three foreigners, unshaven, dirty-cuffed, playing cards in silence like hunters in ambush. She shuddered.

'Yes, but Fritz isn't so bad,' broke in Lissa. She had all this time been wrangling with Zoé.

'No good,' snapped Zoé, 'he's a . . . a *bouche inutile.*' Her pursed-up lips tightened. Fritz was swept away to limbo by her practical French philosophy.

'I like him because he is not useful' said Lissa dreamily. Zoé shrugged her shoulders. Poor fool, this Lissa.

'Who is this Fritz you're always talking about?' asked Victoria.

'He's a . . . you know what they call them,' said Duckie brutally.

'You're a liar,' screamed Lissa jumping up. 'He's . . . oh, Vic, you do not understand. He's the man I care for; he is so handsome, so clever, so gentle . . .'

'Very gentle,' sneered Zoé, 'why did you not take off your long gloves last week, *hein* ? Perhaps you had blue marks ? '

Lissa looked about to cry. Victoria put her hand on her arm.

'Never mind them,' she said, ' tell me.'

' Oh, Vic, you are so good.' Lissa's face twitched, then she smiled like a child bribed with a sweet. 'They do not know ; they are hard. It is true, Fritz does not work, but if we were married he would work and I would do nothing. What does it matter. ? ' They all smiled at the theory, but Lissa went on with heightened colour :

' Oh, it is so good to forget all the others ; they are so ugly, so stupid. It is infernal. And then, Fritz, the man that I love for himself . . .'

' And who loves you for . . ,' began Zoé.

'Shut up, Zoé,' said Duckie, her kindly heart expanding before this idealism, ' leave the kid alone. Not in my line, of course. You take my tip, all of you, you go on your own. Don't you get let in with a landlady and don't you get let in with a man. It's *them* you've got to let in.'

' That's what I say,' remarked Zoé. ' We are successful because we take care. One must be economical. For instance, every month I can . . .' She stopped and looked round suspiciously ; with economy goes distrust, and Zoé was very French. ' Well, I can manage,' she concluded vaguely.

' And you need not talk, Duckie,' said Lissa savagely. ' You drink two quids' worth every week.'

' Well, s'pose I do,' grumbled the cherub. ' Think I do it for pleasure ? Tell you what, if I hadn't got squiffy at the beginning I'd have gone off me bloomin' chump. I was in Buenos Ayres, went off with a waiter to get married. He was in a restaurant, Highgate way, where I was in service. I found out

all about it when I got there. O Lor! Why, we jolly
well *had* to drink, what with those Argentines who're
half monkeys and the good of the house! Oh,
Lor!' She smiled. 'Those were high old times,' she
said inconsequently, overwhelmed by the glamour of
the past. There was silence.

'I see,' said Victoria suddenly. 'I've never seen
it before. If you want to get on, you've got to run
on business lines. No ties, no men to bleed you.
Save your money. Don't drink; save your looks.
Why, those are good rules for a bank cashier! If
you trip, down you go in the mud and nobody'll pick
you up. So you've got to walk warily, not look at
anybody, play fair and play hard. Then you can
get some cash together and then you're free.'

There was silence. Victoria had faced the problem
too squarely for two of her guests. Lissa looked
dreamily towards the garden, wondering where Fritz
was, whether she was wise in loving; Duckie, conscious of her heavy legs and incipient dropsy, blushed,
then paled. Alone, Zoé, stiff and energetic like the
determined business woman she was, wore on her
lips the enigmatic smile born of a nice little sum in
French three per cents.

'I must be going,' said Duckie hoarsely. She
levered herself off the sofa. Then, almost silently,
the party broke up.

CHAPTER XIII

LIFE pursued its even tenour; and Victoria, watching it go by, was reminded of the endless belt of a machine. The world machine went on grinding, and every breath she took was grist thrown for ever into the intolerable mill. It was October again, and already the trees in the garden were shedding fitful rains of glowing leaves. Alone the elder tree stood almost unchanged, a symbol of the everlasting. Now and then Victoria walked round the little lawn with Snoo and Poo, who were too shivery to chase the fat spiders. Often she stayed there for an hour, one hand against a tree trunk, looking at nothing, bathed in the mauve light of the dying year. Already the scents of decay, of wetness, filled the little garden and struck cold when the sun went down.

Every day now Victoria felt her isolation more cruelly. Solitude was no longer negative; it had materialised and had become a solid inimical presence. When the sun shone and she could walk the milky way of the streets, alone but feeling with every sense the joy of living time, there was not much to fear from solitude; there were things to look at, to touch, to smell. Now solitude no longer lurked round corners; at times a gust of wind carried its icy breath into her bones.

She was suffering, too, a little. She felt heavy in the legs, and a vein in her left calf hurt a little in the evening if she had walked or stood much. Soon, though it did not increase, the pain became her daily companion, for even when absent it haunted her. She would await a twinge for a whole day, ready and fearful, bracing herself up against a shock which often found her unprepared. At all times too the obsession seemed to follow her now. Perhaps she was walking through Regent's Park, buoyant and feeling capable of lifting a mountain, but the thought would rush upon her, perhaps it was going to hurt. She would lie awake too, oblivious of the heavy breathing by her side, rested, all her senses asleep, and then though she felt no pain the fear of it would come upon her and she would wrestle with the thought that the blow was about to fall

Sometimes she would go out into the streets, seeking variety even in a wrangle between her Pekingese and some other dog. This meant that she must separate them, apologise to the owner, exchange perhaps a few words. Once she achieved a conversation with an old lady, a kindly soul, the mistress of a poodle. They walked together along the Canal, and the futile conversation fell like balm on Victoria's ears. The freshness of a voice ignorant of double meanings was soft as dew. They were to meet again, but the old lady was a near neighbour and she must have heard something of Victoria's reputation, for when they met again opposite Lord's, the old lady crossed over and the poodle followed her haughtily, leaving Snoo and Poo disconsolate and wondering on the edge of the pavement.

One morning Augusta came into the boudoir about twelve, carrying a visiting card on a little tray.

'Miss Emma Welkin,' read Victoria. 'League of the Rights of Women. What does she want, Augusta?'

'She says she wants to see Mrs Ferris, Mum.'

'League of the Rights of Women? Why, she must be a suffragist.'

'Yes, Mum. She wear a straw hat, Mum,' explained Augusta with a slight sniff.

'And a tweed coat and skirt, I suppose,' said Victoria smiling.

'Oh, yes, Mum. Shall I say go away?'

'M'm. No, tell her to come in.'

While Augusta was away Victoria settled herself in the cushions. Perhaps it might be interesting. The visitor was shown in.

'How do you do?' said Victoria holding out her hand. 'Please sit down. Excuse my getting up, I'm not very well.'

Miss Welkin looked about her, mildly surprised. It was a pretty room, but somehow she felt uncomfortable. Victoria was looking at her. A capable type of feminity this; curious, though, in its thick man-like clothes, its strong boots. She was not bad looking, thirty perhaps, very erect and rather flat. Her face was fresh, clean, innocent of powder; her eyes were steady behind glasses; her hair was mostly invisible, being tightly pulled back. There were firm lines about her mouth. A fighting animal.

'I hope you'll excuse this intrusion,' said the suffragist, 'but I got your name from the directory and I have come to . . . to ascertain your views about the all-important question of the vote.' There was a queer stiltedness about the little speech. Miss Welkin was addressing the meeting.

'Oh? I'm very much interested,' said Victoria. 'Of course I don't know anything about it except what I read in the papers.'

The grey eyes glittered. Evangelic fervour radiated from them. 'That's what we want,' said the suffragist. 'It's just the people who are ready to be our friends who haven't heard our side and who get biassed. Mrs Ferris, I'm sure you'll come in with us and join the Marylebone branch?'

'But how can I?' asked Victoria. 'You see I know nothing about it all.'

'Let me give you these pamphlets,' said the

suffragist. Victoria obediently took a leaflet on the
marriage law, a pamphlet on 'The Rights of Women,'
a few more papers too, some of which slipped to the
floor.

'Thank you,' she said, 'but first of all tell me, why
do you want the vote?'

The suffragist looked at her for a second. This
might be a keen recruit when she was converted.
Then a flood of words burst from her.

'Oh, how can any woman ask, when she sees the
misery, the subjection in which we live. We say
that we want the vote because it is the only means
we have to attain economic freedom . . . we say to
man : " Put your weapon in our hands and we will
show you what we can do." We want to have a voice
in the affairs of the country. We want to say how
the taxes we pay shall be spent, how our children
shall be educated, whether our sons shall go to war.
We say it's wrong that we should be disfranchised
because we are women . . . it is illogical . . . we
must have it.'

The suffragist stopped for a second to regain
breath.

'I see,' said Victoria, 'but how is the vote going
to help?'

'Help?' echoed Miss Welkin. 'It will help because
it will enable women to have a voice in national
affairs.'

'You must think me awfully stupid,' said Victoria
sweetly, 'but what use will it be to us if we do get a
voice in national affairs?'

Miss Welkin ignored the interruption.

'It is wrong that we should not have a vote if we
are reasonable beings; we can be teachers, doctors,
chemists, factory inspectors, business managers,
writers; we can sit on local authorities, and we can't
cast a vote for a member of Parliament. It's preposterous, it's . . .'

'Yes, I understand, but what will the vote do for us? Will it raise wages?'

'It must raise wages. Men's wages have risen a lot since they got the vote.'

'Do you think that's because they got the vote?'

'Yes. Well, partly. At any rate there are things above wages,' said the suffragist excitedly. 'And you know, we know that the vote is wanted especially because it is an education; by inducing women to take an interest in politics we will broaden their minds, teach them to combine and then automatically their wages will rise.'

'Oh, yes.' Victoria was rather struck by the argument. 'Then,' she said, 'you admit men are superior to women?'

'Well, yes at any rate at present,' said the suffragist rather sulkily. 'But you must remember that men have had nearly eighty years training in political affairs. That's why we want the vote; to wake women up. Oh, you have no idea what it will mean when we get it. We shall have fresh minds bearing on political problems, we shall have more adequate protection for women and children, compulsory feeding, endowment of mothers, more education, shorter hours, more sanitary inspection. We shall not be enslaved by parties; a nobler influence, the influence of pure women will breathe an atmosphere of virtue into this terrible world.'

The woman's eyes were wrapt now, her hands tightly clenched, her lips parted, her cheeks a little flushed. But Victoria's face had hardened suddenly.

'Miss Welkin,' she said quietly, 'has anything struck you about this house, about me?'

The suffragist looked at her uneasily.

'You ought to know whom you are talking to,' Victoria went on, 'I am a . . . I am a what you would probably call . . . well, not respectable.'

A dull red flush spread over Miss Welkin's face,

x

from the line of her tightly pulled hair to her stiff white collar; even her ears went red. She looked away into a corner.

'You see,' said Victoria, 'it's a shock, isn't it. I ought not to have let you in. It wasn't quite fair, was it?'

'Oh, it isn't that, Mrs Ferris,' burst out the suffragist, 'I'm not thinking of myself. . . .'

'Excuse me, you must. You can't help it. If you could construct a scale with the maximum of egotism at one end, and the maximum of altruism at the other and divide it, say into one hundred degrees, you would not, I think, place your noblest thinkers more than a degree or two beyond the egotistic zero. Now you, a pure girl, have been entrapped into the house of a woman of no reputation, whom you would not have in your drawing-room. Now, would you?'

Miss Welkin was silent for a moment; the flush was dying away as she gazed round eyed at this beautiful woman lying in her piled cushions, talking like a mathematician.

'I haven't come here to ask you into my drawing-room,' she answered. 'I have come to ask you to throw in your labour, your time, your money, with ours in the service of our cause.' She held her head higher as the thought rose in her like wine. 'Our cause,' she continued, 'is not the cause of rich women or poor women, of good women or bad; it's the cause of woman. Thus, it doesn't matter who she is, so long as there is a woman who stands aloof from us there is still work to do.'

Victoria looked at her interestedly. Her eyes were shining, her lips parted in ecstasy.

'Oh, I know what you think,' the suffragist went on; 'as you say, you think I despise you because you . . . you. . . .' The flush returned slightly. . .

'But I know that yours is not a happy life and we are bringing the light.'

'The light!' echoed Victoria bitterly. 'You have
no idea, I see, of how many people there are who are
bringing the light to women like me. There are
various religious organisations who wish to rescue
us and to house us comfortably under the patronage
of the police, to keep us nicely and feed us on what
is suitable for the fallen; they expect us to sew ten
hours a day for these privileges, but that is by the
way. There are also many kindly souls who offer
little jobs as charwomen to those of us who are too
worn out to pursue our calling; we are offered
emigration as servants in exchange for the power of
commanding a household; we are offered poverty
for luxury, service for domination, slavery to women
instead of slavery to men. How tempting it is!
And now here is the light in another form : the right
to drop a bit of paper into a box every four years or
so and settle thereby whether the Home Secretary
who administers the law of my trade shall live in fear
of buff prejudice or blue.'

The suffragist said nothing for a second. She felt
shaken by Victoria's bitterness.

'Women will have no party,' she said lamely,
'they will vote as women.'

'Oh? I have heard somewhere that the danger of
giving women the vote is that they will vote solid "as
women," as you say and swamp the men. Is that so?'

'No, I'm afraid not,' said the suffragist unguardedly,
'of course women will split up into political parties.'

'Indeed? Then where is this woman vote which
is going to remould the world? It is swamped in
the ordinary parties.'

The suffragist was in a dilemma.

'You forget,' she answered, wriggling on the
horns, 'that women can always be aroused for a noble
cause. . . .'

'Am I a noble cause?' asked Victoria, smiling.
'So far as I can see women, even the highest of them,

despise us because we do illegally what they do legally, hate us because we attract, envy us because we shine. I have often thought that if Christ had said, "Let her who hath never sinned . . ." the woman would have been stoned. What do you think?'

The suffragist hesitated, cleared her throat.

'That will all go when we have the vote, women will be a force, a nobler force; they will realise . . . they will sympathise more . . . then they will cast their vote for women.'

Victoria shook her head.

'Miss Welkin,' she said, 'you are an idealist. Now, will you ask me to your next meeting if you are satisfied as to my views, announce me for what I am and introduce me to your committee?'

'I don't see . . . I don't think,' stammered the suffragist, 'you see some of our committee. . . .'

Victoria laughed.

'You see. Never mind. I assure you I wouldn't go. But, tell me, supposing women get the vote, most of my class will be disfranchised on the present registration law. What will you women do for us?'

The suffragist thought for a minute.

'We shall raise the condition of women,' she said. 'We shall give them a new status, increase the respect of men for them, increase their respect for themselves; besides, it will raise wages and that will help. We shall . . . we shall have better means of reform too.'

'What means?'

'When women have more sympathy.'

'Votes don't mean sympathy.'

'Well, intelligence then. Oh, Mrs Ferris, it's not that that matters; we're going to the root of it. We're going to make women equal to men, give them the same opportunities, the same rights. . . .'

'Yes, but will the vote increase their muscles? will it make them more logical, fitter to earn their living?'

'Of course it will,' said Miss Welkin acidly.

'Then how do you explain that several millions of men earn less than thirty shillings a week, and that at times hundreds of thousands are unemployed?'

'The vote does not mean everything,' said the suffragist reluctantly. 'It will merely ensure that we rise like the men when we are fit.'

'Well, Miss Welkin, I won't press that, but now, tell me, if women got the vote to-morrow, what would it do for my class?'

'It would raise. . . .'

'No, no, we can't wait to be raised. We've got to live, and if you "raise" us we lose our means of livelihood. How are you going to get to the root cause and lift us, not the next generation, at once out of the lower depths?'

The suffragist's face contracted.

'Everything takes time,' she faltered. 'Just as I couldn't promise a charwoman that her hours would go down and her wages go up next day, I can't say that . . . of course your case is more difficult than any other, because . . . because. . . .'

'Because,' said Victoria coldly, 'I represent a social necessity. So long as your economic system is such that there is not work for the asking for every human being—work, mark you, fitted to strength and ability—so long on the other hand as there is such uncertainty as prevents men from marrying, so long as there is a leisured class who draw luxury from the labour of other men ; so long will my class endure as it endured in Athens, in Rome, in Alexandria, as it does now from St John's Wood to Pekin.'

There was a pause. Then Miss Welkin got up awkwardly. Victoria followed suit.

'There,' she said, 'you don't mind my being frank, do you? May I subscribe this sovereign to the funds of the branch? I do believe you are right, you know, even though I'm not sure the millenium is coming.'

Miss Welkin looked doubtfully at the coin in her palm.

'Don't refuse it,' said Victoria, smiling, 'after all, you know, in politics there is no tainted money.'

CHAPTER XIV

VICTORIA lay back in bed, gazing at the blue silk wall.
It was ten o'clock, but still dark; not a sound disturbed dominical peace, except the rain dripping
from the trees, falling finally like the strokes
of time. Her eyes dwelt for a moment
on the colour prints where the nude beauties
languished. She felt desperately tired, though she
had not left the house for thirty-six hours; her
weariness was as much a consequence as a cause of
her consciousness of defeat. October was wearing;
and soon the cruel winter would come and fix its
fangs into the sole remaining joy of her life, the
spectacle of life itself. She was desperately tired,
full of hatred and disgust. If the face of a man rose
before her she thrust it back savagely into limbo;
her legs hurt. The time had come when she must
realise her failure. She was not, as once in the
P. R. R., in the last stage of exhaustion, hunted,
tortured; she was rather the wounded bird crawling
away to die in a thicket than the brute at bay.

As she lay, she realised that her failure had two
aspects. It was together a monetary and a physical
failure. The last three months had in themselves
been easy. Her working hours did not begin before
seven o'clock in the evening; and it was open to her,
being young and beautiful, to put them off for two
or three hours more; she was always free by twelve
o'clock in the morning at the very latest, and then
the day was hers to rest, to read and think. But she

was still too much of a novice to escape the excitement inherent in the chase, the strain of making conversation, of facing the inane; nor was she able without a mental effort to bring herself to the response of the simulator. As she sat in the Vesuvius or stared into the showcase of a Regent Street jeweller, a faint smile upon her face, her brain was awake, her faculties at high pressure. Her eyes roved right and left and every nerve seemed to dance with expectation or disappointment. When she got up now, she found her body heavy, her legs sore and all her being dull like a worn stone. A little more, she felt, and the degradation of her body would spread to her sweet lucidity of mind; she would no longer see ultimate ends but would be engulfed in the present, become a bird of prey seeking hungrily pleasure or excitement.

Besides, and this seemed more serious still, she was not doing well. It seemed more serious because this could not be fought as could be intellectual brutalisation. An examination of her pass books showed that she was a little better off than at the time of Cairns's death. She was worth, all debts paid, about three hundred and ninety pounds. Her net savings were therefore at the rate of about a hundred and fifty a year; but she had been wonderfully lucky, and nothing said that age, illness or such misadventures as she classed under professional risk, might not nullify her efforts in a week. There was wear and tear of clothes too : the trousseau presented her by Cairns had been good throughout but some of the linen was beginning to show signs of wear ; boots and shoes wanted renewing ; there were winter garments to buy and new furs.

'I shall have stone martin,' she reflected. Then her mind ran complacently for a while on a picture of herself in stone martin; a pity she couldn't run to sables. She brought herself back with a jerk to her consideration of ways and means. The situation was really not brilliant. Of course she was extravagant in a way. Eighty-five pounds rent ; thirty pounds in rates and taxes, without counting income tax which might be anything, for she dared not protest ; two servants—all that was too much. It was quite impossible to run the house under five hundred a year, and clothes must run into an extra hundred.

'I could give it up,' she thought. But the idea disappeared at once. A flat would be cheaper, but it meant unending difficulties ; it was not for nothing that Zoé, Lissa and Duckie envied her. And the rose-covered pergola ! Besides it would mean saving a hundred a year or so ; and, from her point of view, even two hundred and fifty a year was not worth saving. She was nearly twenty-eight, and could count on no more than between eight and twelve years of great attractiveness. This meant that, with the best of luck, she could not hope to amass much more than three thousand pounds. And then ? Weston-super-Mare and thirty years in a boarding-house ?

She was still full of hesitation and doubt as she greeted Betty at lunch. This was a great Sunday treat for the gentle P. R. R. girl. When she had taken off her coat and hat, she used to settle in an arm-chair with an intimate feeling of peace and protection. This particular day Betty did not settle down as usual, though the cushions looked soft and tempting and a clear fire burned in the grate. Victoria watched her for a moment. How exquisite and delicate this girl looked ; tall, very slim and rounded. Betty had placed one hand on the mantelpiece, a small long hand rather coarsened at the finger tips, one foot on the fender. It was a little foot, arched and neat in the cheap boot. She had bought new boots for the occasion ; the middle of the raised sole was still white. Her face was a little flushed, her eyes darkened by the glow.

'Well, Betty,' said her hostess suddenly, 'when's the wedding?'

'Oh, Vic, I didn't say . . . how can you . . .' Her face had blushed a tell-tale red.

'You didn't say,' laughed Victoria, 'of course you didn't say, shy bird! But surely you don't think I don't know. You've met somebody in the City and you're frightfully in love with him. Now, honest, is there anybody?'

'Yes . . . there is, but . . .'

'Of course there is. Now, Betty, tell me all about it.'

'Oh, I couldn't,' said Betty, gazing into the fire. 'You see it isn't quite settled yet.'

'Then tell me what you're going to settle. First of all, who is it?'

'Nobody you know. I met him at . . . well he followed me in Finsbury Circus one evening. . . .'

'Oh, naughty, naughty! You're getting on, Betty.'

'You mustn't think I encouraged him,' said Betty with a tinge of asperity. 'I'm not that sort.' She stopped, remembering Victoria's profession, then, inconsequently: 'You see, he wouldn't go away and . . . now . . . .'

'And he was rather nice, wasn't he?'

'Well, rather.' A faint and very sweet smile came over Betty's face. Victoria felt a little strangle in her throat. She too had thought her bold partner at the regimental dance at Lympton rather nice. Poor old Dick.

'Then he got out of me about the P. R. R.,' Betty went on more confidently. 'And then, would you believe it, he came to lunch every day! Not that he was accustomed to lunch at places like that,' she added complacently.

'Oh, a swell?' said Victoria.

'No, I don't say that. He used to go to the Lethes, before they shut up. He lives in the West End too, in Notting Hill, you know.'

'Dear, dear, you're flying high, Betty. But tell me, what is he like? and what does he do? and is he very handsome?'

'Oh, he's awfully handsome, Vic. Tall you know and very, very dark; he's so gentlemanly too, looks like the young man in *First Words of Love*. It's a lovely picture, isn't it?'

'Yes, lovely,' said Victoria summarily. 'But tell me more about him.'

'He's twenty-eight. He works in the City. He's a ledger clerk at Anderson and Dromo's. If he gets a rise this Christmas, he . . . well, he says . . .'

'He says he'll marry you.'

'Yes.' Betty hung her head, then raised it quickly. 'Oh, Vic, I can't believe it. It's too good to be true. I love him so dreadfully . . . I just can't wait for one o'clock. He didn't come on Wednesday. I thought he'd forgotten me and I was going off my head. But it was all right, they'd kept him in over something.'

'Poor little girl,' said Victoria gently. 'It's hard isn't it, but good too.'

'Good! Vic, when he kisses me I feel as if I were going to faint. He's strong, you see. And when he puts his arms round me I feel like a mouse in a trap . . . but I don't want to get away: I want it to go on for ever, just like that.'

She paused for a moment as if listening to the first words of love. Then her mind took a practical turn.

'Of course we shan't be able to live in Notting Hill,' she added. 'We'll have to go further out, Shepherd's Bush way, so as to be on the Tube. And he says I shan't go to the P. R. R. any more.'

'Happy girl,' said Victoria. 'I'm so glad, Betty; I hope . . .'

She restrained a doubt. 'And as you say you can't stay to tea I think I know where you're going.'

'Well, yes, I am going to meet him,' said Betty laughing.

'Yes . . . and you're going to look at little houses at Shepherd's Bush.'

Betty looked up dreamily. She could see a two-storeyed house in a row, with a bay window, and a front garden where, winter or summer, marigolds grew.

After lunch, as the two women sat once more in the boudoir, they said very little. Victoria, from time to time, flicked the ash from her cigarette. Betty did not smoke, but, her hands clasped together in her lap, watched a handsome dark face in the coals.

'And how are you getting on, Vic?' she asked suddenly. Swamped by the impetuous tide of her own romance she had not as yet shown any interest in her friend's affairs.

'I? Oh, nothing special. Pretty fair.'

'But, I mean . . . you said you wanted to make a lot of money and . . .'

'Yes, I'm not badly off, but I can't go on, Betty. I shall never do any good like this.'

Betty was silent for some minutes. Her ingrained modesty made any discussion of her friend's profession intolerable. Vanquished in argument, grudgingly accepting the logic of Victoria's actions, she could not free her mind from the thought that these actions were repulsive, that there must have been some other way.

'Oh? You want to get out of it all . . . .you know . . . I have never said you weren't quite right, but . . .'

'But I'm quite wrong?'

'No . . . I don't mean that . . . I don't like to say that . . . I'm not clever like you, Vic, but . . .'

'We've done with all that,' said Victoria coldly. 'I do want to get out of it because it's getting me no nearer to what I want. I don't quite know how to do it. I'm not very well, you know.'

Betty looked up quickly with concern in her face.

'Have those veins been troubling you again?'

'Yes, a little. I can't risk much more.'

'Then what are you going to do?'

Victoria was silent for a moment.

'I don't know,' she said. 'I never thought of all this when the Major was alive.'

'Ah, there never was anybody like him,' said Betty after a pause.

Victoria sat up suddenly.

'Betty,' she cried, 'you're giving me an idea.'

'I? an idea?'

'There must be somebody like him. Why shouldn't I find him?'

Betty said nothing. She looked her stiffest, relishing but little the fathering upon her of this expedient.

'But who?' soliloquised Victoria. 'I don't know anybody. You see Betty, I want lots and lots of money. Otherwise it's no good. If I don't make a lot soon it will be too late.'

Betty still said nothing. Really she couldn't be expected. . . . Then her conscience smote her; she ought to show a little interest in dear, kind Vic.

'Yes,' she said. 'But you must know lots of people. You never told me, but you're a swell and all that. You must have known lots of rich men when you came to London.'

She stopped abruptly, shocked by her own audacity. But Victoria was no longer noticing her; she was following with lightning speed a new train of thought.

'Betty,' she cried, 'you've done it. I've found the man.'

'Have you? Who is it?' exclaimed Betty. She was excited, unable in her disapproval of the irregular to feel uninterested in the coming together of women and men.

'Never mind. You don't know him. I'll tell you later.'

An extraordinary buoyancy seemed to pervade Victoria. The way out! she had found the way out! And the two little words echoed in her brain as if some mighty wave of sound was rebounding from side to side in her skull. She was excited, so excited that, as she said goodbye to Betty, she forgot to fix their next meeting. She had work to do and would do it that very night.

As soon as Betty was gone she dressed quickly. Then she changed her hat to make sure she was looking her best. She went out and, with hurried steps, made for the Finchley Road. There was the house with the evergreens, as well clipped as ever, and the drive with its clean gravel. She ran up the steps of the porch, then hesitated for a moment. Her heart was beating now. Then she rang. There was a very long pause during which she heard nothing but the pumping of her heart. Then distant shuffling foot-steps coming nearer. The door opened. She saw a slatternly woman . . . behind her the void of an empty house. She could not speak for emotion.

'Did you want to see the house, mum?' asked the woman. She looked sour. Sunday afternoon was hardly a time to view.

'The house?'

'Oh . . . I thought you come from Belfrey's, mum. It's to let.'

The caretaker nodded towards the right and Victoria, following the direction, saw the house agents' board. Her excitement fell as under a cold douche.

'Oh! I came to see. . . Do you know where Mr Holt is?'

'Mr Holt's dead, mum. Died in August, mum.'

'Dead?' Things seemed to go round. Jack was the only son . . . then?

'Yes, mum. That's why they're letting. A fine big 'ouse, mum. Died in August, mum. Ah, you should have seen the funeral. They say he left half a million, mum, and there wasn't no will.'

'Where is Mrs Holt and . . . and Mr Holt's son.'

The caretaker eyed the visitor suspiciously. There was something rakish about this young lady which frightened her respectability.

'I can't say, mum,' she answered slowly. 'I could forward a letter, mum,' she added.

'Let me come in. I want to write a note.'

The caretaker hesitated for a moment, then stood aside to let her pass.

'You'll 'ave to come downstairs mum,' she said, 'sorry I'm all mixed up. I was doing a bit of washing. Git away Maria,' to a small child who stood at the top of the stairs.

In the gaslit kitchen, surrounded by steaming linen, Victoria wrote a little feverish note in pencil. The caretaker watched her every movement. She liked her better somehow.

'I'll forward it all right, mum,' she said. 'Thank you mum. . . . Oh, mum, I don't want you to think—' She was looking amazedly at the half sovereign in her palm.

'That's all right,' said Victoria, laughing loudly. She felt she must laugh, dance, let herself go. 'Just post it before twelve.'

The woman saw her to the door. Then she looked at the letter doubtfully. It was freshly sealed and could easily be opened. Then she had a burst of loyalty, put on a battered bonnet, completed the address, stamped the envelope and, walking to the pillar box round the corner, played Victoria's trump card.

CHAPTER XV

'AND so, Jack, you haven't forgotten me?'

For a minute Holt did not answer. He seemed spellbound by the woman on the sofa. There she lay at full length, lazy grace in every curve of her figure, in the lines of her limbs revealed by the thin sea-green stuff which moulded them. This new woman was a very wonderful thing.

'No,' he said at length, 'but you have changed.'

'Yes?'

'You're different. You used to be simple, almost shy. I used to think you very like a big white lily. Now you're like—like a big white orchid—an orchid in a vase of jade.'

'Poet! artist!' laughed Victoria. 'Ah, Jack, you'll always be the same. Always thinking me good and the world beautiful.'

'I'll always think you good and beautiful too.'

Victoria looked at him. He had hardly changed at all. His tall thin frame had not expanded, his hands were still beautifully white and seemed as aristocratic as ever. Perhaps his mouth appeared weaker, his eyes bluer, his face fairer owing to his black clothes.

'I'm glad to see you again, Kathleen Mavourneen,' she said at length.

'Why did you wait so long?' asked Holt. 'It was cruel, cruel. You know what I said—I would—'

'No, no,' interrupted Victoria fearing an avowal. 'I couldn't. I've been through the mill. Oh, Jack, it was awful. I've been cold, hungry, ill; I've worked ten hours a day—I've swabbed floors.'

A hot flush rose in Holt's fair cheeks.

'Horrible,' he whispered, ' but why didn't you tell me. I'd have helped, you know I would.'

'Yes, I know, but it wouldn't have done. No, Jack, it's no good helping women. You can help men a bit; but women, no. You only make them more dependent, weaker. If women are the poor, frivolous, ignorant things they are, it's because they've been protected or told they ought to want to be protected. Besides, I'm proud. I wasn't coming back to you until I was—well I'm not exactly rich, but—'

She indicated the room with a nod and Holt, following it, sank deeper into wonder at the room where everything spoke of culture and comfort.

'But how—?' he stammered at last, 'how did you—? what happened then?'

Victoria hesitated for a moment.

'Don't ask me just now, Jack,' she said, 'I'll tell you later. Tell me about yourself. What are you doing? and where is your mother?'

Holt looked at her doubtfully. He would have liked to cross-question her, but he was the second generation of a rising family and had learned that questions must not be pressed.

'Mother?' he said vaguely. 'Oh, she's gone back to Rawsley. She never was happy here. She went back as soon as pater died; she missed the tea fights, you know, and Bethlehem and all that.'

'It must have been a shock to you when your father died.'

'Yes, I suppose it was. The old man and I didn't exactly hit it off but, somehow—those things make you realise—'

'Yes, yes,' said Victoria sympathetically. The similarity of deaths among the middle classes!

x

Every woman in the regiment had told her that
'these things make you realise' when Dicky died.
'But what about you? Are you still in—in cement?'

'In cement!' Jack's lip curled. 'The day my
father died I was out of cement. It's rather awful,
you know, to think that my freedom depended on his
death.'

'Oh, no; life depends on death,' said Victoria
smoothly. 'Besides, we are members of one another ;
and when, like you, Jack, we are a minority, we suffer.'

Holt looked at her doubtfully. He did not quite
understand her ; she had hardened, he thought.

'No,' he went on, 'I've done with the business.
They turned it into a limited liability company a
month ago. I'm a director because the others say
they must have a Holt in it ; but directors never do
anything, you know.'

'And you are going to do like the charwoman,
going to do nothing, nothing for ever ? '

'No, I don't say that. I've been writing—verses,
you know, and some sketches.'

'Writing ? You must be happy now, Jack. Of
course you'll let me see them ? Are they published?'

'Yes. At least, Amershams will bring out some
sonnets of mine next month.'

'And are you going to pass the rest of your life
writing sonnets?'

'No, of course not. I want to travel. I'll go
South this winter and get some local colour. I might
write a novel.'

His head was thrown back on the cushion, looking
out upon the blue southern sky, the bluer waters
speckled as with foam by remote white sails.

'You might give me a cigarette, Jack,' said
Victoria. 'They're in that silver box, there.'

He handed her the box and struck a match. As
he held it for her his eyes fastened upon the shapely
whiteness of her hands, her pink polished finger-

nails, the roundness of her forearm. Soft feminine
scents rose from her hair; he saw the dark tendrils
over the nape of her neck. Oh, to bury his lips in
that warm white neck! His hand trembled as he
lit his own cigarette and Victoria marked his
heightened colour.

'You'll come and see me often, Jack, won't you?'

'May I? It's so good of you. I'm not going South
for a couple of months.'

'Yes, you can always telephone. You'll find me
there under Mrs Ferris.'

Holt looked at her once more.

'I don't want you to think I'm prying. But, you
wrote me saying I was to ask for Mrs Ferris. I did,
of course, but, you . . . you're not. . . .?'

'Married? No, Jack. Don't ask me anything
else. You shall know everything soon.'

She got up and stood for a moment beside his
chair. His eyes were fixed on her hands.

'There,' she said, 'come along and let me shew you
the house, and my pictures, and my pack of hounds.'

He followed her obediently, giving its meed of
praise to all her possessions. He did not care for
animals; he lacked the generation of culture which
leads from cement-making to a taste for dogs. The
French engravings on the stairs surprised him a little.
He had a strain of puritanism in him running straight
from Bethlehem, which even the reading of Swinburne
and Baudelaire had not quite eradicated. A vague
sense of the fitness of things made him think that
somehow these were not the pictures a lady should
hang; she might keep them in a portfolio. Otherwise, there were the servants. . . .

'And what do you think of my bedroom?' asked
Victoria opening the door suddenly.

Holt stood nervously on the threshold. He took in
its details one by one, the blue paper, the polished
mahogany, the flowered chintzes, the long glass, the

lace curtains; it all looked so comfortable, so
luxurious as to eclipse easily the rigidly good but
ugly things he had been used to from birth onwards.
He looked at the dressing table too, covered with its
many bottles and brushes; then he started slightly
and again a hot flush rose over his cheeks. With an
effort he detached his eyes from the horrid thing
he saw.

'Very pretty, very pretty,' he gasped. Without
waiting for Victoria he turned and went downstairs.

Within the next week they met again. Jack took
no notice of her for four days, and then suddenly
telephoned asking her to dine and to come to the
theatre. She was still in bed and she felt low-
spirited, full of fear that her trump would not make.
She accepted with an alacrity that she regretted a
minute later, but she was drowning and could not
dally with the lifebelt. Her preparation for the
dinner was as elaborate as that which had heralded
her capture of Cairns, far more elaborate than any she
made for the Vesuvius where insolent beauty is
a greater asset than beauty as such. This time she
put on her mauve frock with the heavily embroidered
silver shoulder straps; she wore little jewellery, merely
a necklet of chased old silver and amethysts, and a
ring figuring a silver chimera with tiny diamond
eyes. As she surveyed herself in the long glass, the
holy calm which comes over the perfectly-dressed
flowed into her soul like a river of honey. She was
immaculate, and from her unlined white forehead to
her jewel-buckled shoes she was beautiful in every
detail. Subtle scent followed her like a train
bearer.

The entire evening was a tribute. From the
moment when Holt set eyes upon her and reluctantly
withdrew them to direct the cabman, until they drove
back through the night, she was conscious of the
wave of adulation that broke at her feet. Men's

eyes followed her every movement, drank in every rise and fall of her breast, strove to catch sight of her teeth, flashing white, ruby cased. Her progress through the dining hall and the stalls was imperial in its command. As she saw men turn to look at her again, women even grudgingly analyse her, as homage rose round her like incense, she felt frightened; for this seemed to be her triumphant night, the zenith of her beauty and power, and perhaps its very intensity showed that it was her swan song. She felt a pain in her left leg.

Jack Holt passed that evening at her feet. A fearful exultation was upon him. The neighbourhood of Victoria was magnetic; his heart, his senses, his æsthetic sense were equally enslaved. She realised everything he had dreamed, beauty, culture, grace, gentle wit. It hurt him physically not to tell that he loved her still, that he wanted her, that she was everything. He revelled in the thought that he had found her again, that she liked him, that he would see her whenever he wanted to, perhaps join his life with hers; then fear gripped his uneven soul, fear that he was only her toy, that now she was rich she would tire of him and cast him into a world swept by the icy blasts of regret. And all through ran the horribly suggestive memory of that which he had seen on the dressing table.

Victoria was conscious of all this storm, though unable to interpret its squalls and its lulls. Without effort she played upon him; alternately encouraging the pretty youth, bending towards him to read his programme so that he could feel her breath on his cheek, and drawing up and becoming absorbed in the play. In the darkness she felt his hand close over hers; gently but firmly she freed herself. As they drove back to St John's Wood they hardly exchanged a word. Victoria felt tired; for in the dark, away from the crowds, the music, the admiration

of her fellows, reaction had full play. Holt found he
could say nothing, for every nerve in his body was
tense with excitement. A hundred words were on
his lips but he dared not breathe them for fear of
breaking the spell.

'Come in and have a whisky and soda before you
go,' said Victoria in a matter of fact tone as he opened
the garden gate.

He could not resist. A wonderful feeling of intimacy
overwhelmed him as he watched her switch on the
lights and bring out a decanter, a syphon and glasses.
She put them on the table and motioned him towards
it, placing one foot on the fender to warm herself
before the glowing embers. His eyes did not leave
hers. There was a surge of blood in his head. One
of his hands fixed on her bare arm; with the other
he drew her towards him, crushed her against his
breast; she lay unresisting in his arms while he
covered her lips, her neck, her shoulders, with hot
kisses, some quick and passionate, others lingering,
full of tenderness. Then she gently repulsed him
and freed herself.

Jack,' she said softly, 'you shouldn't have done
that. You don't know . . . you don't know . . .'

He drew his hand over his forehead. His brain
seemed to clear a little. The maddening mystery of
it all formed into a question.

'Victoria, why are those two razors on your dressing
table?'

She looked at him a brief space. Then, very
quietly, with the deliberation of a surgeon,

'Need yot ask? Do you not understand what
I am?'

His eyes went up towards the ceiling; his hands
clenched; a queer choked sound escaped from his
throat. Victoria saw him suffer, wounded as an
æsthete, wounded in his traditional conception of
purity, prejudieed, ununderstanding. For a second

she hated him as one hates a howiing dog on whose paw one has trodden.

'Oh,' he gasped, 'oh.'

Victoria watched him through her downcast eyelashes. Poor boy, it had to come. Pandora had opened the chest. Then he looked at her again with returning sanity.

'Why didn't you tell me before? I can't bear it. You, whom I thought. . . . I can't bear it.'

'Poor boy.' She took his hand. It was hot and dry.

'I can't bear it,' he repeated dully.

'I had to. It was the only way.'

'There is always a way. It's awful.' His voice broke.

'Jack,' she said softly, 'the world's a hard place for women. It takes from them either hard labour or gratification. I've done my best. For a whole year I worked. I worked ten hours a day, I've starved almost, I've swabbed floors. . . .'

He withdrew his hand with a jerk. He could bear that even less than her confession.

'Then a man came,' she went on relentlessly, 'a good man who offered me ease, peace, happiness. I was poor, I was ill. What could I do? Then he died and I was alone. What could I do? Ah, don't believe mine is a bed of roses, Jack!'

He had turned away, and was looking into the dying fire. His ideals, his prejudices, all were in the melting pot. Here was the woman who had been his earliest dream, degraded, irretrievably soiled. Whatever happened he could not forget; not even love could break down the terrific barrier which generations of hard and honest men of Rawsley had erected in his soul between straight women and the others. But she was the dream still: beautiful, all that his heart desired; such that (and he felt it like an awful taunt) he could not give her up.

He looked at her, at her sorrowful face. No, he

could not let her pass out of his life. He thought of disjointed things. He could see his mother's face, the black streets of Rawsley; he thought of the pastor at Bethlehem denouncing sin. All his standards were jarred. He had nothing to hold on to while everything seemed to slip: ideals, resolutions, dreams; nothing remained save the horrible sweetness of the mermaid's face.

'Let me think,' he said hoarsely, 'let me think.'

Victoria said nothing. He was in hands stronger than hers. He was fighting his tradition, the blood of the Covenanters, for her sake. Nothing that she could say would help him; it might impede him. He had turned away; she could see nothing of his face. Then he looked into her eyes.

'What was can never be again,' he said; 'what I dreamed can never be. You were my beacon and my hope. I have only found you to lose you. If I were to marry you there would always be that between us, the past.'

'Then do not marry me. I do not ask you to.' Her voice went down to a whisper and she put her hands on his shoulders. 'Let me be another, a new dream, less golden, but sweet.'

She put her face almost against his, gazing into his eyes. 'Do not leave this house and I will be everything for you.'

She felt a shudder run through him as if he would repel her, but she did not relax her hold or her gaze. She drew nearer to him, and inch by inch his arms went round her. For a second they swayed close locked together. As they fell into the deep arm chair her loose black hair uncoiled, and, falling, buried their faces in its shadow.

CHAPTER XVI

THE months which followed emerged but slowly from blankness for these two who had joined their lives together. Both had a difficulty in realising, the woman that she had laid the coping stone of her career, the man that he was happy as may be an opium eater. The first days were electric, hectic. Victoria felt limp, for her nerves had been worn down by the excitement and the anxiety of making sure of her conquest. The reaction left her rather depressed than glowing with success. Jack was beyond scruples; he felt that he had passed the Rubicon. He was false to his theories and his ideals, in revolt against his upbringing. At the outset he revelled in the thought that he was cutting himself adrift from the ugly past. It was joyful to think that the pastor in his whitewashed barn would covertly select him as a text. For the first time in his fettered life he saw that the outlaw alone is free; both he and Victoria were outlaws, but she had tasted the bitterness of ostracism while he was still at the stage of welcoming it.

As the weeks wore, however, Victoria realised her position better and splendid peace flowed in upon her. She did not love Holt; she began even to doubt whether she could love any man if she could not love him, this handsome youth with the delicate soul, grace, generosity. It was not his mental weakness that repelled her, for he was virile enough; nor was it the touch of provincialism against which his intelligence struggled. It was rather that he did not attract her. He was clever enough, well read, kind, but he lacked magnetism ; he had nothing of the slumberous fire which distinguished Farwell. His passion was personal, his outlook theoretical and limited ; there was nothing purposeful in his ideas. He had no message for her. In no wise did he repel her, though. Sometimes she would take his face between her hands, look awhile into the blue eyes where there always lurked some wistfulness, and then kiss him just once and quickly, without knowing why.

'Why do you do that, Vicky?' he asked once.

She had not answered but had merely kissed his cheek again. She hardly knew how to tell him that she sighed because she could only consent to love him instead of offering to do so. While he was sunk in his daily growing ease she was again thinking of ultimate ends and despised herself a little for it. She had to be alone for a while before she could regain self-control, remember the terrible tyranny of man and her resolve to be free. Gentle Jack was a man, one of the oppressors, and as such he must be used as an instrument against his sex. The very ease with which she swayed him, with which she could foresee her victory, unnerved her a little. When she answered his hesitating question as to how much she needed to live, she had to force herself to lie, to trade on his enslavement by asking him for two thousand a year. She dared to name the figure, for ' Whitaker ' told her that the only son of an intestate takes two-thirds of the estate ; the book had also put her on the track of the registration of joint-stock companies. A visit to Somerset House enabled her to discover that some three hundred thousand shares of Holt'ʳ Cement Works, Ltd., stood in the name of John Holt ; as they were quoted in the paper something above par he could hardly be worth less than fifteen thousand a year.

She had expected to have to explain her needs, to have to exaggerate her rent, the cost of her clothes, but Holt did not say a word beyond 'all right.' She had told him it hurt her to take money from him ; and that, so as to avoid the subject, she would like him to tell his bankers to pay the monthly instalments into her account. He had agreed and then talked of their trip to the South. Clearly the whole matter was repugnant to him. As neither wanted to talk about it the subject was soon almost forgotten.

They left England early in December after shutting up the house. Victoria did not care to leave it in charge of Laura, so decided to give her a three months' holiday on full pay ; Augusta accompanied them. The sandy-haired German was delighted with the change in the fortunes of her mistress. She felt that Holt must be very rich, and doubted not that her dowry would derive some benefit from him. Snoo and Poo were left in Laura's charge. Victoria paid a quarter's rent in advance, also the rates ; insured against burglary, and left England as it settled into the winter night.

The next three months were probably the most steadily happy she had ever known. They had taken a small house known as the Villa Mehari just outside Algiers. A French cook and a taciturn Kabyl completed their establishment. The villa was a curious compromise between East and West. Its architect had turned out similar ones in scores at Argenteuil and Saint Cloud, saving the minaret and the deep verandah which faced the balmy west. From the precipitous little garden where orange and lime trees bent beneath their fruit among the underbrush of aloes and cactus, they could see, far away, the estranging sea.

The Kabyl had slung a hammock for Victoria between a gate-post and a gigantic clump of palm trees. There she passed most of her days, lazily

swinging in the breeze which tumbled her black hair;
while Jack, lying at her feet in the crisp rough grass,
looked long at her sun-warmed beauty. The days
seemed to fly, for they were hardly conscious of the
recurrence of life. It was sunrise, when it was good
to go into the garden and see the blue green
night blush softly into salmon pink, then burst
suddenly into tropical radiance; then, vague occupations, a short walk over stony paths to a café where
the East and West met; unexpected food; sleep
in the heat of the day under the nets beyond which
the crowding flies buzzed; then the waning of the
day, the heat settling more leaden; sunset, the cold
snapping suddenly, the night wind carrying little
puffs of dust, and the muezzin, hands aloft, droning,
his face towards the East, praises of his God.

Holt was totally happy. He felt he had reached
Capua, and not even a thought of his past life could
disturb him. He asked for nothing now but to live
without a thought, eating juicy fruit, smoking for
an hour the subtle narghilé; he loved to bask in the
radiance of the African sun of Victoria's beauty, which
seemed to expand, to enwrap him in perfume like a
heavy narcotic rose. In the early days he tried to
work, to attune himself to the pageant of sunlit
life. His will refused to act, and he found he could
not write a line; even rhymes refused to come to him.
Without an effort almost he resigned himself into the
soft hands of the East. He even exaggerated his
acceptance by clothing himself in a burnous and
turban, by trying to introduce Algerian food, couscous,
roast kid, date jam, pomegranate jelly. At times they
would go into Algiers, shop in the Rue Bab-Azoum,
or search for the true East in what the French called
the high town. But Algiers is not the East; and they
quickly returned to the Villa Mehari, stupefied by the
roar of the trams, the cries of the water and chestnut
vendors, all their senses offended by the cafés on the

wharf where sailors from every land drank vodka, arrack, pale ale, among zouaves and chasseurs d'Afrique.

Sometimes Holt would go into Algiers by himself and remain away all day. Victoria stayed at the villa careless of flying time, desultorily reading Heine or sitting in the garden where she could play with the golden and green beetles. Her solitude was complete, for Holt had avoided the British consul and of course knew none of the Frenchmen. She watched the current of her life flow away, content to know that all the while her little fortune was increasing. England was so far as to seem in another world. Christmas was gone ; and the link of a ten pound note to Betty, to help to furnish the house at Shepherd's Bush, had faded away. When she was alone, those days, she could not throw her mind back to the ugly, brutish past, so potently was the influence of the East growing upon her being. Then in the cool of the evening Jack would return, gay, and anxious to see her, to throw his arms round her and hold her to him again. Those were the days when he brought her some precious offering, aqua-marines set in hand-wrought gold, or chaplets of strung pearls.

'Jack,' she said to him one day as he lay in the grass at her feet, 'do you then love me very much?'

'Very much.' He took her hand and, raising himself upon his elbow, gravely kissed it.

'Why?'

'Because you're all the poetry of the world. Because you make me dream dreams, my Aspasia.'

She gently stroked his dark hair.

'And to think that you are one of the enemy, Jack!'

'One of the enemy? what do you mean?'

'Man is woman's enemy, Jack. Our relation is a war of sex.'

'It's not true.' Jack flushed; the idea was repulsive.

'It is true. Man dominates woman by force, by

man-made law; he restricts her occupations; he
limits her chances; he judges of her attire; he denies
her the right to be ugly, to be old, to be coarse, to
be vicious.'

'But you wouldn't—'

'I'd have everything the same, Jack.'

Holt thought for a moment.

'Yes, I suppose we do keep them down. But
they're different. You see, men are men and—'

'I know the rest. But never mind, Jack dear,
you're not like the others. You'll never be a
conqueror.'

Then she muzzled him with her hand, and, kissing
its scented palm, he thought no more of the stern
game in which they were the shuttlecocks.

The spring was touching Europe with its wings; and
here already the summer was bursting the seed pods,
the sap breaking impatiently through the branches.
All the wet warmth of the brief African blooming ran
riot in thickening leaf. The objective of Jack's life,
influenced as he was by the air, was Victoria and the
ever more consuming love he bore her; the minutes
only counted when he was by her side, watching her
every movement, inhaling, touching her. All his
energies seem to have been driven into this narrow
channel. He was ready to move or to remain as
Victoria might direct; he spoke little, he basked.
Thus he agreed to extending their stay for a month;
he agreed to shorten it by a fortnight when Victoria,
suddenly realising that her life force was wasting
away in this enervating atmosphere, decided to go
home.

Victoria's progress to London was like the march of
a conqueror. She stopped in Paris to renew her
clothes. There Jack knew hours of waiting in the
hired victoria while his queen was trying on frocks.
He showed such a childish joy in it all that she indulged her fancy, her every whim; dresses, wraps, lace

veils, furs, hats massive with ostrich feathers, aigrettes, delicate kid boots, gilt shoes, amassed in their suite. Jack egged her on ; he rioted too. Often he would stop the victoria and rush into a shop if he saw something he liked in the window, and in a few minutes return with it, excitedly demanding praise. He did not seem to understand or care for money, to have any wants except cigarettes. He followed, and in his beautiful dog-like eyes devotion daily grew.

They entered London on a bustling April day. A biting east wind carried rain drops and sunshine. As it stung her face and whipped her blood, Victoria found the old fierce soul reincarnating itself in her. She opened her mouth to take in the cold English air, to bend herself for the finishing of her task.

CHAPTER XVII

It was in London that the real battle began. In Algiers the scented winds made hideous and unnatural all thoughts of gain. On arriving in London Victoria ascertained with a thrill of pleasure that her bank had received a thousand pounds since October. After disposing of a few small debts and renewing some trifles in the house, she found herself a capitalist: she had about fifteen hundred pounds of her own. The money was lying at the bank and it only struck her then that the time had come to invest it. Her interview with the manager of her branch was a delightful experience; she was almost bursting with importance, and his courteous appreciation of his increasingly wealthy client was something more than balm. It was a foretaste of the power of money. She had known poor men respected, but not poor women; now the bank manager was giving her respectful attention because she had fifteen hundred pounds.

'You might buy some industrials,' he said.

'Industrials? What are they?'

'Oh, all sorts of things. Cotton mills, iron works, trading companies, anything.'

'Cement works?' she asked with a spark of devilry.

'Yes, cement works too,' said the manager without moving a muscle.

'But do you call them safe?' she asked, returning to business.

'Oh, fairly. Of course there are bad years and good. But the debentures are mostly all right and some of the prefs.'

Victoria thought for a moment. Reminiscences of political economy told her that there were booms and slumps.

'Has trade been good lately?' she asked suddenly.

'No, not for the last two years or so. It's picking up though. . . .'

'Ah, then we're in for a cycle of good trade. I think I'll have some industrials. You might pick me out the best.'

The manager seemed a little surprised at this knowledge of commercial crises but said nothing more, and made out a list of securities averaging six per cent net.

'And please buy me a hundred P. R. R. shares,' added Victoria.

She could have laughed at the manager's stony face because he did not see the humour of this. He merely said that he would forward the orders to a stockbroker.

Victoria felt that she had put her hand to the plough. She was scoring so heavily that she never now wished to turn back. Holt was every day growing more dreamy, more absorbed in his thoughts. He never seemed to quicken into action except when his companion touched him. He grew more silent too; the hobbledehoy was gone. He was at his worst when he had received a letter bearing the Rawsley postmark. Victoria knew of these, for Holt's need of her grew greater every day; he was now living at Elm Tree Place. He hardly left the house. He got up late and passed the morning in the boudoir, smoking cigarettes, desultorily reading and nursing the Pekingese which he now liked better. But on the days when he got letters from Rawsley, letters so bulky that they were sometimes insufficiently

z

stamped, he would go out early and only return at
night. Then, however, he returned as if he had been
running, full of some nameless fear ; he would strain
Victoria to him and hold her very close, burying his
face below the bedclothes as if he were afraid. On one
of those days Victoria accidentally saw him come out of
a small dissenting chapel near by. He did not see
her, for he was walking away like a man possessed ;
she said nothing of this but understood him better,
having an inkling that the fight against the Rawsley
tradition was still going on.

She did not, however, allow herself to be moved by
his struggle. It behoved her to hold him, for he was
her last chance and the world looked rosy round her.
As the spring turned into summer he became more
utterly hers.

'You distil poison for me,' he said one day as they
sat by the rose-hung pergola.

'No, Jack, don't say that, it's the elixir of life.'

'The elixir of life. Perhaps, but poison too. To
make me live is to make me die, Victoria ; we are
both sickening for death and to hasten the current of
life is to hasten our doom.'

'Live quickly,' she whispered, bending towards
him ; ' did you live at all a year ago ? '

'No, no.' His arms were round her and his lips
insistent on hers. He frightened her a little, though.
She would have to take him away. She had already
confided this new trouble to Betty when the latter
came to see her in April, but Betty, beyond suggesting cricket, had been too full of her own affairs.
Apparently these were not going very well. Anderson
& Dromo's had not granted the rise, and the marriage
had been postponed. Meanwhile she was still at the
P. R. R., and very, very happy. Betty too, her baby,
her other baby, frightened Victoria a little. She was
so rosy, so pretty now, and there was something
defiant and excited about her that might presage

disease. But Betty had not come near her for the last two months.

About the middle of June she took Jack away to Broadstairs. He was willing to go or stay, just as she liked. He seemed so neutral that Victoria experimented upon him by presenting him with a sheaf of unpaid bills. He looked at them languidly and said he supposed they must be paid, asked her to add them up and wrote a cheque for the full amount. Apparently he had forgotten all about the allowance, or did not care.

Broadstairs seemed to do him good. Except at the week end the Hotel Sylvester was almost empty. The sea breeze blew stiffly from the north or the east. His colour increased and once more he began to talk. Victoria encouraged him to take long walks alone along the front. She had some occupation, for two little girls who were there in charge of a Swiss governess had adopted the lovely lady as their aunt. A new sweetness had come into her life, shrill voices, the clinging of little hands. Sometimes these four would walk together, and Holt would run with the children, tumbling in the sand in sheer merriment.

'You seem all right again, Jack,' said Victoria on the tenth morning.

'Right! Rather, by jove, it's good to live, Vicky.'

'You were a bit off colour, you know.'

'I suppose I was. But now, I feel nothing can hold me. I wrote a rondeau this morning on the pier. Want to see it?'

'Of course, silly boy. Aren't you going to be the next great poet?'

She read the rondeau, scrawled in pencil on the back of a bill. It was delicate, a little colourless.

'Lovely,' she said, 'of course you'll send it to the *Westminster.*'

'Perhaps . . . hulloa, there are the kiddies.' He

ran off down the steps from the front. A minute after Victoria saw him helping the elder girl to bury her little sister in the sand.

Victoria felt much reassured. He was normal again, the half wistful, half irresponsible boy she had once known. He slept well, laughed, and his crying need for her seemed to have abated. At the end of the fortnight Victoria was debating whether she should take him home. She was in the hotel garden talking to the smaller girl, telling her a wonderful story about the fairy who lived in the telephone and said ping-pong when the line was engaged. The little girl sat upon her knee; when she laughed Victoria's heart bounded. The elder girl came through the gate leading a good-looking young woman in white by the hand.

'Oh, mummie, here's auntie,' cried the child, dragging her mother up to Victoria. The two women looked at one another.

'They tell me you have been very kind . . .' said the woman. Then she stopped abruptly.

'Of course, mummie, she's not *really* our auntie,' said the child confidentially.

Victoria put the small girl down. The mother looked at her again. She seemed so nice and refined . . . yet her husband said that the initials on the trunks were different . . . one had to be careful.

'Come here, Celia,' she said sharply. 'Thank you,' she added to Victoria. Then taking her little girls by the hand she took them away.

Jack willingly left Broadstairs that afternoon when Victoria explained that she was tired and that something had made her low-spirited.

'Right oh!' he said. 'Let's go back to town. I want to see Amershams and find out how those sonnets have sold.'

He then left her to wire to Augusta.

Their life in town resumed its former course,

interrupted only by a month in North Devon. Jack's
cure was complete; he was sunburnt, fatter; the joy
of life shone in his blue eyes. Sometimes Victoria
found herself growing younger by contagion, slough-
ing the horrible miry coat of the past. If her heart
had not been atrophied she would have loved the boy
whom she always treated with motherly gentleness.
His need of her was so crying, so total, that he lost all
his self-consciousness. He would sit unblushing by
her side in the bow of a fishing smack, holding her
hand and looking raptly into her grey eyes; he was
indifferent to the red brown fisherman with the
Spanish eyes and curly black hair who smiled as the
turtle doves clustered. His need of her was as mental
as it was physical; his body was whipped by the salt
air to seek in her arms oblivion, but his mind had
become equally dependent. She was his need.

Thus when they came back to town the riot continued; and Victoria, breasting the London tide,
dragged him unresisting in her rear. She hated
excitement in every form, excitement that is of the
puerile kind. Restaurant dining, horse shows, flower
shows, the Academy, tea in Bond Street, even the
theatre and its most inane successes, were for her
a weariness to the flesh.

'I've had enough,' she said to Jack one day. 'I'm
sick of it all. I've got congestion of the appreciative
sense. One day I shall chuck it all up, go and live
in the country, have big dogs and a saddle horse,
dress in tweeds and read the local agricultural rag.'

'Give up smoking, go to church, and play tennis
with the curate, the doctor and the squire's flapper,'
added Holt. 'But Vicky, why not go now?'

'No, oh, no, I can't do that.' She was frightened
by her own suggestion. 'I must drain the cup of
pleasure so as to be sure that it's all pain; then I'll
retire and drain the cup of resignation . . . unless,
as I sometimes think, it's empty.'

Jack had said nothing to this. Her wildness surprised and shocked him. She was so savage and yet so sweet.

Victoria realised that she must hold fast to the town, for there alone could she succeed. In the peace of the country she would not have the opportunities she had now. Jack was in her hands. She never hesitated to ask for money, and Jack responded without a word. Her account grew by leaps and bounds. The cashier began to ask whether she wanted to see the manager when she called at the bank. She could see, some way off but clearly, the beacons on the coast of hope.

All through Jack's moods she had suffered from the defection of Betty. On her return from Broadstairs she had written to her to come to Elm Tree Place, but had received no answer. This happened again in September; and fear took hold of her, for Betty had, ivy-like, twined herself very closely round Victoria's heart of oak. She went to Finsbury; but Betty had gone, leaving no address. She went to the P.R.R. also. The place had become ghostly, for the familiar faces had gone. The manageress was nowhere to be seen; nor was Nelly, probably by now a manageress herself. Betty was not there, and the girl who wonderingly served the beautiful lady with a tea-cake said that no girl of that name was employed at the depot. Then Victoria saw herself sitting in the churchyard of her past, between the two dear ghosts of Farwell and Betty. The customers had changed, or their faces had receded so that she knew them no more: they still played matador and fives and threes, chess too. Alone the chains remained which the ghosts had rattled. Silently she went away, turning over that leaf of her life for ever. Farwell was dead, and Betty gone—married probably— and in Shepherd's Bush, not daring to allow Victoria's foot to sully the threshold of ' First Words of Love.'

Her conviction that Betty was false had a kind of tonic effect upon her. She was alone and herself again ; she realised that the lonely being is the strong being. Now, at last, she could include the last woman she had known in the category of those who threw stones. And her determination to be free grew apace.

She invented a reason every day to extract money from Holt. He, blindly desirous, careless of money, acceded to every fresh demand. Now it was a faked bill from Barbezan Soeurs for two hundred pounds, now the rent in arrear, a blue rates notice, an offhand request for a fiver to pay the servants, the vet's bill or the price of a cab. Holt drew and overdrew. If a suspicion ever entered his mind that he was being exploited, he dismissed it at once, telling himself that Victoria was rather extravagant. For a time letters from Rawsley synchronised with her fresh demands, but repetition had dulled their effects: now Holt postponed reading them ; after a time she saw him throw one into the fire unread. Little by little they grew rarer. Then they ceased. Holt was eaten up by his passion, and Victoria's star rose high.

All conspired to favour her fortune. Perhaps her acumen had helped her too, for she had seen correctly the coming boom. Trade rose by leaps and bounds ; every day new shops seemed to open ; the stalks of the Central London Railway could be seen belching clouds of smoke as they ground out electric power ; the letter-box at Elm Tree Place was clogged with circulars denoting by the fury of their competion that trade was flying as on a great wind. Other signs too were not wanting : the main streets of London were blocked by lorries groaning under machinery, vegetables, stone ; immense queues formed at the railway stations waiting for the excursion trains ; above all, rose the sound of gold as it hissed and sizzled as if molten on the pavements, flowing into the pockets of merchants, bankers and share-

holders. All the women at the Vesuvius indulged in
new clothes.

Victoria's investments were seized by the current.
She had not entirely followed the bank manager's
advice. Seeing, feeling the movement, she had
realised most of her debentures and turned them into
shares. One of her ventures collapsed, but the
remainder appreciated to an extraordinary extent. At
last, in the waning days of the year her middle-class
prudence reasserted itself. She knew enough of
political economy to be ready for the crash; she
realised. One cold morning in November she counted
up her spoils. She had nearly five thousand pounds.

Meanwhile, while her blood was aglow, Holt sank
further into the dullness of his senses. A mania was
upon him. Waking, his thought was Victoria; and
the cry for her rose everlasting from his racked body.
She was all, she was everywhere; and the desire for
her, for her beauty, her red lips, soaked into him like
a philtre, narcotic and then fiery but ever present,
intimate and exacting. He was her thing, her toy,
the paltry instrument which responded to her every
touch. He rejoiced in his subjection; he swam in
his passion like a pilgrim in the Ganges to find brief
oblivion; but again the thirst was on him, ravaging,
ever demanding more. More, more, ever more, in
the watches of the night, when ice seizes the world
to throttle it—among all, in turmoil and in peace—he
tossed upon the passionate sea; with one thought,
one hope.

CHAPTER XVIII

'I'M glad we're going away, Jack,' said Victoria leaning back in the cab and looking at him critically. 'You look as if you wanted a change.'

'Perhaps I do,' said Jack.

Victoria looked at him again. He had not smiled as he spoke to her, which was unusual. He seemed thinner and more delicate than ever, with his pale face and pink cheekbones. His black hair shone as if moist; and his eyes were bigger than they had ever been, blue like silent pools and surrounded by a mauve zone. His mouth hung a little open. Yet, in spite of his weariness, he held her wrist in both his hands, and she could feel his fingers searching for the opening in her glove.

'You are becoming a ⁄responsibility,' she said smiling. 'I shall have to be a mother to you.'

A faint smile came over his lips.

'A mother? After all, why not? Phedra. . . .' His eyes fixed on the grey morning sky as he followed his thought.

The horse was trotting sharply. The winter air seemed to rush into their bodies. Jack, well wrapped up as he was in a fur coat, shrank back against the warm roundness of her shoulder. In an access of gentleness she put her free hand in his.

'Dear boy,' she said softly bending over him.

But there was no tenderness in Jack's blue eyes, rather lambent fire. At once his grasp on her hand tightened and his lips mutely formed into a request.

Casting a glance right and left she kissed him quickly on the mouth.

Up on the roof their bags jolted and bumped one another ; milk carts were rattling their empty cans as they returned from their round ; far away a drum and file band played an acid air. They were going to Ventnor in pursuit of the blanketed sun ; and Victoria rejoiced, as they passed through Piccadilly Circus where moisture settled black on the fountain, to think that for three days she would see the sun radiate, not loom as a red guinea. They passed over Waterloo Bridge at a foot pace ; the enormous morning traffic was struggling in the neck of the bottle. The pressure was increased because the road was up between it and Waterloo Station. On her left, over the parapet, Victoria could see the immense desert of the Thames swathed in thin mist, whence emerged in places masts and where massive barges loomed passive like derelicts. She wondered for a moment whether her familiar symbol, the old vagrant, still sat crouching against the parapet at Westminster, watching rare puffs of smoke curling from his pipe into the cold air. The cab emerged from the crush, and to avoid it the cabman turned into the little black streets which line the wharf on the east side of the bridge, then doubled back towards Waterloo through Cornwall Road. There they met again the stream of drays and carts ; the horse went at a foot pace, and Victoria gazed at the black rows of houses with the fear of a lost one. So uniformly ugly these apartment houses, with their dirty curtains, their unspeakable flowerpots in the parlour windows. Here and there cards announcing that they did pinking within ; further, the board of a sweep ; then a good corner house, the doctor's probably, with four steps and a brass knocker and a tall slim girl on her hands and knees washing the steps.

The cab came to an abrupt stop. Some distance ahead a horse was down on the slippery road ; shouts came from the crowd around it. Victoria idly watched the girl, swinging the wet rag from right to left. Poor thing. Everything in her seemed to cry out against the torture of womanhood. She was a picture of dumb resignation as she knelt with her back to the road. Victoria could see her long thin arms, her hands red and rigid with cold, her broken-down shoes with the punctured soles emerging from the ragged black petticoat.

There was a little surge in the crowd. The girl got up, and with an air of infinite weariness stretched her arms. Then she picked up the pail and bucket and turned towards the street. For the space of a second the two women looked into one another's faces. Then Victoria gave a muffled cry and jumped out of the cab. She seized with both hands the girl's bare arms.

'Betty! Betty!' she faltered.

A burning blush covered the girl's face and her features twitched. She made as if to turn away from the detaining hands.

'Vicky, what are you doing . . . what does this mean?' came Jack's voice from the cab.

'Wait a minute, Jack. Betty, my poor little Betty. Why are you here? Why haven't you written to me?'

'Leave me alone,' said Betty hoarsely.

'I won't leave you alone. Betty, tell me, what's this? Are you married?'

A look of pain came over the girl's face, but she said nothing.

'Look here, Betty, we can't talk here. Leave the bucket, come with me. I'll see it's all right.'

'Oh, I can't do that. Oh, let me alone; it's too late.'

'I don't understand you. It's never too late. Now just get into the cab and come with me.'

'I can't. I must give notice . . .' She looked about to weep.

'Come along.' Victoria increased the pressure on the girl's arms. Jack stood up in the cab. He seemed as frightened as he was surprised.

'I say, Vicky . . .' he began.

'Sit down, Jack, she's coming with us. You don't mind if we don't go to Ventnor?'

Jack's eyes opened in astonishment but he made no reply. Victoria pulled Betty sharply down the steps.

'Oh, let me get my things,' she said weakly.

'No. They'd stop you. There, get in. Drive back to Elm Tree Place, cabman.'

Half an hour later, lying at full length on the boudoir sofa, Betty was slowly sipping some hot cocoa. There was a smile on her tear-stained face. Victoria was analysing with horror the ravages that sorrow had wrought on her. She was pretty still, with her china blue eyes and her hair like pale filigree gold; but the bones seemed to start from her red wrists, so thin had she become. Even the smile of exhausted content on her lips did not redeem her emaciated cheeks.

'Betty, my poor Betty,' said Victoria, taking her hand. 'What have they done to you?'

The girl looked up at the ceiling as if in a dream.

'Tell me all about it,' her friend went on, 'what has happened to you since April?'

'Oh, lots of things, lots of things. I've had a hard time.'

'Yes, I see. But what happened actually? Why did you leave the P.R.R.?'

'I had to. You see, Edward . . .' The flush returned.

'Yes?'

'Oh, Vic, I've been a bad girl and I'm so, so unhappy.' Betty seized her friend's hand to raise herself and buried her face on her breast. There Victoria let her sob, gently stroking the golden hair. She understood already, but Betty must not be questioned yet. Little by little, Betty's weeping grew less violent and confidence burst from her pent up soul.

'He didn't get a rise at Christmas, so he said we'd have to wait . . . I couldn't bear it . . . it wasn't his fault. I couldn't let him come down in the world, a gentleman . . . he had only thirty shillings a week.'

'Yes, yes, poor little girl.'

'We never meant to do wrong . . . when baby was coming he said he'd marry me . . . I couldn't drag him down . . . I ran away.'

'Betty, Betty, why didn't you write to me?'

The girl looked at her. She was beautiful in her reminiscence of sacrifice.

'I was ashamed . . . I didn't dare . . . I only wanted to go where they didn't know what I was. . . . I was mad. The baby came too early and it died almost at once.'

'My poor little girl.' Victoria softly stroked the rough back of her hand.

'Oh, I wasn't sorry . . . it was a little girl . . . they don't want any more in the world. Besides I didn't care for anything; I'd lost him . . . and my job. I couldn't go back. My landlady wrote me a character to go to Cornwall road.'

'And there I found you.'

'I wonder what we are going to do for you,' she went on. 'Where is Edward now?'

'Oh, I couldn't go back; I'm ashamed. . . .'

'Nonsense, you haven't done anything wrong. He shall marry you.'

'He would have,' said Betty a little coldly, 'he's square.'

'Yes, I know. He didn't beg you very hard, did he? However, never mind. I'm not going to let you go until I've made you happy. Now I'll tuck you up with a rug, and you're going to sleep before the fire.'

Betty lay limp and unresisting in the ministering hands. The unwonted sensations of comfort, warmth and peace soothed her to sleepiness. Besides, she felt as if she had wept every tear in her racked body. Soon her features relaxed, and she sank into profound, almost deathlike slumber.

Victoria meanwhile told her story to Jack, who sat in the dining room reading a novel and smoking cigarettes. He came out of his coma as Victoria unfolded the tale of Betty's upbringing, her struggle to live, then love the meteor flashing through her horizon. His cheeks flushed and his mouth quivered as Victoria painted for him the picture of the girl half distraught, bearing the burden of her shame, unable to reason or to forsee, to think of anything except the saving of a gentleman from life on thirty bob a week.

'Something ought to be done,' he said at length, closing his book with novel vivacity.

'Yes, but what?'

'I don't know.' His eyes questioned the wall; they grew vaguer and vaguer as his excitement decreased, as a ship in docks sinks further and further on her side while the water ebbs away.

'You think of something,' he said at length, picking up his book again. 'I don't care what it costs.'

Victoria left him and went for a walk through the misty streets seeking a solution. There were not many. She could not keep Betty with her, for she was pure though betrayed; contact with the irregular would degrade her because habit would induce her to condone that which she morally condemned. It would spoil her and would ultimately throw her into a life for which she was not fitted because gentle and unspoiled.

'No,' mused Victoria as she walked, 'like most women, she cannot rule : a man must rule her. She

is a reed, not an oak. All must come from man,
both good and evil. What man has done man
must undo.'

By the time she returned to Elm Tree Place she
had made up her mind. There was no hope for
Betty except in marriage. She must have her own
fireside ; and, from what she had said, her lover was
no villain. He was weak, probably ; and, while he
strove to determine his line of conduct, events had
slipped beyond his control. Perhaps, though, it was
not fair to deliver Betty into his hands bound and
defenceless, bearing the burden of their common
imprudence. She was not fit to be free, but she
should not be a slave. It might be well to be the
slave of the strong, but not of the weak.

Therefore Victoria arrived at a definite solution.
She would see the young man ; and, if it was not
altogether out of the question, he should marry Betty.
They should have the little house at Shepherd's Bush,
and Betty should be made a free woman with a
fortune of five hundred pounds in her own right,
enough to place her for ever beyond sheer want. It
only struck Victoria later that she need not, out of
quixotic generosity, deplete her own store, for Holt
would gladly give whatever sum she named.

' Now, Betty,' she said as the girl drained the glass
of claret which accompanied the piece of fowl that
composed her lunch, ' tell me your young man's name
and Anderson & Dromo's address. I'm going to see
him.'

' Oh, no, no, don't do that.' The look of fear
returned to the blue eyes.

' No use, Betty, I've decided you're going to be
happy. I shall see him to-day at six, bring him
here to-morrow at half past two, as it happens to be
Saturday. You will be married about the thirtieth
of this month.'

' Oh, Vic, don't make me think of it. I can't do

it . . . it's no good now. Perhaps he's forgotten me, and it's better for him.'

'I don't think he's forgotten you,' said Victoria. 'He'll marry you this month, and you'll eat your Christmas dinner at Shepherd's Bush. Don't be shy, dear—you're not going empty handed; you're going to have a dowry of five hundred pounds.'

'Vic! I can't take it; it isn't right . . . you need all you've got . . . you're so good, but I don't want him to marry me if . . . if. . . .'

'Oh, don't worry, I shan't tell him about the money until he says yes. Now, no thanks; you're my baby, besides it's going to be a present from Mr Holt. Silence,' she repeated as Betty opened her mouth, 'or rather give me his name and address and not another word.'

'Edward Smith, Salisbury House, but. . . .'

'Enough. Now, dear, don't get up.'

The events of that Friday and Saturday formed in later days one of the sunbathed memories in Victoria's dreary life. It was all so gentle, so full of sweetness and irresolute generosity. She remembered everything, the wait in the little dark room into which she was ushered by an amazed commissionaire who professed himself willing to break regulations for her sake and hand Mr Smith a note, the banging of her heart as she realised her responsibility and resolved to break her word if necessary and to buy a husband for Betty rather than lose him, then the quick interview, the light upon the young man's face.

'Where is she?' he asked excitedly. 'Oh, why did she run away? You can't think what I've been going through.'

'You should have married her,' said Victoria coldly, though she was moved by his sincerity. He was handsome, this young man, with his bronzed face, dark eyes, regular features and long dark hair.

'Oh, I would have at once if I'd known. But I

couldn't make up my mind; only thirty bob a week. . . .'

'Yes, I know,' said Victoria softly, 'I used to be at the P. R. R.'

'You?' The young man looked at her incredulously.

'Yes, but never mind me. It's Betty I've come for. The baby is dead. I found her cleaning the steps of a house near Waterloo.'

'My God,' said the young man in low tones. He clenched his hands together; one of his paper cuff protectors fell to the floor.

'Will you marry her now?'

'Yes . . . at once.'

'Good. She's had a hard time, Mr Smith, and I don't say it's entirely your fault. Now it's all going to be put square. I'm going to see she has some money of her own, five hundred pounds. That will help won't it?'

'Oh, it's too good to be true. Why are you doing all this for us? You're. . . .'

'Please, please, no thanks. I'm Betty's friend. Let that be enough. Will you come and see her to-morrow at my house? Here's my card.'

On the last day of November these two were married at a registry office in the presence of Victoria and the registrar's clerk. A new joy had settled upon Betty, whose shy prettiness was turning into beauty. Victoria's heart was heavy as she looked at the couple, both so young and rapt, setting out upon the sea with a cargo of glowing dreams. It was heavy still as the cab drove off carrying them away for a brief week-end, which was all Anderson and Dromo would allow. She tasted a new delight in this making of happiness.

Holt had not attended the ceremony, for he felt too weak. His interest in the affair had been dim, for he looked upon it as one of Victoria's whims. He was ceasing to judge as he ceased to appreciate, so much

2A

was his physical weakness gaining upon him ; all his faculty of action was concentrated in the desire which gnawed at his very being. Victoria reminded him of his promise, and, finding his cheque book for him, laid it on the table.

'Five hundred pounds,' she said. 'Better make it out to me. It's very good of you, Jack.'

'Yes, yes,' he said dully, writing the date and the words 'Mrs Ferris.' Then he stopped. Concentrating with an effort he wrote the word 'five.'

'Five . . . five . . .' he murmured. Then he looked up at Victoria with something like vacuousness.

A wild idea flashed through her brain. She must act. Oh, no, dreadful. Yet freedom, freedom. . . . He could not understand . . . she must do it.

'Thousand,' she prompted in a low voice.

'Thousand pounds,' went Jack's voice as he wrote obediently. Then, mechanically, reciting the formula his father had taught him: 'Five, comma, 0, 0, 0, dash, 0, dash, 0. John Holt.'

Victoria put her hands down on the table to take the cheque he had just torn out. All her fingers were trembling with the terrible excitement of a slave watching his fetters being struck off. As she took it up and looked at it, while the figures danced, Holt's eyes grew more insistent on her other hand. Slowly his fingers closed over it, raised it to his lips. With his eyes closed, breathing a little deeper, he covered her palm with lingering kisses.

CHAPTER XIX

THE endowment of Betty was soon completed. Advised by the bank manager to whom she confided something of the young couple's improvident tendencies, Victoria vested the money in a trust administered by an insurance company. The deed was so drafted that it could not be charged; the capital could not be touched, excepting the case of male offspring who, after their mother's death, would divide it on their respective twenty-fifth birthdays; as she distrusted her own sex and perhaps still more the stock from which the girls might spring, she bound their proportion in perpetuity; failing offspring she provided that, following on his wife's decease, Mr Edward Smith should receive one fifth of the capital, four fifths reverting to herself.

Victoria revelled somewhat in the technicalities of the deed; every clause she framed was a pleasure in itself; she turned the 'hereinbefores' and the 'predecease as aforesaids' round in her mouth as if they were luscious sweets. The pleasure of it was not that of Lady Bountiful showering blessings and feeling the holy glow of charity penetrate her being. Victoria's satisfaction was more vixenish; she, the outlaw, the outcast, had wrested from Society enough money to indulge in the luxury of promoting a marriage, converting the illegal into the legal, creating respectability. The gains that Society term infamous were being turned towards the support of that Society; still more, failing her infamous help, Betty and

Edward Smith would not have achieved their coming together with the approval of the Law, their spiritual regeneration and a house at Shepherd's Bush.

She was now the mistress of a fortune of over ten thousand pounds, a good half of which was due to her final stratagem. The time had now come for her to retire to the house in the country when she could resume her own name, piece together for the sake of the county her career since she left India for Alabama, and read the local agricultural rag. Her plans were postponed, however, owing to Holt's state of health, which compelled her, out of sheer humanity, to take him to a sunnier clime. She dismissed Algiers as being too far; she asked Holt where he would like to go to, but he merely replied 'East Coast,' which in December struck her as being absurd. Finally she decided to take him to Folkestone, as it was very near and he would doubtless like to sit with the dogs on the Leas.

Folkestone was bright and sunny. The sting in the glowing air brought fresh colour to Victoria's cheeks, a deeper brilliancy to her grey eyes; she felt well; her back was straighter; when a lock of dark hair strayed into her mouth driven by the high wind it tasted salt on her lips. Sometimes she could have leaped, shouted, for life was rushing in upon her like a tide. Most days, however, she was quiet, for Holt was not affected by the sea. His listlessness was now such that he hardly spoke. He would walk by her side vacuously, looking at his surroundings as if he did not see them. At times he stopped, concentrated with an effort and bought a bun from a hawker to break up for the dogs.

Victoria noticed that he was slipping, with ununderstanding fear. The phenomenon was beyond her. Though the guests at the hotel surrounded her with an atmosphere of admiration, Holt's condition began to occupy all her thoughts. He was thin now to the point of showing bone under his coat, pale and hectic, generally listless, sometimes wild-eyed. He never read, played no games, talked to nobody. Indeed nothing remained of him save the half physical, half emotional power of his passion. Victoria called in a doctor, but found him vague and shy ; beyond cutting down Holt's cigarettes he prescribed nothing.

Victoria resigned herself to the role of a nurse. At the beginning of January she noticed that Holt was using a stick to walk. The sight filled her with dread. She watched him on the Leas, walking slowly, resting the weight of his body on the staff, stopping now and then to look at the sea, or worse, at a blank wall. A terrible impression of weakness emanated from him. He was going down the hill. One morning in the middle of January, Holt did not get up. When questioned he hardly answered. She dressed feverishly without his moving, and went out to find the doctor herself, for she was unconsciously afraid of the servants' eyes. When she returned with the doctor Holt had not moved ; his head was thrown back, his mouth a little open, his face more waxen than usual.

'Oh, oh. . . .' Victoria nearly screamed, when Holt opened his eyes. The doctor threw back the bedclothes and examined his patient. As Victoria watched him inspecting Holt's mouth, the inside of his eyelids, then his finger nails, a terror came upon her at these strange rites. She went to the window and looked out over the sea ; it was choppy, grey and foamy like a river in spate. She strove to concentrate on her freedom, but she could feel the figure on the bed.

'Got any sal volatile ? ' said the doctor's voice.

'No, shall I. . . .? '

'No, no time for that, he's fainting ; get me some salts, ammonia, anything.'

Victoria watched him forcing Holt to breathe the

ammonia she used to clean ribbons. Holt opened his eyes, coughed, struggled ; tears ran down his face as he inhaled the acrid fumes. Still he did not speak. The doctor pulled him out of bed, crossed his legs, and then struck him sharply across the shin, just under the knee, with the side of his hand. Holt's leg hardly moved. The doctor hesitated for a moment, then pushed him back into the bed.

'I . . . Mrs. . . . ?'

' Holt.'

' Well, Mrs Holt, I'm afraid your husband is in a serious condition. Of course I don't say that with careful feeding, tonics, we can't get him round, but it'll be a long business, and . . . and . . . you see . . . How long have you been married ? '

' Over a year,' said Victoria with an effort.

' Ah. Well Mrs Holt, it will be part of the cure that you leave him for six months.'

Victoria gasped. Why? Why? Could it be . . .? The thought appalled her. Dimly she could hear the doctor talking.

' His mother . . . if he has one . . . today . . . phosphate of . . .'

Then the doctor was gone. A telegram had somehow been sent to Rawsley Cement Works. Then the long day, food produced on the initiative of the hotel servants, the room growing darker, night.

It was ten o'clock, and two women stood face to face by the bed. One was Victoria, beautiful like a marble statue, with raven black hair, pale lips. The other a short stout figure with tight hair, a black bonnet, a red face stained with tears.

' You've killed him,' said the harsh voice.

Victoria looked up at Mrs Holt.

' No, no.'

' My boy, my poor boy ! ' Mrs Holt was on her knees by the side of the motionless figure.

Victoria began to weep, silently at first, then

noisily. Mrs Holt started at the sound, then jumped
to her feet with a cry of rage.

'Stop that crying,' she commanded. 'How dare
you? How dare you?'

Victoria went on crying, the sobs choking her.

'A murderess,' Mrs Holt went on. 'You took my
boy away; you corrupted him, ruined him, killed
him. You're a vile thing; nobody should touch
you, you. . . .'

Victoria pulled herself together.

'It's not my fault,' she stumbled. 'I didn't know.'

'Didn't know,' sneered Mrs Holt, 'as if a woman of
your class didn't know.'

'That's enough,' snarled Victoria. 'I've had
enough. Understand? I didn't want your son. He
wanted me. That's all over. He bought me, and
now you think the price too heavy. I've been heaven
to him who only knew misery. He's not to be pitied,
unless it be because his mistress hands him over to
his mother.'

'How dare you?' cried Mrs Holt again, a break
in her voice as she pitied her outraged motherhood.

'It's you who've killed him; you, the family,
Rawsley, Bethlehem, your moral laws, your religion.
It's you who starved him, ground him down until he
lost all sense of measure, desired nothing but love
and life.'

'You killed him, though,' said the mother.

'Perhaps. I didn't want to. I was . . . fond of
him. But how can I help it? And supposing I did?
What of it? Yes, what of it? Who was your son
but a man?'

'My son?'

'Your son. A distinction, not a title. Your son
bears part of the responsibility of making me what
I am. He came last but he might have come first,
and I tell you that the worker of the eleventh hour
is guilty equally with the worker of the first. Your

son was nothing and I nothing but pawns in the game, little figures which the Society you're so proud of shifts and breaks. He bought my womanhood; he contributed to my degradation. What else but degradation did you offer me?'

Mrs Holt was weeping now.

'I am a woman, and the world has no use for me. Your Society taught me nothing. Or rather it taught me to dance, to speak a foreign language badly, to make myself an ornament, a pleasure to man. Then it threw me down from my pedestal, knowing nothing, without a profession, a trade, a friend, or a penny. And then your Society waved before my eyes the lily-white banner of purity, while it fed me and treated me like a dog. When I gave it what it wanted, for there's only one thing it wants from a woman whom nothing has been taught but that which every woman knows, then it covered me with gifts. A curse on your Society. A Society of men, crushing, grinding down women, sweating their labour, starving their brains, urging them on to the surrender of what makes a woman worth while. Ah . . . ah. . . .'

Breath failed her. Mrs Holt was weeping silently in her hands in utter abandonment.

'I'm going,' said Victoria hoarsely. She picked up a handkerchief and dabbed her eyes.

As she opened the door the figure moved on the bed, opened its eyes. Their last lingering look was for the woman at the door.

CHAPTER XX

THE squire of Cumberleigh was not sorry that 'The Retreat' had found a tenant at last. The house belonged to him, and he might have let it many times over; but so conservative and aristocratic was his disposition that he preferred to sacrifice his rent rather than have anyone who was undesirable in the neighbourhood. Yet, in the case of the lady who had now occupied the house for some three weeks, though the strictest enquiries had been made concerning her, both in Cumberleigh and the surrounding district, nothing could be ascertained beyond the scanty facts that she was a widow, well-to-do and had been abroad a good deal. The squire had seen her on two separate occasions himself and could not but admit that she was far from unprepossessing; she was obviously a lady, well-bred and educated, and, if her frock and hat had been a trifle smarter than those usually seen in a country village, she had owned up to having recently been to Paris to replenish her wardrobe. It was curious, when he came to reflect upon it, how little she had told him about herself, and yet, what was more curious, she had no sooner left him after the second visit than he had betaken himself to his solicitor to get him to make out the lease. She had received and signed it the following day, showing herself remarkably business-like, but not ungenerous when it came to the buying of the fixtures and to the vexed question of outdoor and indoor repairs.

As the squire climbed the hill that gave upon the village from the marshes, one cold March evening, he did not regret his decision; for, standing in front of 'The Retreat,' he felt bound to admit that there was something cheering and enlivening in the fact that the four front windows now flaunted red curtains and holland blinds, where they had been so dark and forbidding. In the lower one on the left, where the lamps had not yet been lighted or the blinds drawn down, in the light of the dancing fire, he could see distinctly a woman's workbox on a small inlaid table, a volume of songs on the cottage piano, and, at the back of the room, a hint of china tea cups, glistening silver and white napery. Presently a trim maid came out to bolt the front door, followed by two snuffling yellow dogs who took the air for a few moments in tempestuous spirits, biting each other about the neck and ears and rushing round in giddy circles on the tiny grass plot until, in response to a call from the maid, they returned with her to the house. They were foreigners evidently, these dogs! The squire could not remember the name of the breed, but he thought he had seen one of the kind before in London. He was not quite sure he approved of foreign dogs; they were not so sporting or reliable as those of the English breeds; still, these were handsome fellows, well kept and (from the green ribbons that adorned their fluffy necks) evidently made much of. He was still looking after the dogs when he was joined by the curate coming out of the blacksmith's cottage opposite and stopping to light a match in the shelter of the high wall of 'The Retreat.'

'First pipe I have had to-day,' said the new-comer as he puffed at it luxuriously. 'It's more than you can say, squire, I'll be bound.'

'Twenty-first, that's more like it,' said the squire with a laugh. 'How is Mrs Johnson?' This in allusion to the curate's call at the smithy.

'Dying. Won't last the night out, I think. She is quite unconscious. Still I am glad I went. Johnson and his daughters seemed to like to have me there, though of course there was nothing for me to do.'

'Quite so, quite so,' said the squire approvingly, for the village was so small that he took a paternal interest in all its inhabitants. 'Any more news?'

'Mrs Golightly has had twins, and young Shaw has enlisted. That's about all, I think. Oh, by the by, I paid a call here to-day.' And he indicated 'The Retreat.' 'It seemed about time you know, and one mustn't neglect the new-comers.'

'Of course not,' the squire assented with conviction. 'Was she . . . did she in any way indicate that she was pleased to see you?'

'She was very gracious, but she seemed to take my call quite as a matter of course. A nice woman I should think, though a little reserved. However she is going to rent one seat in church if not more, and she said I might put her name down for one or two little things I am interested in at present.'

'In fact you made hay while the sun shone. Well, after all, why not? She didn't tell you anything about herself I suppose, or her connections?'

'No, she never mentioned them. I understood or she implied she had been abroad a good deal and that her husband had died some years ago. Still I really don't think we need worry about her; the whole thing, if I may say so, was so obviously all right, the house I mean and all its appointments. She is a quiet woman, a little shy and retiring perhaps, belongs to the old-fashioned school.'

'Well she is none the worse for that,' said the squire with a grunt. 'We don't meet many of that kind nowadays. Even the farmers' daughters are quite ready to set you right whenever they get a chance. This modern education is a curse, I have said so from the very beginning. Still they haven't robbed us of our Church schools yet, if that is any consolation. Coming back to dine with me to-night, Seaton?'

The young man shook his head. 'Very sorry, squire, it's quite impossible to-night. It is Friday night, choir practice you know, and there is a lantern lecture in the mission hall. I ought to be there already, helping Griffin with the slides.'

'All right, Sunday evening then, at the usual time,' said the squire cordially as the curate left him, and, as he looked after him, he criticised him as a busy fellow, not likely to set the Thames on fire perhaps, but essentially the right man in the right place.

His own progress was a good deal slower; not that he found the hill too steep, for, in spite of his fifty years, he was still perfectly sound of wind and limb, as was shown by his athletic movements, the fresh healthy colour on his cheeks, and the clear blue of his eyes, but rather because he seemed loth to tear himself away from 'The Retreat' and his new tenant. Even when he had reached the little post office that crowned the summit, he did not turn off towards his own place till he had spent another five minutes contemplating the stack of chimney-pots sending out thick puffs of white smoke into the quiet evening sky, and listening attentively to the cheerful sound of a tinkling piano blended with the gentle lowing of the cattle on the marsh below. After all, he told himself, he was very glad Seaton had called, for apart from his duty as a clergyman it was only a kind and neighbourly thing to do.

It was a pity that there were not more of his kind in the neighbourhood, for in spite of his own preference for the country, he could imagine that a woman coming to it fresh from London at such a season might find it dull and a little depressing. He wondered if Mrs Menzies, of Hither Hall, would call if he asked her to do so. Of course she would in a moment if he put it on personal grounds, but that was not the point. All he wished was to be kind and hospitable to a stranger; and Mrs Menzies, much as he respected and admired her, had never been known to err on the side of tolerance, nor did one meet in her drawing-room anyone whose pedigree would not bear a thorough investigation. Yes, there was no doubt about it, though the laws that governed social intercourse were on the whole excellent and had to be kept, there were here, as everywhere else in life, exceptions to the rule, occasions when anyone of a kindly disposition must feel tempted to break them. And Mrs Menzies was certainly a little stiff: witness her behaviour in the case of Captain Clinton's widow and the fuss she had made because the unfortunate lady had forgotten to tell her of her relationship to the Eglinton Clintons and had only vouchsafed the fact that her father's people had been in trade. Why, it had taken weeks if not months to clear the matter up; and it had been very awkward for everybody, the Eglinton Clintons included when the truth had transpired. No, on second thoughts he would not ask Mrs Menzies to call; he would far rather make the first venture himself than risk a snub for this lonely defenceless stranger.

He turned into the gates of Redland Hall with a half-formed intention of doing so immediately. He dined alone as usual; it was very rare that the dining-room of Redland Hall extended its hospitality to anybody nowadays; for the squire, like most men over forty, had lost the habit of entertaining and did not know how to recover it. A bachelor friend spent a night with him from time to time; the curate supped with him every Sunday; and his sister came for a week or two during the summer, when she invariably told him that the house was too uncomfortable to live in, and he ought to have it thoroughly done up and modernised. He invariably promised

to set about it immediately, with the full intention
of doing so; but his resolution began to weaken the
day on which he saw her off at the station, and
degenerated steadily for the remainder of the year.
That night, however, for the first time for many
months he made a voyage of discovery into his own
drawing-room. Yes, there was no doubt about it,
Selina was quite right in calling it draughty and
uncomfortable; the gilt French furniture was shabby
and tarnished, the Aubusson carpet worn, the wall
paper faded, the whole room desolate in its suggestion
of past glory. He crossed over to the enormous grand
piano, opened it and struck a yellow key gently with
one finger. Was he wrong, he wondered, in thinking its
tone was lamentably thin and poor? A rat scampered
and squeaked in the waincoting, the windows rattled
in their loose sashes; he shut the piano abruptly and
left the room. It would cost a good deal to have
it thoroughly done up, of course; but that was not
the point. Who would superintend the decorations?
He did not trust his own taste and had no faith
in that of any upholsterer. Selina would come and
help him if he asked her, though she would think it
strange, for she had paid her annual visit in August,
and it was now only March; besides, if she brought
her delicate little girls with her at such a time the
whole house would be upset in arranging for their
comfort. Still, Selina or no, he had quite made up
his mind to have the room done up and to buy a
new piano immediately; it was ridiculous to harbour
an instrument which was merely a nesting place for
mice. He returned to the dining-room, poured
himself out a stiff whiskey and soda, and dozed over
his *Spectator* for the rest of the evening. Yet, next
morning, even in the unromantic light of day, he
was surprised to find that his plan of doing up the
drawing-room still held good.

He had intended to ride into Wetherton that day

to try his new mare across country, for the gates were high in that direction and good enough to test her powers as a jumper. A glance at the glistening frost on the grass soon sufficed, however, to tell him that his scheme could not be carried out ; nor was he sorry until, having spent the morn'ng on his farms and inspected everything and everyb dy at his leisure, it occurred to him with a despe ate sense of conviction that there was still the afterr oon to be filled in somehow. About three he set off in the direction of the village, looked in at the church and had a brief colloquy with Seaton regarding the new pews which were being put up, interviewed the postmaster, condoled with the blacksmith upon the death of his wife, and even ventured down as far as the marsh to see if the new carrier who had taken the place of old Dick Tomlinson was likely to fulfil his duties properly. About four o'clock he found himself once more opposite ' The Retreat.' It was on the main road certainly, but it was only recently that he had become aware of its importance in the landscape. One could not get to the marsh or come back from it without passing it. The windows looked as trim as ever—trimmer perhaps, for short muslin curtains interspaced with embroidery seemed to have sprung up in the night. They were very decorative in their way ; at the same time they quite shut out all prospect of the interior, and there was no workbox, piano, or suggestion of tea things to be seen to-day. The foreign dogs were snuffling in the garden as he passed the second time, and one of them nosed its way through the iron gate and ventured a few yards down the road, but just as the squire had made up his mind it was his duty to take it back, it returned of its own accord. He watched the trim maid come out and call them as she had done the day before, and saw them rush after her frolicking round her skirt,

Suddenly he crossed the road, looked up and down to make sure there was no acquaintance within sight, opened the iron gate of 'The Retreat,' and passed up the gravel pathway into the porch.

'Mrs Fulton is at home,' said the trim maid demurely, in answer to his question.

www.ingramcontent.com/pod-product-compliance
Lightning Source LLC
Chambersburg PA
CBHW030354030726
47497CB00002B/332